ILYA VINITSKY

Ghostly Paradoxes

Modern Spiritualism and Russian Culture in the Age of Realism

UNIVERSITY OF TORONTO PRESS
Toronto Buffalo London

© University of Toronto Press 2009
Toronto Buffalo London
utorontopress.com

Reprinted in paperback 2018

ISBN 978-0-8020-9935-8 (cloth)   ISBN 978-1-4875-2365-7 (paper)

Library and Archives Canada Cataloguing in Publication

Vinitsky, Ilya
Ghostly paradoxes: modern spiritualism and Russian culture in the age of realism/Ilya Vinitsky.

Includes bibliographical references and index.
ISBN 978-0-8020-9935-8 (cloth)   ISBN 978-1-4875-2365-7 (paper)

1. Russian literature – 19th century – History and criticism. 2. Literature and spiritualism – Russia. 3. Realism in literature. I. Title.

PG3096.R4V55 2009   891.709′003   C2008-908154-4

University of Toronto Press acknowledges the financial assistance to its publishing program of the Canada Council for the Arts and the Ontario Arts Council, an agency of the Government of Ontario.

Canada Council
for the Arts

Conseil des Arts
du Canada

ONTARIO ARTS COUNCIL
CONSEIL DES ARTS DE L'ONTARIO
an Ontario government agency
un organisme du gouvernement de l'Ontario

Funded by the   Financé par le
Government   gouvernement
of Canada   du Canada

GHOSTLY PARADOXES

Modern Spiritualism and Russian Culture in the Age of Realism

The culture of nineteenth-century Russia is often seen as dominated by realism in the arts, as exemplified by the novels of Leo Tolstoy and Ivan Turgenev, the paintings of 'the Wanderers,' and the historical operas of Modest Mussorgsky. Paradoxically, nineteenth-century Russia was also consumed with a passion for spiritualist activities such as table-rappings, seances of spirit communication, and materialization of the 'spirits.' *Ghostly Paradoxes* examines the surprising relationship between spiritualist beliefs and practices and the positivist mindset of the Russian Age of Realism (1850–80) to demonstrate the ways in which the two disparate movements influenced each other.

Foregrounding the important role that nineteenth-century spiritualism played in the period's aesthetic, ideological, and epistemological debates, Ilya Vinitsky challenges literary scholars who have considered spiritualism to be archaic and peripheral to other cultural issues of the time. *Ghostly Paradoxes* is an innovative work of literary scholarship that traces the reactions of Russia's major realist authors to spiritualist events and doctrines and demonstrates that both movements can be understood only when examined together.

ILYA VINITSKY is an associate professor in the Department of Slavic Languages and Literatures at the University of Pennsylvania.

Contents

Acknowledgments   vii
Preface   ix
Abbreviations   xix

Introduction: A New World – Modern Spiritualism in Russia,
1853–1870s   3

**PART ONE   TABLE TALKS: SEANCE AS CULTURAL
METAPHOR   21**

1 Seance as Test, or, Russian Writers at a Spiritualist Rendezvous   23

2 Russian Glubbdubdrib: The Shade of False Dimitry and Russian
Historical Imagination in the Age of Realism   43

3 Dead Poets' Society: Pushkin's Shade in Russian Cultural
Mythology of the Second Half of the Nineteenth Century   57

**PART TWO REALIST EXORCISM: SPIRITUALISM AND
THE RUSSIAN LITERARY IMAGINATION
OF THE 1860s TO 1880s   87**

4 Flickering Hands: The Spiritualist Realism of Nikolai Vagner   89

5 The Middle World: The Realist Spiritualism of
Saltykov-Shchedrin   107

6 The Underworld: Dostoevsky's Ontological Realism   119

7   The (Dis)infection: Art and Hypnotism in Leo Tolstoy   136

Epilogue: The Spirit of Literature – Reflections on Leskov's Artistic
Spiritualism   156

Notes   165
Works Cited   219
Index   241

Acknowledgments

This book was conceived some ten years ago as a continuation of my work on Vasily Zhukovsky and Russian Romantic spiritualism. I was intrigued by the transformation undergone by the Romantic ghosts in the realistic and positivist second half of the nineteenth century. Unlike the 'traditional' apparitions, who walked by night to frighten the mortals, revealing terrible secrets or demanding revenge, the ghosts of the 1850s to 1880s dutifully appeared at the public's request and politely responded through mediums to questions from the curious. These 'tamed' talkative ghosts, which for various reasons attracted many Russian authors of the age, may seem trivial and perhaps comic to the observer; however, as I hypothesized, they reveal important paradoxes in the cultural mindset that characterized the period, among them a surprising *spectralization* of social and political 'realities,' which the realists claimed to 'mirror' in their works. I thus became, as Caryl Emerson wittily observed, a phantomologist of Russian Realist culture.

I would like to thank my friends and colleagues who have helped me materialize my ideas in the present book. First and foremost, I owe a debt to Caryl Emerson for her encouragement and intellectual generosity throughout the writing of this book. For important suggestions on previous drafts of individual chapters, I am most thankful to Mark Grigorievich Altshuller, Boris Gasparov, Irene Masing-Delic, Hugh McLean, Gary Saul Morson, Donna Orwin, Nina Perlina, Nadya Peterson, Kevin M.F. Platt, David Powelstock, Simon Richter, William Mills Todd III, Andrew Baruch Wachtel, and Alexander Zholkovsky. I am grateful to the members of the University of Pennsylvania Nineteenth-Century Study Group for the stimulating discussion of two chapters of this manuscript and of my argument in general. My very special thanks are to Oliver Ready, Jim Tonn, Timothy J. Portice, Kristen Lodge, and Chloe Kitzinger for their excellent translations and smart editorial suggestions. I need especially to thank my editors Jill McConkey, Barbara Porter, Daniel Quinlan, and Matthew Kudelka for their professional help and support. Thanks are due to my friends Mikhail Liustrov, Alexander Kobrinsky, Peter Thomas, Seth Graham, Ilya Kukulin, Maria Maiofis, and Michael Denner, who helped in various ways. I cannot imagine having completed this book without my parents' enormous support. My daughter Anna, with her sceptical mind, sense of humour, and twelve imaginary friends, was a genuine source for my scholarly inspiration. My greatest debt is to my wife, Svetlana, for her love, patience, and faith that someday I would return to reality from my intellectual business trip to the ghost world.

As for material reality, I am most grateful to the University of Pennsylvania for its generous financial support. Finally, in the spirit of this study, I wish to thank Alexander Sergeevich Pushkin, Edgar Allan Poe, and Ivan Semyonovich Barkov for their permission to reproduce their posthumous writings transmitted through mediums.

Chapters 1 and 6 of this book first appeared in, respectively, *The Russian Review* 67, no. 1 (2008): 88–109; and *The Slavic Review* 65, no. 3 (2006): 523–43, and are reprinted below with the kind permission of the publishers. An earlier version of what later became chapter 4 appeared in Russian in *Novoe Literaturnoe Obozrenie* 78 (2006): 171–98, and I appreciate the permission to reprint it. The introduction and chapters 2, 3, 4, and 5 were translated from Russian by Oliver Ready, the preface by Kristen Lodge, chapters 1 and 6 by James Tonn, chapter 7 by Timothy Portice, and the epilogue by Chloe Kitzinger.

Note to the Reader

In the body of the text I have used the popular transliteration scheme (e.g., Mayakovsky rather than Maiakovskii, Solovyov rather than Solov'ev, Helene Blavatsky rather than Elena Blavatskaia), since this book is intended for a relatively wide audience, not necessarily readers with a knowledge of Russian. In the footnotes and works cited, however, I have used the Library of Congress system of transliteration: Gogol', Dostoevskii, Solov'ev, Mariia, Vasilii, Iurii, and so on. Poetic citations of primary text are given not in transliterated form but in Cyrillic.

In quotations, [...] indicates my own omission of a portion of the original. Italics in quotations are from the original unless otherwise noted.

For English citations of Russian works, I have used existing English-language translations, modified occasionally when a more literal rendition is important to my argument. Otherwise, the translations are mine.

Unless otherwise stated, extracts from the works of Fyodor Dostoevsky, Alexander Pushkin, Leo Tolstoy, and Mikhail Saltykov-Shchedrin are given in the text from the following editions, with an indication of volume and page in parenthesis:

F.M. Dostoevskii, *Polnoe sobranie sochinenii v 30 tomakh* (Leningrad: Nauka, 1972–90).

A.S. Pushkin, *Polnoe sobranie sochinenii v 19 tomakh* (Moscow: Voskresen'e, 1994–7).

L.N. Tolstoi, *Polnoe sobranie sochinenii v 90 tomakh (Iubileinoe izdanie)* (Moscow: Gosudarstuennoe Izdatel'stvo Khudozhestennai Literatura, 1928–59).

M.E. Saltykov-Shchedrin, *Sobranie sochinenii v 20 tomakh* (Moscow: Khudozhestennai Literatura, 1965–77).

Preface

You have certainly had occasion, dear reader, to be present at debates on the substance of the soul and its dependence on the body. It is usually a young man who is arguing with an elderly man, if they are both naturalists, or two young men, if one of them is more preoccupied with the problem of matter and the other, with the problem of spirit [...] Grandiloquent phrases, far-reaching opinions, and bright thoughts crackle and rain down like someone's rockets. The debate will make the flesh creep for some listeners – young, timid enthusiasts; others will listen with bated breath; still others will break out in a sweat. But the performance will inevitably come to an end. Terrifying columns of flame will blaze up to the sky, break up, and be extinguished ... and only a peaceful memory of bright apparitions will remain in the soul. That is usually the fate of all private debates among dilettantes. They agitate the imagination for a time, but they do not persuade anyone.

I.M. Sechenov, *Reflexes of the Brain*

'Sasa, ay ... ay ...,' he repeated several times. It was impossible to understand his words. The doctor thought he understood and, repeating his words, asked, 'The princess is afraid?' He shook his head and repeated the same thing. 'His soul is in pain,' Princess Mary guessed. He bellowed affirmatively, took her hand, and started to press it against different parts of his chest, as though looking for the right place for it.

L.N. Tolstoy, *War and Peace*[1]

Dead and Living Souls

The 1850s through the 1880s, known in Russia as the Age of Realism and dominated by materialist and positivist tendencies, was also a time that saw the flourishing of various spiritualist and mystical circles that were opposed to both materialism and the official Church. Yet literary scholars generally consider this spiritualist trend to be archaic, marginal, or peripheral in relation to the fundamental cultural issues of the time. Mystics and seekers of contact with spirits were constantly ridiculed in plays, novels, and serious and comic journals. Nevertheless, closer investigation shows that the spiritualist trend played a significant role in the ideological and social life of the realist age. The reality of the soul – its dependence on the body (matter), the means of acquiring knowledge about it, and the possibility of its continued existence after death – was a major issue of the time. Physicists, physiologists, theologians, mystics, and, of course, writers all took part in this debate.[2] Passionate arguments about the soul amounted to a battle among ideologies for the souls of contemporaries, who were seeking someone to believe, something to have faith in. Spiritualists' attempts to resolve this debate by radical means – by summoning and interrogating the dead! – fostered a fascinating and ideologically rich public scandal, one that I investigate in this book.

In this study, I draw attention to two aspects of the cultural communication between 'spirits' and 'reality': (1) the semiotic and epistemological significance of Modern Spiritualism (a positivist modification of mystical spiritualism, one that maintains that the ultimate reality is spirit) for the realist consciousness of the age; and (2) the paradoxical refraction of various spiritualist ideas and doctrines in realist literature. Simply put, the former approach considers spiritualism as the (comic) shadow of Russian culture in the Age of Realism, while the latter goes 'inside' the realistic mind and text and presents realism as haunted by numerous spectres.[3] I have therefore divided this study into two parts, constructed around several plots (texts) that 'play out' – or, to use a word from the spiritualist lexicon, 'materialize' – the relevant ideological, epistemological, and aesthetic conflicts. I hope that a discussion of (latent) spiritualism in the realist imagination will be able to bridge the gap with the more widely researched mysticism and spiritualism of the Romantic and Modernist periods.

The Shade of Realism

The main character of Part One of this book (in the literal, figurative, symbolic, mythological, scholarly, historical, aesthetic, and religious senses) is the ghost, or spectre – that is, the only material evidence acceptable by positivists that an immaterial world exists. My study relies on three categories of research: philosophical and ideological interpretations of the phenomenon of the ghost and the trope of spectrality in Western culture;[4] studies of the history of modern spiritualism (spiritism) as a social movement;[5] and studies of the role played by spiritualist models in literature.[6] Despite radical differences in their approaches, these works are unified by a common aspiration to 'make or let a spirit speak'[7] about the religious, cultural, psychological, ideological, and aesthetic conflicts that it 'materializes' or veils. The ghost appears here as a metaphor for a 'sick' reality (ideological, psychological, socio-historical), one that yields to scholarly decoding (deconstructionist, Freudian, sociological, or New Historical). As Helen Sword has aptly observed, the contemporary critic acts as a cultural medium who interprets 'voices from a remote "other world": of literature, the unconsciousness, the past.'[8] I see my task in this context as that of 'listening to' the Russian ghost, whose troubled fate in the realist era I will reconstruct as the story develops. I will be interpreting the ghost not as an Other revealing secrets about a world unknown to the man of the Age of Realism, nor as a metaphor for his mourning, but as his own echo or shade, dependent on him, reflecting and exaggerating his own questions and pursuits.

   In Part One I focus on the most influential (and most ridiculed) spiritualist movement of the realist era: Modern Spiritualism (or spiritism), a doctrine that espoused individual immortality and the possibility of regular communication with the souls of the dead through mediums – that is, through people gifted with special psychic talents. The adepts of Modern Spiritualism understood it not simply as an alternative to materialist science, the Church, and philosophy, but as a synthesis of knowledge and truth, psychology and mystical understanding, empiricism and idealism – in sum, as a shortcut to the ultimate answer to all questions. This synthetic claim made by spiritualism, which naturally evoked indignation among the institutions that did not want to be 'synthesized,' is especially attractive to those today who research the ideological conflicts of that time. Also, spiritualism attracted many

Russians of that era because of its performative character: the seance was a kind of scientific–religious mystery play in which the ideas agitating society were staged. Spiritualism is intriguing to me not so much as a doctrine which responded in a unique way to the religious yearnings of an 'age of doubt' and which expressed contemporaries' hope that the power of science would satisfy those yearnings, but as a peculiar reflection of the culture of that time – one that gathered, materialized, and parodied the many utopian goals and practices that characterized the realist period.

The Reality of Shades

The spiritualist metaphor allows one to see and analyse only the general principles of the mindset of the realist epoch. In Part Two of this book I discuss how the spiritualist controversy of the Age of Realism was reflected in concrete literary practices. In a sense, realism itself is a ghost: scholars call it elusive or even deny its existence, but they cannot do without it. Here, I do not undertake a summarizing discussion of a lengthy critique of realism (itself an interesting case of exorcism!) or suggest my own definition of realism. Instead I focus on a single feature of realism, one that according to George Levine represents an attempt 'to embrace the reality that stretched beyond the reach of language.'[9] This attempt, I believe, makes down-to-earth realism akin to its celestial opposite, spiritualism, which also claimed the ability to embrace the other world by means of words. To achieve this utopian goal – that is, to 'cover the transition from the real world, in which the writing and reading of the text are located, to the fictive world' of the literary characters or spirits – both realism and spiritualism relied on 'empirical data.'[10]

Many studies have examined the role of mystical and spiritualist ideas and doctrines in nineteenth- and early twentieth-century Russian literature. Yet when scholars talk about the influence of the Western mystical legacy on Russian literature, they usually refer to only two periods – Romanticism and Modernism – and to a limited number of writers within these periods: Alexander Pushkin (almost exclusively in his *Queen of Spades*), Mikhail Lermontov, Prince Vladimir Odoevsky, Nikolai Gogol, Vladimir Solovyov, Aleksandr Blok, Andrei Belyi, and Vyacheslav Ivanov.[11] During these two periods, public interest in mysticism was overwhelming and literature itself was often perceived as a powerful means of mystically transforming and transfiguring the world. Yet echoes of various mystical and theosophical doctrines appear surprisingly often in the major works of Russian literature from the Golden Age of Realism: Fourierian visions in Nikolai Cherny-shevsky's utopian novel *What Is To Be Done?*; the pneumatology of J.-H. Jung-Stilling and the philosophy of Allan Kardec in the anti-nihilistic and 'god-seeking' works of Leskov; Schopenhauerian mysticism in the works of Leo Tolstoy and Ivan Turgenev; and Swedenborg's philoso-phy in Fyodor Dostoevsky's *oeuvre*.

I suggest that it is in the very epistemology of realism that we must seek the reasons for the interest of realist writers in various spiritualist phenomena and teachings. Realism strives to create a verbal image of reality 'as it is' (Roland Barthes's 'reality effect') by imitating a 'scien-tific' method; yet at the same time, it constantly senses the impossi-bility of attaining this utopian goal. As George Levine observes: 'The impelling energy in the quest for world beyond words is that the world be there, and meaningful and good; the persistent fear is that it is merely monstrous and mechanical, beyond the control of human meaning.'[12]

In this regard, the history of Russian Realism, which originated in the late 1840s, is especially telling.[13] From the start, the radical theore-ticians of this literary movement – Vissarion Belinsky (1811–48) and Nikolai Dobrolyubov (1836–61) – considered its mission to be the struggle against romantic idealism and phantoms in the name of an objective, truthful 'reflection' of social reality. However, the ghosts of Romanticism did not disappear as a result of this realist exorcism; rather, they were tamed, absorbed by positivist rationalism,[14] or they were 'hidden' in the depths of the work.[15] I contend that realist writ-ers, either consciously or unconsciously, sought in various spiritualist doctrines of their time epistemological models that resonated with their literary practice and ideological intuition and that permitted them to express and explain repressed feelings of metaphysical uncer-tainty and hope. Indeed, one of the central themes of Russian Realism is the languishing of the human mind in the material world. This suf-fering may be attributed to various natural causes (social, biological, or economic), but the essence of the conflict does not change: the external world (a provincial town, a village, St Petersburg, or all of Russia) is a ward in a madhouse or a Gothic dungeon from which the suffering protagonist attempts in vain to escape. It is no coincidence that real-ists of that era constantly characterized social reality using words such as 'oppressive,' 'agonizing,' 'illusive,' 'miserable,' and 'dark,' and deliverance from the 'darkness' using words such as 'ray,' 'light,' and 'awakening' (recall Dobrolyubov's influential article 'The Ray of Light in the Dark Kingdom,' 1859). Moreover, the more consistent and militant the realist's obsession with the matter, the more pronounced this gnostic conflict became in his work (recall here Mikhail Saltykov-Shchedrin, Alexey Pisemsky, and Gleb Uspensky).

The 'realist mode' (as well as contemporaneous society) is thus characterized by an intense interaction between two opposing tendencies: an overtly materialist trend (which emphasizes the objective depiction of social reality as perceived through experience) and a hidden spiritualist trend (which strives to find an escape for the mind suffering in the real world).[16] Of course, the correlation of these tendencies is represented differently in the works of different authors, but *neither absolutely outweighs the other.* I contend that it was in this peculiar balance of irreconcilable forces that Dostoevsky saw the unhealthiness and 'fantastic' character of the realist consciousness.[17]

Finally, this gravitation towards spiritualist doctrines derives from the Realist ontology of authorship. The artistic world created by the realist is not a mere verbal illusion of (elusive) reality; rather, its continuation in a new status, a neighbouring world of shades, is 'naturally' produced and 'scientifically' described by the author–medium. This world is inhabited by fictional characters – that is, by ordinary people in their new, purified, literary, and meaningful existence. They are suffering and tested like the human souls of the Catholic purgatory or of the 'middle world' of spiritualism. They haunt readers' imaginations, 'ask' for their compassion and forgiveness, and 'depend' on their readers' moral and spiritual progress, since the better the people become the 'easier' and 'brighter' the characters' destiny in this spirit world of literature will be. This inner kinship of the realist teleology with spiritualism (above all, with doctrines of the progress of the soul in the world beyond) is reflected in various works of the age, from Gogol's conception of *Dead Souls* (1842) as a three-volume narrative of spiritual progress to the futurology of Chernyshevsky's *What Is To Be Done?* (1863) and Dostoevsky's tribulations of the soul in *The Brothers Karamazov* (1880).

In conclusion, I will say a few words about the structure of this book. The Introduction gives a history of the spiritualist movement in Russia from the 1850s through to its culmination in the mid-1870s. Part One, 'Table Talks: Seance as Cultural Metaphor,' examines cultural conflicts, problems, and phenomena that came to light in the polemics on experimental spiritualism in the 1870s: the epistemological contest between spiritualists, scientists, and writers as 'psychic investigators' (chapter 1), the 'spiritualist' ontology of Russian historical imagination in the Age of Realism (chapter 2), and the phenomenon of the omniscient 'dead author' in Russian realist consciousness (chapter 3).

In Part Two, 'Realist Exorcism: Spiritualism and the Russian Literary Imagination of the 1860s to 1880s,' I focus on four different strategies of realist disenchantment:[18] the 'spiritualist realism' of the distinguished Russian scientist, writer, and ardent propagator of mediumism Nikolai Vagner (chapter 4), the 'realist spiritualism' of the satirist and materialist Mikhail Saltykov-Shchedrin (chapter 5), the 'ontological realism' of Fyodor Dostoevsky (chapter 6), and the 'artistic hypnotism' of Leo Tolstoy (chapter 7). By no means do I insist on the necessity of all of these isms; I use them as tools for analysis rather than out of an enthusiasm for the classification that was so characteristic of theoreticians of both realism and spiritualism. I conclude my story about realist spirit hunting on an optimistic note (since I am an optimist) with a discussion of a provocative 'pneumatological joke' by Nikolai Leskov, which I interpret as a parable concerning the reality and nature of the spirit of literature itself.

There were certainly other prominent Russian writers who reflected on spiritualism in their work, among them, Ivan Turgenev. Though I will not discuss their positions at length (as the Russian literary phantom Kozma Prutkov wisely observed, it is impossible to embrace the unembracable), the ghosts of these authors, as well as other important participants in the contemporary debate (from scientists Ivan Sechenov and Dmitry Mendeleev to philosophers Alexander Aksakov, Pamfil Yurkevich, and Nikolai Strakhov and to literary critics Dmitry Pisarev and Nikolai Chernyshevsky) will be constant companions in this book.

Abbreviations

BZ	*Bibliograficheskie zapiski* (Bibliographical Notes)
DB	*Domashniaia beseda* (Household Talk)
Gr	*Grazhdanin* (Citizen)
MV	*Moskovskie vedomosti* (Moscow Gazette)
NLO	*Novoe literaturnoe obozrenie* (New Literacy Review)
OR RGB	Otdel Rukopisei Rossiiskoi gosudarstvennoi biblioteki (The Manuscript Division of the Russian State Library)
OZ	*Otechestvennye zapiski* (Fatherland Notes)
RA	Russian Archive (Russian Archive)
Rb	*Rebus*
RI	*Russkii invalid* (Russian Veteran)
RS	*Russkaia starina* (Russian Antiquity)
RV	*Russkii vestnik* (Russian Herald)
SEEJ	*Slavic and East European Journal*
SPbV	*Sankt-Peterburgskie vedomosti* (St Petersburg Gazette)
SPch	*Severnaia pchela* (Northern Bee)
VE	*Vestnik Evropy* (Herald of Europe)

GHOSTLY PARADOXES

Realistic fiction is written to give the effect that it represents life and the social world as it seems to the common reader, evoking the sense that its characters might in fact exist and that such things might well happen.

M.H. Abrams, 'Realism,' *Glossary of Literary Terms*

There are more things in heaven and earth, Horatio,
Than are dreamt of in your philosophy.

William Shakespeare, *Hamlet*

'It goes on, you know,' the Hatter continued, 'in this way: –
'Up above the world you fly,
Like a tea-tray in the sky.
Twinkle, twinkle – ...'

Lewis Carroll, 'A Mad Tea-Party'

Introduction: A New World – Modern Spiritualism in Russia, 1853–1870s

Among current items of news, primacy must be accorded, without dispute, to that mystery which nature has hitherto hidden from men and whose traces are only now beginning to be discerned.

Moscow Gazette, 30 April 1853

Stout Lady. He took me by my hair!
Leonid Fyodorovich [*in a whisper*]. Don't be afraid! It won't hurt! Give him your hand! His hand is generally cold, but I like it.
Stout Lady [*hiding her hands*]. Not for the world!
Sakhatov. Yes, it is strange, it is strange.

Leo Tolstoy, *The Fruits of Enlightenment*

Spiritualism as a Practice

Spiritualism (Modern Spiritualism, *spiritisme*) is a religious movement founded on the observation and study of occurrences that, according to its devotees, testify to the existence of an afterlife and to the possibility of making contact with the dead through mediums. The movement is usually separated into two strands: the philosophical strand (*spiritisme*), which interprets spiritualist phenomena in mystical–religious terms; and the experimental strand (Modern Spiritualism, or mediumism, as some of the spiritualists preferred), which takes as its aim the scientific description and investigation of the physical manifestation of spiritual forces. Spiritualism arose in America in 1848 with the 'Rochester rappings,' during which unusual phenomena – including raps, other noises, and the movement of furniture with no visible cause – caught society's interest. It was observed that these phenomena regularly took place in the presence of certain individuals (mediums). The discoveries resulted in experiments with 'turning' or 'dancing' tables.

These mysterious phenomena were initially explained as the effects of galvanic current, animal magnetism, or the unconscious influence on the table of the participants' hands. Spiritualists, however, quickly pointed out that the observed phenomena could not be explained naturally, as the consequence of physical laws such as magnetism; the explanation had to involve some rational will that, for whatever reason, wished to make itself known. This gave rise to the theory that 'invisible beings' were announcing their presence through signals. These beings entered into 'telegraphic' contact with the participants of the seances by tapping out messages on a table leg according to a fixed code. Initially, the taps were considered to signify only yes and no; later, it was judged that they corresponded to the letters of the alphabet. This method of communication became known as 'table talking.' The beings with whom contact had been established announced that they were 'spirits belonging to the invisible world' and that they wished to use their knowledge to help the living.

At first, messages were transmitted 'typtologically' (via the alphabetical code), but this took a great deal of time. The crucial refinement in communication with spirits was the invention of the planchette – a small table with three legs and a pencil in the place of the fourth. When the participants placed their hands on the table, it would begin to move and write under the direction of the will of the spirit called up by the medium. 'From this moment, the exchange of messages and thoughts with spirits became as quick and as easy as between living people,' wrote the Russian spiritualist Apollon Boltin. 'This discovery of a new world offered a vast field for research. Just as the microscope revealed the world of the infinitesimally small, so have turning tables disclosed to us the world of the invisible.'[1]

By the mid-1850s, spiritualism was becoming an influential movement in the religious and social life of France, Britain, and the United States, boasting its own prophets and spirit-seers, leaders and famous mediums, canonical books, catechisms, institutions (associations, centres, conferences), media (magazines, newspapers), publishing houses, rituals, holidays, and schools and lyceums.[2] It was accepted as a contemporary religion by diverse social groups and ideological tendencies, whether monarchist, reformist, or radical. In practice, the 'spirits' provided a convenient means by which seance goers could have their convictions confirmed; in this way, the battleground of contemporary opinion was projected onto the other world. Spiritualism's success drew stinging criticism from sceptics, who viewed attempts to communicate with spirits as futile and spiritualism itself as a senseless superstition. The movement was attacked by theologians and Christian mystics, who saw in the need for material proofs of immortality signs of 'weakness of faith' and in the summoning of spirits a readiness to toy with demonic forces (modern sorcery). It was also heavily criticized by doctors, who explained the rappings and other phenomena as collective hallucinations (a modern pathology) and who warned of the dangers that seances posed to the psyche.[3]

The Age of Table Turning

In ideological and organizational terms, the ground for spiritualism in Russia had been prepared by the philosophical and mystical circles that had existed since the time of Alexander I and that sought to reconcile faith with knowledge through the 'rational mysticism' represented by the pneumatology of Emanuel Swedenborg and Johann Heinrich Jung-Stilling, the animal magnetism of Franz Mesmer, the phrenology of Franz Joseph Gall, and the mystical psychology of Justinus Kerner. In the 1830s and 1840s, society was especially curious about so-called clairvoyants; it was thought that, while in a state of trance or mystical ecstasy, these people were able to penetrate the spiritual world, see the past and the future, converse with spirits, prophesize, and cure the sick. As in the West, Russia's cult of clairvoyance took on chivalrous and mystical overtones. These young, sickly, and melancholically disposed Pythias (many clairvoyants were all but children) were the forebears of the female mediums of the spiritualist movement.[4]

The new movement was also fertilized by the wealth of mystical folklore that had accumulated in the 1830s and 1840s and that abounded in stories of supernatural occurrences, which were avidly discussed within families and among friends.[5] Finally, as in the West, printed texts (especially newspapers) played a decisive role in the spread of spiritualism, informing the public about astonishing phenomena and the various attempts made to explain them.[6] During the last years of Nicholas I's reign, spiritualism (in the form of table turning) was almost the only Western social and religious movement to enter Russia. Even then, it was only semilegal.

The public history of spiritualism in Russia began on 13 April 1853, when Faddei Bulgarin's *Severnaia pchela* (Northern Bee) published an article titled 'Moving Tables,' devoted to a sensational story from Bremen. 'For nigh on a week,' wrote the paper's correspondent in Germany, 'this venerable Hanseatic town has been in an unusual state of agitation, absorbed by a phenomenon that could scarcely have been imagined before the *Washington* sailed in from New York.' The topic was table turning, which had been brought to Europe from America.[7] 'The task now,' wrote the *Bee*, 'is to discover what kind of force this is, which gushes from the hands of a known quantity of people and endows wood [...] with the capacity for rapid movement.'[8]

Bulgarin's newspaper took on the role of propaganda organ for the new phenomenon and entered into heated debate with sceptics. It immediately refuted the suggestions made in other publications that the sensational events in Bremen were a fraud, or a joke invented by the foreign press. 'If this had been reported by American newspapers, we would have taken it for a joke ourselves,' the reporter pointed out; surely, he added, serious Germans would hardly stoop to such frivolity. The *Bee* then related the successful experiments conducted with tables by its employees, recalling Hamlet's words to Horatio – 'There are more things in heaven and earth, Horatio, than are dreamt of in your philosophy' – and speculating that research into table turning would in time lead humanity to great discoveries.[9]

Throughout the spring and summer of 1853, the *Bee* regularly printed reports about moving tables in St Petersburg and various towns in the Russian Empire, as well as in India and China; accounts by respectable readers about their experiments with tables and hats; translations of articles about table turning from the Western (usually French) press; and letters from scholars offering explanations. These included galvanic currents, the involuntary pressure of fingers on the table, animal magnetism, and so on – in short, the entire spectrum of early interpretations of table turning in the West.

Moskovskie vedomosti (the Moscow Gazette) was just as quick off the mark, being the first to indicate the possible role of supernatural forces in phenomena such as dancing tables, plates, and hats. Referring to the *Revue Britannique*, the newspaper described a book recently published in Paris under the 'strange title' *Des esprits et les leurs manifestations fluidiques.* 'This book,' noted the *Gazette*, 'is written with such conviction and logic [...] that it can scarcely be viewed as the product of hallucination.

The author saw and heard with his own senses, verified the latter with his reason, compared and considered. He belongs to no academy, but this does not hinder him from believing the evidence of his eyes and from giving greater weight to facts than to the prejudices of science, for science, like ignorance, also has its prejudices.'[10] The book in question was by the marquis Eudes de Mirville, who interpreted mysterious phenomena as the actions of a Satanic force. In France, his book was received as a manifesto of the Catholic critique of *spiritisme*. [11]

The debate on table turning that gripped France at the dawn of the Second Empire remained firmly in the sights of the Russian press. In 1853 and 1854, Russian newspapers published the views of members of the Parisian Academy of Sciences, who had investigated occurrences of table turning and had established that the tables did in fact move (the commission, however, produced no definitive report). Censorship laws precluded discussion in the Russian press of the stream of mystical speculations about the 'unknown force' that had appeared in France (by Gasparin, Thury, Güldenstubbe, and others); nevertheless, the various theories of *spiritisme* infiltrated Russia, where they were quickly absorbed by educated society. By the winter of 1853–4, seances were being held in St Petersburg and Moscow. Spirits were summoned and requests yielded answers, advice, and even literary works.

According to the reminiscences of one observer, tables moved and played tricks 'at the hands of inspired forgers'; they even wrote 'diverse dicta in every language, and the credulous witnesses of the table-writing sought prophecies in these largely incoherent phrases, or else the innermost secrets of persons present and absent.' The first seances were intended simply for family entertainment, but by the second half of the 1850s serious spiritualist circles were being formed, with their own mediums (usually young women), ideology (usually founded on various modifications of Mesmerism and Swedenborgian theosophy), and regular meetings and offices (such as the circle of V.I. Dal' in Nizhnii Novgorod).[12]

In the autumn of 1853, Russian journals entered the debate on rotating tables. *Moskvitianin* (The Muscovite) devoted two articles to the new fashion: 'On Living Tables' and 'A Few Words on Tables Which Merely Move and Tables Which Predict the Future, Divine the Past, and Reply in Writing to Sundry Questions.' In the journal's view, moving tables represented an innocent amusement that might eventually benefit science. Even so, experiments with tables that wrote and divined were dangerous, since they influenced 'people's health, morality, and intellectual capabilities.'[13] By the end of 1853, table divining and table writing had gained so much popularity that Metropolitan Filaret (Drozdov) found it necessary to speak out about the perils of 'contemporary sorcery.' In 'On Table Divining,' a letter published as a separate pamphlet, Metropolitan Filaret called on frequenters of seances to give careful thought to the question of 'whom they are dealing with, and from whom they wish to learn that which is hidden.'[14]

Scholarly criticism of spiritualism first appeared in the mid-1850s. Various journals, including *The Muscovite* and *Sovremennik* (The Contemporary) acquainted readers with psychological interpretations of spiritualist phenomena (the 'hallucinatory' theories of Lelut and Brierre de Boismont)[15] and with the positivist view of spiritualism, which was represented early on by the the leading positivist Émile Littré in his article 'Tables That Talk and Spirits That Rap' (1856), published in *The Contemporary*.[16] The article poured scorn on spiritualism's claims to originality (in Littré's view, all of these phenomena, together with their explanations, had been known since antiquity) and on its scientific status.

How can the success of table turning and table divining in Russian society of that decade be explained? The sceptics of the time pointed to simple curiosity and the desire of idle minds to kill time. Sociologists saw the popularity of spiritualism as a consequence of apathy in society, as a form of ideological escapism for the educated class. Spiritualists for their part, whether Western or Russian, were inclined to see in the discovery of an unknown force 'the dawn of a new era' in which scientific knowledge would be reconciled with faith in the immortality of the soul, and in which humanity would draw closer to its final goal.[17] The 'world war' that began in the Crimea in 1853 had catalysed eschatological and millenarian sentiments in Europe. During his years of exile on Jersey, for example, Victor Hugo appealed to spirits for information about forthcoming historical events and the imminent decline of the empire of 'Napoléon le Petit.'[18] In Russia, the tables were supplying Fyodor Tyutchev with persuasive evidence of the approaching victory of the Orthodox army and the consolidation of the Slavonic Empire, whose capital would be Constantinople. Even in distant Pittsburgh, Pennsylvania, the spirits were announcing the global consequences of the Crimean War. Early spiritualism, in other words, was accompanied by a sense that history was on the march and that great change was about to come.

The Age of Systems

In the ideological context of the 1860s, a decade of reforms, materialism and positivism were strangely intertwined with a range of spiritualist systems, from the pneumatology of Swedenborg and Andrew Jackson Davis to the 'progressive' sightings of the afterlife experienced by the socialists Charles Fourier, Robert Owen, and Pierre Leroux. Mystical propensities were bound up with the scientific imagination and moral idealism. It was supposed that certain spiritually gifted individuals were able to foresee humanity's ideal future and, in accordance with these visions, to direct contemporaries on the path towards perfection. Thus, even as principled an opponent of the fanciful and the metaphysical as Dmitry Pisarev posited that the mystical hallucinations of the reincarnationalist Leroux were founded on a passionate love of humanity and on faith in mankind's infinite perfectibility.[19] Leroux, Pisarev affirmed, 'understands and feels most profoundly that humanity is outgrowing its cradle, that something is slowly maturing in the powerful collective mind, something new and massive, something in which all the truths of obsolete and obsolescent philosophical systems will be combined.'[20] Such visionaries, in Pisarev's view, were plainly mad. But in certain cases their madness was akin to the ecstatic condition of humanity's great poets and reformers, who had always appeared at crucial moments in world history.[21]

The enthusiasm for the otherworldly shown by Russian society in the late 1850s and 1860s had had no parallel in Russia since the reign of Alexander I. The mystical wave swept before it every estate in the empire, engendering – rather, reviving – the tradition of high-society mysticism and, consequently, a deeply strained relationship between spiritualist aristocrats and the Orthodox Church. Following the example of other European monarchs, the Tsar himself, Alexander II, sought contact with the enigmatic spirit world, via the renowned Anglo-American medium Daniel Dunglas Home (1833–86).[22]

The *spiritisme* of the French mystic Allan Kardec (born Léon-Dénizarth-Hippolyte Rivail, 1804–69) gained especially wide circulation in 1860s Russia. Kardec introduced his teaching in *Le livre des esprits* (1857), *Le livre des médiums* (1861), and other writings allegedly dictated to him by 'higher spirits' in response to questions prepared in advance. Kardec was also the founder, in 1858, of the monthly periodical *Revue spirite*, which became the mouthpiece for his teachings.[23]

Kardecist spiritualism is 'a teaching founded on the existence, manifestation, and exhortation of spirits.' At the heart of this spiritual philosophy is the doctrine of reincarnation as the law of the gradual development of the spirit. A human soul is a reincarnated spirit, striving for moral betterment. A single corporeal existence does not suffice 'to acquire every intellectual and moral quality'; a whole succession of reincarnations is required, each giving the spirit the opportunity 'to take several steps forward on the path of progress.'

In the intervals between reincarnations, the spirits abide in a 'wandering' condition, housed in a semimaterial envelope that Kardec called *perisprit*. These spirits constitute an 'entire population thronged about us'; they see us and constantly collide with us. They are distinguished from one another 'by degrees,' in accordance with the level of perfection each has achieved. But even the lowest and most impure spirits should in time attain the higher levels of development. This spiritualist model of the world, therefore, has no place for the doctrine of hell and eternal punishment, nor for Satan, demons, or even angels. Kardec interpreted Jesus Christ as the human reincarnation of the perfect spirit and affirmed that the Earth is only one of an infinite number of worlds in the cosmos (and a far from ideal one at that). At the same time, Kardec held that the future Messiah was 'already growing, unknown,' and would soon appear 'to remake mankind.' He perceived the contemporary moral task of *spiritisme* to be the preaching of mercy, limitless religious tolerance, and freedom of thought.[24] In the precise formulation of David Hess, Kardec saw his doctrine not as an empirical science about the spiritual world, 'but a science that bridged the gap between "is" and "ought" by taking what he interpreted as the facts of spirit communication and transforming them into the moral principles of Spiritist doctrine.'[25]

Kardec's Russian apostle was General Apollon Petrovich Boltin, former vice governor of Viatka and Vladimir. In the early 1860s, Boltin translated Kardec's fundamental works into Russian and wrote several interpretations of his doctrine. Naturally, the religious censors refused to permit their publication, but manuscripts of the translations (and even a lithograph) spread quickly in society, continuing the tradition of mystical *samizdat* that dated back to the Masonic Translators' Seminary of the 1780s.[26]

Kardecist societies, complete with 'writing' and 'hearing' mediums, caught on quickly in both capitals and in the provinces.[27] According to a contemporary witness, many families had their own 'domestic advisers,' who controlled the seances. Messages were dictated by Saint Augustine and Saint Ludovic (spirits who cooperated with Kardec himself), and also by native spirits – Serafim Sarovsky, the martyr Ekaterina, and others.[28] The spirits of historical figures were also summoned: Peter the Great, Nicholas I, Tsarevich Dimitry, Ivan the Terrible,[29] and famous writers such as Pushkin, Zhukovsky, Belinsky, and Gogol. The spiritualist airwaves, meanwhile, were forever being polluted by nonsensical messages, false information, and malicious jokes by the 'lower' spirits (buffoon-spirits, in the terms of Kardec's hierarchy).

Rigid censorship meant that spiritualism assumed an idiosyncratic form in Russia and was concentrated almost exclusively in the salons of the aristocracy and the drawing rooms of the intelligentsia. The mystical and experimental circles of the 1850s to 1870s had no press organs of their own, nor a common centre.[30] Translations of fundamental spiritualist texts spread in manuscript form or were printed in the West. Meanwhile, any mention of the activities of Russian spiritualists in journals or newspapers was invariably hostile. A Russian spiritualist, Prince Emil Wittgenstein, sadly remarked that:

> the great enemy of Spiritualism in Russia [...] is the Church. I think myself it should be the friend of its power, for without it, the Church may *say*, but it cannot *prove* anything, and with it, it is built upon *facts* which no rival Church can disprove ... [Spiritualism] loosens the chains of ecclesiastical tyranny; breaks open the doors of the Inquisition, puts out its fires, or uses them to burn up priestly passports to heaven or hell, besides making of every one his own priest. Of course this won't suit the ecclesiastics who live by the people's slavery; nor their freedom, – hence, although Spiritualism is known and believed in, alike by peer and peasant, it must be believed in against authority, – and be assured, my friend, it has a warm place in the hearts of thousands who dare not openly avow their convictions.[31]

Compared to American and French spiritualism, Russian 'writing' spiritualism was far more temperate and exact: local spirits did not communicate any new doctrines (despite attempts to make them do so); they were politically reliable, even conservative; and they were distinguished by their practical cast of mind.[32] Furthermore, whereas Western spiritualism employed a variety of methods, whether 'psychic' or 'physical,' to receive compositions from beyond the grave,[33] in Russia similar texts were obtained almost exclusively by means of tables and planchettes, right up to the end of the nineteenth century.[34] This was the cheapest and most accessible method, since it did not require the participation of professional mediums. Moreover, it endowed the resulting text, in the view of the spiritualists, with stronger objective and scientific credentials since the personality of the medium was rendered less important than in other methods, such as an improvisation in a state of trance. Also, it was associated with traditional Russian clerical employment. Consider this characteristic conversation about table writing from the early 1850s, recorded by the actor and playwright P.A. Karatygin:

'You can tell me, like Galileo: the earth (the table) really does turn! But I'm a stubborn sort, and I refuse to attribute the table's movement to spirits.'
    'Perhaps you don't even believe that a table can write?'
    'Even less.'
    'Well I believe it,' remarked N.I. Bakhtin phlegmatically. 'In departments and in offices in general, "tables" write memoranda, reports, references, etcetera. That's the only method of table-writing I accept. Putting paper on a table to write makes sense; putting table on paper for this same purpose may be original, but it makes no sense at all.'[35]

Sample Case 1: A 'Writing' Circle

The memoirs and private correspondence of contemporaries confirm the existence in the 1850s and 1860s of numerous spiritualist circles, together with their 'offices.' But the contents of these offices have, by all accounts, been lost.[36] Thus, for example, the copious archive of the Russian Kardecist General V.I. Felkner, which included regular accounts of seances and notes on manifestations, was entirely destroyed after his death. 'I did not preserve the manuscripts,' admitted the brother of the deceased, 'but simply burned all this useless rubbish, recognizing its contents to be the ravings of the mentally infirm.'[37] Pushkin's close friend P.V. Nashchokin destroyed his own spiritualist archive out of religious considerations.

Against this background, N.P. Vagner's little book *Nabliudeniia nad mediumizmom* (Observations on Mediumship, 1902) holds particular interest. Devoted to the history of a spiritualist circle, and written by a prominent participant in the movement, this book describes seances of the 1880s while casting light on the spiritualist gatherings of previous decades.

Between 1883 and 1887 the circle of Doctor Ivan Bibinov met regularly in St Petersburg. Its members belonged to the intelligentsia: doctors, scholars, literary types. The medium was N.D. Strablin (a pseudonym), a military man who possessed astonishing psychic powers. This was a 'writing circle' – that is, its aim was to receive written messages from 'higher' spirits, be they in prose or in verse. Sheets of paper bearing these messages would usually float down from above, in darkness, to be read and discussed by candlelight. The group's ideology was a variation on the Kardecist doctrine of communication with spirits of varying degrees of perfection. The 'spirit control' (a powerful spirit that organizes the appearance of other spirits at a seance and that defends the sitters from unclean forces) was John [Ioann] Damaskin, the spiritualist pseudonym for Doctor Bibinov's uncle, who had died at Polotsk.

The spirits present at the seances communicated the secrets of the kingdom of Abveka, the 'Spirit of Spirits.' Thus, one remorseful spirit sent the circle a description in verse of the afterlife:

Пред лицом Абвеки
Стою я в смущении
И плачу и жадно
Молю о прощении.
А гордые духи
Других измерений
Проходят, не слыша
Моих песнопений...
Внизу, подо мною
Отщепенцы мира
Безумные ищут
Инаго кумира.
Над мною сияет
Святыня в просторе,
Внизу, подо мною,
Греховное море.

Before great Abveka
I stand in confusion.
I cry and I beg,
I hunger for pardon.
The proud spirits pass
From other dimensions
And little they hear

Of my lamentations ...
Below, far below me,
The rebels of the world
Are seeking like madmen
Another false idol.
Above me there shines
The sacred in space,
Below, far below me,
The sea of man's sins.[38]

Other spirits, most of them representing deceased friends of the circle, courteously shared their wisdom in worldly affairs. Thus, the spirit of the former university doctor Uversky provided one woman with a prescription for an incipient abscess, and also wrote out 'in a firm and steady hand' the correct diagnosis of her husband's illness, advising him: 'Visit the doctors. Whoever reaches this diagnosis, let that man treat you. As proof, give your urine to be tested: it will contain many cells of epithelium.'[39]

The circle was also addressed by representatives of the 'negative powers,' bearing the pseudonyms Pug-Dog, Abramka, Beelzebub, and Tredyakovsky, as well as Khariton, Evil Katia, Pig-and-Piglets, Toad, Cock, Goat, Owl, and others. These 'infernal' and 'mischievous' spirits (in Kardec's terminology) sought to confuse the members of Bibinov's circle, giving them false information about the afterlife or simply mocking them. Vagner relates, in all seriousness, several instances of such spiritualistic hooliganism, dismissing out of hand any possible mystification on the part of the medium: 'Not even the most skilful, most gifted actor would have been able to impersonate successfully, for hours on end, all these individuals.'[40]

Be that as it may, there is no denying the theatrical and mystagogic nature of the Kardecist meetings.

Debate

The first debate in the Russian press about 'philosophical spiritualism' was held in 1864. The publication of Archpriest G. Debolsky's critical analysis of Kardecist doctrine in *Raduga* (The Rainbow)[41] was followed by a response from Apollon Boltin and extensive commentary to this response by the journal's editor, Byurger. Shortly afterwards, Boltin launched a journalistic campaign against materialism, publishing (first as an article, then as a separate pamphlet) his critique of I.M. Sechenov's *Reflexes of the Brain* (1863) – the manifesto of the new, 'nihilistic' epoch. Boltin declared the materialist and physiological understanding of psychic life to be mistaken and attacked his opponents' 'borrowing' and corruption of spiritualist terminology: 'How do you define the soul? [...] Why do you take your words from the vocabulary of the spiritualists? Why, for example, do you say *psychic life*, or *the soul is the organ of the brain*? From the spiritualist point of view, these expressions are precise and bear meaning; but from the materialist point of view they bear none, especially when you replace the word *soul* with *product of brain activity*, to which, in your view, it is equivalent.'[42]

In the second half of the 1860s, *spiritisme* was subjected to the sharpest censure in journals both secular and ecclesiastical. The cause of this heightened interest was the rapidly increasing popularity of Kardec's teachings and consequent fears that a new sect might evolve.[43] In 1869 the founder of this doctrine died (or passed over into the world of the spirits), and spiritualist circles were thick with recordings of his 'posthumous' prophecies of the imminent appearance of the Spirit of Truth (the Messiah) and the definitive transformation of humanity. 'In our midst [...] entire societies are occupied with the systematic study of the mysteries of the kingdom beyond the grave, with conversations with the long-deceased, and with similar nonsense,' *Vsemirnaia illiustratsiia* (Worldwide Illustration) noted bitterly in an article devoted to Kardec's life and death (the piece was accompanied by a portrait of the mystic bearing this caption: 'A Famous Spiritualist Charlatan').[44] Readers were informed of the efforts of spiritualists in St Petersburg to establish their own club as well as a journal similar to that of Kardec.[45]

Spiritualism came under fire from all sides: materialist, medical, scientific–rationalistic, moral, and Christian–mystical. Positivists on the left, such as V.V. Lesevich, perceived it as a dangerous phenomenon that testified to a serious social crisis and to the malady of the age.[46] The Church interpreted spiritualist zeal as 'modern sorcery' and a form of idolatry pernicious to the faithful (Filaret's letter, mentioned above, was reprinted in the 1860s). In his 'Sermon on the Perceptible and Spiritual Vision of Spirits' (1863), Bishop Ignaty (Brianchaninov) instructed: 'The general rule for all is to resist at every cost the attraction of phenomena from the Spirit world, and to acknowledge every such phenomenon as a grave temptation [...] It is a great calamity to engage with demons, to bear their imprint upon oneself, and even to submit oneself to their mere influence, which has a particular effect if it is drawn by man's own will.'[47] As models of moral fortitude, he recalled the examples of saints who had been tempted by demons.

The fullest theological critique of spiritualist teachings was contained in M. Lebedev's article, 'Spiritualists and Spiritualism,' published in *Khristianskoe chtenie* (Christian Reading) in 1866. Despite its Western roots, spiritualism was the fruit, in the author's view, 'of a common soil, it lives and breathes the atmosphere of society and of the age.' In the spiritualist project for a 'great moral revolution' in humanity, and in its search for 'palpable authorities' in the 'imaginary souls of the dead,' Lebedev found 'vulgar deception and self-blinding, the impudent mockery of everything sacred and redemptive.'[48] It was a 'false, self-styled "new religion,"' deprived of the mysteries of faith and appealing 'not to faith, but directly to knowledge.' Spiritualism bore no relation to Christian mysticism, for 'the essence of a miracle does not consist in the contradiction between arbitrary action and nature's laws, but in its expression of supernatural causality in harmony with nature.'[49]

The reasons for the popularity of spiritualism in Russian society, and the task of any effective struggle against this heresy, were discussed in a series of articles on spiritualism by Nikolai Leskov.[50] The theologians' fundamental error, Leskov argued, lay in their failure to take due account of the 'mystical side of the doctrine' in their efforts 'to render spiritualism vulgar in the eyes of the people.' Spiritualism might seem ludicrous and 'garrulous,' but it was in fact a fully serious phenomenon, with its own dogma (anti-Christian though it undeniably was) and its own mission and flock. Its success resided mainly in the universal, dominating 'urge to elevate and liberate the human personality from all that strikes it as remotely unjust or constricting.' Spiritualists appealed to the weak in faith through their social activities and good deeds. They

> build almshouses, take in abandoned children, run Christian schools, and concern themselves with the teaching therein of God's law [...] They build churches and martyr themselves for Orthodoxy in the south and north-west of Russia; they set the tone and direction for numerous endeavours and entire administrative fields; any and everywhere they harness ever-more proselytes who believe in independent morality, in our role as guests on the earth, in our unending path to complete perfection in a plural existence, in the necessity of unceasing concern for this perfection and in the completeness [*zakonchennost'*] of the fullest tolerance towards the manners of all those brought together for the short span of mortal life in a shared drawing-room.[51]

Leskov was convinced that the Russian clergy could succeed in its
struggle against spiritualism only by means of vigorous explanatory
activity, asceticism, and selflessness. But the Church demonstrated no
such behaviour; thus spiritualism flourished.

The enlightened theological view of spiritualism as an error and a
religious 'wobble' drew an irate response from N.I. Potulov, a writer
for the ultra-Orthodox *Domashniaia beseda* (Household Talk). In his
numerous articles on spiritualism, this admirer of the Catholic philosopher de Mirville affirmed that spiritualist phenomena were far from
being a ruse or a form of self-deceit. They were real, but they were produced not by the souls of the dead (as spiritualists thought), but by
devils. Spiritualism, Potulov thought, was an 'infernal doctrine,'
whose followers bore the 'vivid mark of the Antichrist.' The Antichrist
had yet to arrive, but the spiritualists were already busy preparing the
ground for his reign.[52] Characteristically, Potulov grouped the spiritualists with revolutionaries and nihilists – a theme picked up by Leskov
in his novel *Na Nozhakh* (At Daggers Drawn, 1870–1) and, many years
later, by Vladimir Solovyov (the Antichrist in the tract 'Three Conversations' is a devoted Spiritualist). Alluding to W.H. Dixon's *New America* (1867), Potulov described the meetings of the doctrine's adepts in
the West as infernal gatherings attended by spirits from hell, long-
haired men, and close-cropped women.[53]

Sample Case 2: The Problem of Identification

The question of how to test and identify representatives of the
'unknown force' that made itself known at seances was of crucial significance for spiritualists. Consider, by way of illustration, the case of
the famous lexicographer and writer Vladimir Dal', who developed
an enthusiasm for table divining in the 1850s. According to the memoirs of Nikolai Berg, Dal' would tell the story of how a spirit made
contact with him at a seance, taking the name of his friend, the
famous poet Vasily Zhukovsky (1783–1852).[54] Dal' told him: 'If you
truly are Zhukovsky's spirit, then tell us something which only two
people know: I and Zhukovsky!' 'Very well,' the spirit replied. 'In the
course of the journey of the Sovereign Heir (now our prosperously
ruling Tsar) through Orenburg in 1837, we met for the first time. You,
a still young and fervent dreamer, brought me a notebook full of
poems and requested my opinion: were they any good and had you
any poetic talent? After running my eyes over the poems, I said that
you would make a poor poet, that you should give it up and take up

prose!' That, according to Dal', was exactly what happened.[55] For Berg, the episode was a curious incident that illustrated the spiritualist enthusiasms of a distant time and the credulity of Dal'.

The incident was interpreted in a quite different manner in *Household Talk* by Potulov, that sworn adversary of the spiritualist heresy. Potulov and Dal' had been at school together[56] and had remained on friendly terms. In the course of one of their meetings, Dal' related how he had tested Zhukovsky's spirit. The spirit, he said, had given an accurate answer, though he had incorrectly named the station at which Zhukovsky had slighted his friend's poems. The medium, Dal' affirmed, could hardly have found out about this conversation from a third party, since he had not spoken of it to anyone, not even his wife. The story led Dal' and the Orthodox mystic Potulov to contrasting conclusions. According to Dal', the spirit's accurate reply testified to the fact that it really was the departed Zhukovsky. According to Potulov, the broadly accurate reply was evidence of a Satanic spell, for the evil spirits 'may have an excellent knowledge of all our secrets.' Dal''s experience of spiritualism thus came to serve as the arena for opposing mystical interpretations that had been introduced into public debate. Mystical doubts could only be resolved in this context by faith, not proof.

The Age of Experiments

Leskov felt that spiritualism's future lay in its 'philosophical-mystical' orientation. However, the successes of the natural sciences in the 1870s were a powerful tonic for the development of experimental (or Anglo-American) spiritualism, the aim of which was the scholarly investigation (rather than the religio-mystical interpretation) of spritualist phenomena: drops of water, raps, accordion playing, levitations, partial and full materializations, and so on. 'This isn't sectarianism, of course, like the new American church, and it isn't Kardec,' noted *Tserkovnyi vestnik* (The Church Herald) in an article of 1875 on spiritualist experiments in St Petersburg. The task of experimental spiritualism was different: 'to fill in existing gaps in our knowledge of natural science through the discovery of a new *natural* force.'[57] Spiritualist phenomena, according to this approach, were not miraculous. Rather, they were manifestations of those laws of nature that scientists had yet to uncover.

One tireless advocate of scientific and empirical spiritualism in Russia was the philosopher and translator Alexander Aksakov. In the early

1870s he attempted the scientific emancipation of spiritualism in Russia by bringing it into the context of contemporary arguments on psychology, the construction of the physical world, biological evolution, and the limits of human cognition. His translations into Russian of spiritualist classics by Robert Hare and William Crookes introduced a new discourse into the debate on mysterious phenomena: the reviewing of methodology, terminology, and technical tools used during experiments; references to scientific authorities and contemporary theoretical physics; detailed accounts of the data yielded by observation, in the correct sequence; and conclusions. If the seances of the Kardecists could be compared to theatrical performances, the experimental seances of the 1870s represented model laboratories.

At Aksakov's invitation, the 'king of mediums' Daniel Dunglas Home visited St Petersburg again in 1870 to give a lecture on mediumship, which prompted a few professors to organize a seance in a university building. Though it ended in failure, the seance stimulated widespread interest in the investigation of psycho-physical phenomena. In 1874, another medium, the Frenchman Camille Brédif, organized twenty-five seances in the capital, after which two professors at the university, by Aksakov's calculation, came to believe in the appearances of spirits. Society's interest in spiritualist experiments was also stimulated by the European *scandale* of 1874–5 generated by the spiritualist photographs of the French Kardecist Édouard Isidore Bouget.[58]

The press responded to empirical spiritualism just as harshly as it had to the philosophical variety (indeed, the two were often confused). In articles and feuilletons of the 1870s it was described not only as 'the greatest absurdity,' but also as a vivid illustration of various crisis-ridden historical, ideological, cultural, and religious processes in contemporary society: as 'mental apathy, fatigue caused by a series of fundamental reforms of our daily lives' (Markov); as 'passionate religious craving' (Rachinsky); and as sorrow for 'lost truth' (Dostoevsky). In 1876 the philosopher Nikolai Strakhov published an extensive critique of spiritualism as a basically positivist superstition (*Three Essays on Spiritualism*).[59] Leo Tolstoy, by his own account, intended to write an article on spiritualism.[60] Indeed, the stormy 'spiritualist season' of 1875 (discussed below) began with the publication (in the January issue of the *Russian Herald*) of the first part of *Anna Karenina*, in which the rationalist Tolstoy inveighed (through his hero, Levin) against spiritualist experiments in high society as activities contrary to the laws of nature, good sense, and morality: 'I consider [...] this attempt by the spiritualists to explain their miracles as the work of some new force to be a complete failure. They speak directly of spiritual power yet wish to subject it to material testing.'[61]

Conclusion

Modern spiritualism and related spiritualist doctrines became widespread in Russia on the eve of and after the Great Reforms of the 1860s and remained constantly within the field of vision of the cultural elite. Sometimes they were fiercely criticized and ridiculed by materialists and theologians; sometimes they were the objects of scientific interest, especially in the field of social psychology; sometimes they were a source of inspiration for idealist writers attempting to oppose the materialistic 'spirit of the time.' In response, the spiritualism of the 1850s through the 1870s resorted to positivist jargon and teleology, constantly proclaiming itself to be a new empirical science capable of solving the age-old debate about the material and spiritual origins of humankind and the world.

PART ONE

Table Talks: Seance as Cultural Metaphor

Друзья! Не знаете вы ада,
Сего пристанища умов,
Где ждет веселая награда
И пьяниц и сорвиголов.
Хоть вправду здесь живет 'лукавый',

Но здесь Гомер - любимец славы.

Здесь Пушкин, гениальный Росс,
В своем величии возрос
И снова нас дарит стихами.

Языков - в Бахусе, мой друг,
Увеселяет наш досуг
Высокосветлыми строфами.
Здесь нежный Гете и Шекспир

По-прежнему волнуют мир.

My friends! You know not hell,
That refuge for independent minds,
Where a cheerful reward
Is waiting for drunkards and madcaps.
Though it's true that the evil one lives here,
Here also resides Homer, glory's favorite;
Here Pushkin, a Russian of genius,
Rose up in grandeur
And presents us with his poems once again;
Here Iazykov, my friend in Bacchus,
Makes our leisure gay
With his lofty, radiant stanzas;
And here tender Goethe and Shakespeare
Still move the world as once they did

...

The Restless Spirit of Ivan Barkov, 'Hellish Poem'

1 Seance as Test, or, Russian Writers at a Spiritualist Rendezvous

Spiritualist phenomena are things that take place at seances, which are performed most often in the evenings, in the darkness, in the presence of special persons called mediums; these phenomena have among their common features a resemblance to so-called tricks, and therefore give the appearance of mystery, of uncommonness, of nonrepeatability under normal conditions.

D.I. Mendeleev, 'Public Lecture on Modern Spiritualism'

What is this? In half-light, half-darkness, people sit around a block of wood [*okolo dereva*], hold out their hands to it, and in a silence that is not only external but internal, as if in a silence of human reason, await a revelation of some kind, of someone, for something. (As Hosea says with shame on behalf of the God of Israel: My people consult with their wooden idol [*drevo*], 4:12). How does the wood [*drevo*] answer? The wood [*derevo*], of course, cannot understand the seekers and give appropriate answers to their questions. Who, then, through the wood, is responding to the seekers? It is impossible to say for sure, but should we not recall here something sure that was revealed to us regarding a certain tree, *the tree of knowledge,* through which a certain personage tempted, seduced, and destroyed mankind?

Father N.A. Sergievsky, 'Sermon at the Church of Moscow University, January 14, 1876'

May each tell, on the question of spiritualism, all that he has personally experienced, without resorting to any affectation, not masking his

motives. Then there will accumulate, at least, factual material, not tinged
by any onesidedness, which only complicates the matter.

P.N. Boborykin, 'Neither Backward nor Forward'

Introduction

On 1 April 1875 a renowned zoologist at St Petersburg University, Professor Nikolai Petrovich Vagner, published a letter, 'On the Subject of
Modern Spiritualism,' in *Vestnik Evropy* (Herald of Europe) enthusiastically describing the mediumistic phenomena he had heard and seen
at seances of the French medium Camille Brédif in 1874. These phenomena (rapping, sounds, partial materialization of spirits, and so
on), Vagner asserted, not only bore witness to the fact that life beyond
the grave was a reality but also opened new horizons for science,
which, he argued, should begin to study manifestations from the spiritual world.[1]

Vagner's letter drew an indignant reaction from journalists of both
the left and right camps, but was supported by another well-known
scholar, the chemist Alexander Mikhailovich Butlerov, who had long
been interested in Modern Spiritualism. On 6 May 1875, their famous
colleague Dmitry Ivanovich Mendeleev presented a lecture at a session
of the Physics Society of St Petersburg University about the urgency of
scientific examinations of so-called mediumistic (spiritualist) phenomena and suggested establishing a special scientific commission to
investigate them. Mendeleev and his colleagues regarded the promo-
tion of Modern Spiritualism by 'authoritative naturalists' as a violation
of scholarly ethics: Vagner and Butlerov were not presenting their
hypotheses in scientific societies, 'where analysis and verification of
new, still unknown facts take place, where an investigation is conducted and regulated with methods based in science,' but had
bypassed this route and appealed directly to society.[2] Mendeleev perceived as his mission the unmasking of modern superstition, the exorcism of spirits from the cathedral of science, and the attraction of
society – especially its youth – to the exploration of the *real* mysteries of
nature (the scientist was himself occupied at that time with problems
of meteorology).

In spite of Mendeleev's patently antispiritualist attitude, his opponents agreed to collaborate with his commission, which comprised
twelve scholars. In the 'interests of science,' the spiritualists first called

in two professional British mediums, the brothers Joseph and William Petty. Then, after the failure of experiments, they summoned an amateur English medium who worked under the pseudonym Madame St Claire.[3] The latter arrived in St Petersburg on 7 January 1876.

Throughout this time, in journals, salons, drawing rooms, and private correspondence, the controversy over Modern Spiritualism continued to grow. Seances had become a socially significant experience, and to take part in them was practically a ritual task for the modern thinking man, who sought to 'come to a conclusion' (or at least to 'form an impression') about mysterious phenomena.[4]

The basic questions in the debate about Modern Spiritualism were these: How are the observed phenomena produced? What is the force that moves the table? Is it of a physical or spiritual origin? In his lecture, Mendeleev identified six hypotheses representing the spectrum of interpretations then being discussed: organic (sounds, resembling ventriloquy, produced within the human body); mechanical (vibration of the table as the result of contact with a part of the body); animal-magnetic (the action of the 'nervous fluid'); hallucinatory (sensory impressions caused by the seance surroundings); spiritualist (the action of spirits); and, finally, the hypothesis of deception, of which Mendeleev was convinced from the very beginning.[5] It should be noted that the 'mystical' hypothesis against which the academic fought was not unified: the 'spirit hypothesis' (the action of souls of the dead) stood in opposition to the 'devil hypothesis' (the interference of unclean forces) espoused by the Church and some secular mystics.

Thus society was presented with a fascinating problem, one that anyone might try to solve using his or her own experience. It goes without saying that none of the hypotheses could persuade all sides. Hence a feeling of dissatisfaction and confusion emerged, and a certain intellectual fog enveloped the medium's table – a characteristic feeling for that positivist era.[6]

The spiritualist seance proved to be a hermeneutic trap in which not dead souls, but living people, were caught. In this sense, the numerous descriptions and interpretations of seances by contemporaries represented a *text*, one especially attractive (and convenient) for 'spectral analysis' of the intense intellectual and spiritual life of the 1870s, with its arguments about the soul and matter, the limits of cognition, natural and metaphysical methods, the psychological and physical-biological origins of man, realism and idealism, and so on. This 'spiritualist text,' which balanced scientific and supernatural interpretations of the observed phenomena, was interesting also to literary critics, inasmuch as it was a background (an ideological and esthetic medium) for many works written during this period, such as the 'strange tales' of Turgenev, the 'mystical anecdotes' of Leskov, and the 'fantastic' short stories of Dostoevsky.[7]

I have chosen to begin this Part with a discussion of one remarkable seance that took place during the 'spiritualist season' of 1875–6. I will treat this seance as a cross-section of various views on spiritualism that were being expressed by the writers Pyotr Boborykin, Nikolai Leskov, and (in greater detail) Fyodor Dostoevsky, who gathered one night in a drawing room for a seance that was to determine their attitude towards spiritism. Though I will examine the ways in wich the seance was contested and then elaborated on by each of the writers, I will focus primarily on the impact it had on Dostoevsky's experimental approach to investigating the depths of the human soul.[8] After introducing the major participants of the seance and discussing their attitudes towards Modern Spiritualism, I will review the course of this seance and discuss Dostoevsky's role in it. I will then consider Dostoevsky's account of spiritualist phenomena in the context of his fellow writers' responses. Finally, I will discuss the strange kinship and bitter rivalry between spiritualist practices and Dostoevsky's own artistic method. In later chapters I will expand on the ways in which the spiritualist (and, more widely, spiritual) theme was refracted in the works of some of the participants of this seance as well as several other authors of the Age of Realism.

Writers' Conference

On Friday, 13 February 1876, during Shrovetide, in the apartment of A.N. Aksakov at Nevsky Prospekt 6, a spiritualist seance was held under the guidance of Madame St Claire. The renowned writers Pyotr Dmitrievich Boborykin, Nikolai Semyonovich Leskov, and Fyodor Mikhailovich Dostoevsky took part, as well as the host and his spiritualist followers: professors Nikolai Petrovich Vagner and Alexander Mikhailovich Butlerov. Aksakov, Butlerov, and Vagner, who were constantly being criticized in journals, were extremely interested in the potentially sympathetic opinion of the influential literary men.[9] The writers, for their part, came to the seance not only with an interest in spiritualist phenomena, but also, in a sense, with a professional assignment: to attempt to express the position of the writers' guild with respect to this issue, which was so engrossing to society. This was essentially an attempt at a writers' conference – one that might contend with Mendeleev's scientific commission. In the 1870s fierce competition was entirely common among the different 'experts on the human soul' (in Dostoevsky's words) – theologians and philosophers, physiologists, spiritualists, and finally, writers.[10] The spiritualist seance proved to be a place where the interests and methods of these groups intersected.

I will now introduce in greater detail the participants of the 13 February seance and briefly characterize their attitudes towards spiritualism.

Madame Claire (or St Claire) was an English medium, recommended to Aksakov by the well-known advocate of Modern Spiritualism William Crookes.[11] Madame Claire's specialty consisted in demonstrating spiritual manifestations in daylight – specifically, 'levitation of a table and other objects with and without contact, changes in the weight of objects, rapping at the table, floor, and other parts of the room,' and 'spontaneous' sounds from an accordion. Her real name was Mary Marshall (neé Brodie; 1842–84), and she was a remarkable figure in the history of English spiritualism. Like a number of other female mediums of that era, she was also an actor (her stage name was St Claire). Her life story (unknown to the most of the Russian observers) merits a brief discussion. In the late 1850s, Mary Brodie secretly married her cousin Emmanuel Marshall. In the 1860s and early 1970s she gave seances together with her aunt and mother-in-law, the eminent London medium Mrs Marshall, and her husband, who participated as a 'drawing medium.' In the 1860s, reports about the Marshalls' seances regularly appeared in press, starting with a harsh critique of their activities as shameless hoaxes in an 1860 article in Charles Dickens's *All the Year Round* ('Modern Magic') and a sympathetic account of the seances published the same year in Thackeray's *Cornhill* ('More Than Science').[12] The Marshalls' seances were attended by many distinguished men of the time, including the naturalist Alfred Russel Wallace, the playwright Robert Bell, and the prominent Pre-Raphaelite ideologue William Michael Rossetti. In the mid-1870s, Mary Marshall received a large inheritance and left the profession of medium. She came to St Petersburg at the invitation of A.N. Aksakov, not from financial motives (she did not take money for her seances), but rather as a 'lover of truth, for its attainment.'[13]

Much was written about her in the Russian press, most of it derisive. According to Boborykin's description, Madame Claire was a middle-aged woman who looked more like an American than an Englishwoman[14] and was 'as if compressed, contained, [she] scarcely moved in her heavy silk dress with its large tail and vast skirt.' She had a 'low, wheezing' voice, spoke in 'domestic English jargon,' and did not shy from very strong language.[15] Seances with Madame Claire continued all through the winter of 1876. Mendeleev's commission considered the mediumistic phenomena that occurred in her presence to be fraudulent and suggested that the noises were produced by some spring (*pruzhinka*) hidden under the medium's skirt. The fact that Claire was a woman, however, prevented anyone from verifying this suspicion.[16]

A.N. Aksakov (1832–1902), a nephew of the famous writer and Slavophile S.T. Aksakov, was a philosopher and prominent figure in the international spiritualist movement. Mendeleev called him an 'apostle of spiritualism' and considered him responsible for the seduction of naive Russian sholars. In the local press he was called 'the great all-Russian priest [*zhrets*] of spiritualism.'[17] Aksakov was related (by his sister's marriage) to the great Anglo-American medium Daniel Dunglas Home.

Aksakov first became acquainted with table turning and took an interest in communication with spirits in the early 1850s in the home of the writer and lexicographer Vladimir Dal' in Nizhny Novgorod. In the second half of the 1860s, Aksakov translated several books by the Swedish theosophist and seer Emmanuel Swedenborg,[18] in whom he saw the herald of a new era of human knowledge. Earlier he had become interested in the spiritualist philosophy of Andrew Jackson Davis, who had played an important role in the American spiritual awakening. Aksakov had given his word that he would absorb himself in 'the history of spiritualism and the detailed exposition of its doctrine,'[19] but decided before long that it would be better to occupy himself with 'the simple logic of facts' than with philosophical speculation. He believed that 'the day will come when even in this field of study a universal truth will shine from the mass of accumulated knowledge, and will illuminate the science of man with a new light.' That day, however, was still far off, and accordingly, 'our work is to devote ourselves to the thankless job' of identifying and verifying mediumistic facts.[20] In other words, by the end of the 1870s Aksakov had 'subdued' his millenarist presentiments, which were entirely characteristic of early Modern Spiritualism, and become a supporter of the so-called scientific trend of this movement, whose goal was to authenticate mediumistic phenomena, apart from any dogma associated with them, by means of purely experimental methods.[21]

In 1871–2, Aksakov translated into Russian the seminal works of famous European scientists 'who have turned to Modern Spiritualism': the Englishman William Crookes's *Spiritualism and Science: Experimental Researches on the Psychic Force*, and the American Robert Hare's *Experimental Investigations of the Spirit Manifestations* (the latter translation was executed jointly with Vladimir Dal'). In 1874 he began to publish the monthy *Psychische Studien* in Leipzig, in which he regularly printed translations of important spiritualist works, accounts of the activities of various spiritualist societies, and information about the state of Modern Spiritualism in Russia.[22] Aksakov was associated with nearly all prominent spiritualists of the time, from Andrew Jackson Davis to Helene Blavatsky, and enjoyed considerable prestige in the Movement.[23]

In January 1876 Aksakov published in *Russkii Vestnik* (Russian Herald) the article 'Mediumism and Philosophy: Recollections of Moscow University Professor Yurkevich,' in which he described the attitude of the late philosopher (a fierce critic of materialistic doctrine) towards Modern Spiritualism.[24] According to Aksakov, Yurkevich considered the 'optimistic' Modern Spiritualism of the American seer Andrew Jackson Davis, the positivism of the Frenchman Auguste Comte, and the pessimism of the German Arthur Schopenhauer to be the three vectors of modern philosophy. Aksakov's article carried the public discussion of Modern Spiritualism into the philosophical sphere.

A.M. Butlerov (1828–86) was a prominent chemist, an academician of the Imperial Academy of Sciences (since 1874), and the creator of the theory of chemical structure (1861). He was introduced to spiritualist phenomena in 1869 by A.N. Aksakov, his wife's cousin. When Daniel Dunglas Home visited Russia he usually stayed in Butlerov's apartment. In November 1875, Butlerov published in *Russian Herald* his seminal article 'Mediumistic Phenomena,'[25] in which he asserted that the study of spiritual phenomena would 'illuminate psychophysiology with a new light' and introduce 'radical changes in our understanding of matter, of energy, and their interrelationships.'[26] Butlerov's works on mediumism represented a scientistic, physical trend in Modern Spiritualism, concerning, as they did, the problem of the existence of a spiritual essence of the physical world.[27] In the 1870s and 1880s, Butlerov waged a fierce polemical battle with the philosopher Nikolai Strakhov regarding mediumism, natural laws, and the fourth dimension. It was

Butlerov who introduced Modern Spiritualism to Vagner, who at first regarded the phenomena critically but, as I have already mentioned, later came to believe in their validity.

N.P. Vagner (1829–1907) was a zoologist, ardent evolutionist, and creator of the theory of pedogenesis (the larval reproduction of insects), as well as a children's writer under the pseudonym Kot Murlyka ('Kitty Cat'). One characteristic feature of his world view – a strange blend of the 'scientific religion' of Charles Darwin and the unbridled fantasy of Hans Christian Andersen and E.T.A. Hoffmann – was a belief in the material reality of the miraculous and the physical coexistence between the living and the dead in God's world. Thus in one of his stories from the early 1870s, 'Bozh'ia niva' (God Furrow), he portrayed the cemetery as a *living cemetery*, ready to reveal its secrets to the initiated.

Vagner came to believe in spirits in 1874 and dedicated the rest of his life to analysing and promoting 'psychic investigations.'[28] In a sensational letter to *Herald of Europe*, he described in detail his own conversion to spiritualist faith, thus becoming the first Russian materialist scholar to declare himself a disciple of this new doctrine. It was Vagner who brought Dostoevsky to the seance (at the latter's request).[29]

P.D. Boborykin (1836–1921) was a prolific writer and a supporter of the French positivism of Auguste Comte. In the mid-1870s he developed a reputation as a 'realist empiricist' with a strong interest in social psychology.[30] His literary agenda, which was close to the naturalism of Émile Zola, centred on the pursuit of an accurate depiction of reality in its sociological dimension, the identification of new tendencies in the social and spiritual life of society, and the objective description of modern mores, interests, and prejudices.[31] Boborykin displayed an interest in Modern Spiritualism as early as the 1860s. In his sensational novel *Zhertva vecherniaia* (Vespertine Sacrifice, 1868), he portrayed a St Petersburg spiritualist seance as seen through the eyes of the heroine. At first, spiritualism seems to her a silly and pitiable occupation of old maids, but before long she observes that at its heart lie feelings that she, a clever but disillusioned woman, is lacking – love and hope: 'Widows, mothers, daughters … cannot come to terms with the death of their husbands, fathers, sons. It is not in the least bit silly. For them it is indeed a consolation.'[32] Boborykin repeatedly addressed the theme of Modern Spiritualism in his articles, seeking to approach its phenomena from the viewpoint of an outside observer. In 1876 he attended three seances of Madame Claire and published a detailed account of them in *Sankt-Peterburgskie Vedomosti* (St Petersburg Gazette).[33]

N.S. Leskov (1831–95) was the well-known author of the novels *Nekuda* (No Way Out, 1864), *Na nozhakh* (At Daggers Drawn, 1870–1), and *Soboriane* (Cathedral Folk, 1872), and the stories 'Smekh i gore' (Laughter and Grief, 1871), 'Zapechatlennyi angel' (The Sealed Angel, 1873), and 'Ocharovannyi strannik' (The Enchanted Pilgrim, 1873). Leskov had a long-standing interest in spiritual phenomena dating back to the late 1860s, when he grew close to a circle of secular mystics who were at that time occupied with 'spiritualism, magnetism, divine inspirations, and the abuse of nihilists.'[34] At this point Leskov also became acquainted with the spiritualist doctrine of Allan Kardec. In his antispiritualist articles of 1869, Leskov critically pulled apart this teaching, pausing at length on the topics of 'independent morality' and the absence of an eternal hell, as well as pointing out the sectarian character of this new faith.[35] However, certain aspects of Kardecian *spiritisme* appealed to Leskov's mystical sense and literary interests: a belief in a spiritual world and in the manifestation of its invisible forces in the material world; the vision of death as the liberation of the soul from the material shell of the body; and the perspective that earthly life is a painful stage on the soul's path to perfection. The ambivalence of Leskov's position with respect to mystical spiritualism was especially noticeable in his antinihilist novel *At Daggers Drawn*. In it, together with a satirical portrayal of the French *spiritistes* and their cynical Russian imitators (the nihilists Glafira and Iosaf Vislenev), Leskov creates an image (on the basis of the pneumatology of Kardec's *Book of Spirits*) of the true *spiritiste* Svetozar Vladenovich Vodopianov – a mysterious character who appears at climactic moments in order to half-open the material curtain that conceals the spiritual teleology of the unfolding action. Leskov wasted no time writing an account of 13 February seance for *Grazhdanin* (Citizen), in which he (to Boborykin's displeasure) named the participants of the gathering.[36]

F.M. Dostoevsky (1821–81) had long been interested in spiritualist phenomena.[37] The writer attentively followed the controversy over Modern Spiritualism that was unfolding in the Russian press.[38] People whom he trusted (such as Vsevolod Solovyov and Apollon Maikov) would describe to him the amazing phenomena (rapping, levitation, and so forth) that they had observed in their own family seances.[39] In 'Modern Spiritualism: Something about Devils: The Extraordinary

Cleverness of Devils, If Only These Are Devils,' published in *A Writer's Diary* in January 1876, Dostoevsky portrayed Modern Spiritualism as a phenomenon that, while comical at first glance, was nonetheless deeply characteristic of this time of spiritual preoccupation, not to mention dangerous because of its implications – namely, its capacity to encourage vulgar materialism, to act as a surrogate for faith, to promote sectarianism, and to flirt with forces hostile to man.[40] In the ironic and paradoxical manner unique to him, Dostoevsky took the spiritualists' hypothesis to its logical conclusion: clever devils (and spirits, for Dostoevsky, are no more than devils) were trying to bring humanity to moral ruin. Modern Spiritualism, for Dostoevsky, was a Western, foreign phenomenon that had emerged from materialistic America and that threatened to create both a schism in educated Russian society and – if it should become widespread – sectarian unrest among the people.

Clearly, it was going to be difficult to develop a unified response to the spiritualist issue from such diverse positions.

The Incident

What, then, took place on 13 February 1876 in Aksakov's apartment? We find descriptions of the seance in three sources: the detailed 'factual' accounts of Leskov (29 February)[41] and Boborykin (16 March)[42] and Dostoevsky's April article about Modern Spiritualism (as well as his preparational materials for it) in his *Writer's Diary* (XXII:126–32). On the basis of these accounts I will attempt to reconstruct the course of the seance.

First, the medium Claire, using the English alphabet, which Aksakov recited, found out from the 'unseen presences' (*nezrimye deiateli*) that, of all the attendees at the seance, the 'most convenient for mediumistic intercourse' was Dostoevsky (the least suitable turned out to be Boborykin). The presences also indicated through rapping 'that this evening the table might be lifted into the air, that chosen dates and names might be guessed; that little bells placed under the table might ring; an accordion placed under the table might play; and that those present might be touched by the unseen presences.'[43]

For the first experiment, Dostoevsky wrote down seven names in French, marking one of them (his own) on a separate piece of paper, which he kept in his hand. Then he slowly drew his pencil along the collective list, and when he brought it to the chosen name, three affirmative knocks issued from the unseen presences. They had guessed correctly. Unfortunately, the same experiment, when carried out by Boborykin, did not come off. In the case of Leskov – again success. Then the attendees wrote down some dates, which the medium did not see. Dostoevsky chose 1849 (because it was the date of his exile, according to Leskov). The unseen presences answered correctly. In turn, the dates chosen by Boborykin and Leskov were incorrectly identified.[44]

Then the table turning began. According to Leskov, the table lifted quite high and stayed up for a long time. According to Boborykin, however, it was scarcely an instant. After this they proceeded to 'sound imitation' (*zvukopodrazhanie*). Butlerov, Boborykin, Dostoevsky, and Leskov 'made random figures on the table with an iron key and after a few instants these strokes and sounds were repeated with complete accuracy, but extremely quietly.'[45]

Then the sound of little bells came from under the table, but 'each time their sound was preceded by some quiet noise as if a kitten were moving the bells with its paws.'[46] To Leskov, however, the sound was 'clean and natural.'

Physical contact came next. Boborykin felt as though someone 'drew a finger along his leg, and also touched him slightly with the heel of a bare foot.' What (or who) this was remained unclear.

The experiment with the accordion only partly succeeded. In Aksakov's hand it produced a few sounds; in Dostoevsky's, it was silent. Presently the medium suggested to Dostoevsky that he put down the accordion and cover it with a handkerchief. He took out a handkerchief and, 'having dropped it under the table, held it by the tip at the surface of the table.' After a few moments he declared that someone was 'pulling aside' his handkerchief. Here, according to Leskov's testimony, 'a slight misunderstanding took place, the explanation of which ended our seance.'[47]

In his account of the seance, Boborykin discloses the nature of the misunderstanding. Dostoevsky had joked that he 'refused to account for such a phenomenon as anything but the dexterity of the medium.' Then, though 'it was said in such a way that, if Madame Claire had understood Russian, she would only have laughed at this perfectly harmless joke,' on hearing Dostoevsky's words translated into English, she for some reason 'instantly took offense, blushed (to whatever extent this was possible for her), her eyes began to flash,' and Boborykin 'quite clearly heard a violent phrase, in English, which plainly showed her anger.' The participants of the seance tried in vain to calm the medium. She 'stubbornly withdrew into her dignity, which no one had wounded, took her hands off the table,' and 'ceased all mediumistic participation.'[48] 'I made the medium angry,' observed Dostoevsky in his notebook (XXIV:150).

As we can see, the seance, which was characterized by ambiguous results, ended in a minor scandal, the initiator of which turned out to be the 'most suitable' participant from the point of view of the 'unseen presences' – Dostoevsky.

Three Visions

The general opinion of the writers who participated in the seance of 13 February was directed against the 'mocking' conclusions of Mendeleev, which the latter made haste to proclaim before the commission's work had been completed (in his public lecture in Solianoi Gorodok on 15 December 1875). Leskov, Boborykin, and Dostoevsky all acknowledged (to Mendeleev's displeasure) that some unexplained phenomena had taken place, but also agreed that their meaning and the means by which they had been produced had not been determined. They were also united in the conviction that the conclusions of the academic commission would not succeed in changing anyone's mind, insofar as the matter was one of faith and not of scientific truth. Nor did the writers accept the hypothesis of the spiritualists (to the displeasure of Vagner, Butlerov, and Aksakov). The title of a series of articles by Boborykin about spiritual seances, 'Neither Backward nor Forward,' conveyed the general feeling: dissatisfaction, frustration, and ambivalence.

Yet each of the writers who participated in the seance understood this ambivalence in his own way, according to his own convictions and aspirations, and as a result reacted in his own way to the 'wonders' that had taken place before his eyes, whether with mystical curiosity, rational scepticism, or religious fear.[49]

Leskov, clearly, was attracted at the seance by the opportunity to penetrate into the spiritual world and to communicate with the dead. It is known that the writer believed in providential coincidences, omens, and visions. He took the spiritual manifestations at Aksakov's very seriously and, as Boborykin indicates, even somewhat exaggerated their scale afterwards. It is also revealing that in his account, Leskov noted that the 'unseen presences' immediately guessed the chosen name of his recently deceased friend, 'Michel.'[50] Leskov's letter to *Citizen* concluded with a characteristic declaration: 'Not being a spiritist and to the utmost desiring that the investigation of unusual phenomena of this type be conducted with the most precise critical methods, I consider it a responsibility to speak about that to which I was witness.'[51] Later he repeatedly returned to the theme of spiritualist phenomena in his work, regarding them as hints that there existed a secret life of the spirit, and contrasting vulgar materialistic spiritualism (*spiritizm*) with true spiritualism (*spiritualizm*), which was based on deep moral feeling and a belief in the final triumph of the soul over impotent substance.[52]

For the 'empiricist' Boborykin, the seance was interesting first and foremost from the sociological and psychological perspectives. His attention was focused on the medium: on her appearance and aspects of her national character – in a word, on the *'habitus* of this mediumistic figure.' In his essays on the seances of Madame Claire, Boborykin, following his positivist agenda, portrayed a typology (*tipologiia*) of spiritualists and discussed the masculine and feminine varieties of the Russian adepts of this doctrine, as well as the reasons underlying the spiritualist mania in the civilized world. For this naturalist writer, the seance was attractive as a place where the material world ended and where socially and psychologically motivated fantasies began. At the same time, Boborykin emphasized the impossibility, using available empirical methods, for science or external observation to 'arrive at the absolute truth' about what had been seen (one could nor, for example, ask the lady to undress in order to ascertain whether she was concealing any 'devices').[53]

Dostoevsky clearly had a very different perspective. As mentioned earlier, he dedicated a caustic article to Modern Spiritualism in his January *Diary.* Not going so far as to attempt a detailed analysis of this 'seriocomic and deeply ambivalent' article,[54] I will at least note that Dostoevsky principally referred to the figures behind seances, in accordance with Orthodox beliefs concerning communication with the other world, as devils (in contrast to Leskov, who took the hypothesis about souls of the dead seriously!).[55] In the Orthodox tradition, demons have always been vanquished through defiant mockery and rudeness by the tempted towards the tempter, the purpose being to unmask his devilish tricks. It is clear that the joking tone of Dostoevsky's article concealed a religious–mystical position:[56] if these phenomena were real, then they were produced by enemies of the human race who were driving society to schism, religious wars, disbelief, and, as a consequence the reign of the Antichrist.[57] In other words, Dostoevsky saw in Modern Spiritualism's vogue a sign of the approaching end – the sorcery of the Antichrist. At the same time – as a man of the secular nineteenth century – Dostoevsky had doubts about the reality of these phenomena and, it follows, their origins ('If Only These Are Devils'). The article about devils in the January edition of his diary represented a peculiar fantastical extravaganza that disguised his metaphysical doubt and terror.[58] The ambivalence of Dostoevsky's position was noted by critics. A.M. Skabichevsky wrote in a review of the January *Diary* that the reader could not determine 'who is before you – whether he's a mystic pretending to be a skeptic, or a skeptic pretending to be a mystic' (XXII:295).[59]

The January article on devils offered, so to speak, a literary and theoretical examination of this unresolved question. It seems that Dostoevsky went to the February seance in order to verify his conjectures with personal experience. Instead of fleeing from temptation (or from the utter foolishness of contemporaries who had been taken in – if it indeed was all a matter of deception), he had willingly exposed himself to it (and later, despite the insistent advice of Konstantin Petrovich Pobedonostsev not to write about this seance, he printed an article on it in the *Diary*). It would not be an exaggeration to say that the spiritualist seance was for Dostoevsky a psychological and metaphysical experiment, a test of his own beliefs and doubts.

Theatre of the Soul

On a symbolic level, the seance recalls a medieval mystery play insofar as it acts as a boundary zone where revelations, sorcery, and science, the material and spiritual worlds, life and death, belief and disbelief collide. In this context the liminal experience of the seance participant is related to the experience of the dying or condemned man (it is interesting that the date which Dostoevsky thought of in order to test the devils [1849] could be interpreted not only as the year of his exile but also as the year of his mock execution). In the article 'Just a Bit More about Spiritualism,' in the April issue of his *Diary*, the writer explained how one result of this moral experiment was his discovery of the 'law of disbelief.' I will allow myself to quote at length from this article:

> I think that whoever wants to put his faith in spiritualism will not be
> stopped by lectures or even by entire commissions, while those who do

not believe, at least if they truly do not want to believe, will not be swayed by anything. That was precisely the conviction I took away from the February seance at Aksakov's; it was, at least, my first strong impression then. Up to that time I had simply rejected spiritualism, i.e., in essence I was perturbed only by the mystical sense of its doctrine. (I was never able completely to reject spiritualist phenomena, with which I had had some acquaintance even before the seance with the medium, nor can I now – especially now – after having read the report of the Scientific Commission on Spiritualism.) But after that remarkable seance I suddenly surmised – or rather, I suddenly discovered – not only that I do not believe in spiritualism but that I haven't the least wish to believe in it, so that there is no evidence that will ever cause me to change my views. That is what I took away from the seance and later came to understand. And, I confess, this impression was almost gratifying because I had been a little apprehensive on my way to the seance. I might add that this is not merely a personal matter: I think there is something that applies to us all in this observation of mine. I have a sense of some special law of human nature, common to all and pertaining specifically to faith and disbelief in general. I somehow came to understand then – specifically through this experience, specifically through this seance – what power disbelief can uncover and develop within you at a given moment, absolutely despite your own will, although it may be in accordance with your secret desire … The same thing is probably true of faith. That's what I wanted to talk about. (XXII:127–8)[60]

This commentary was preceded by a more concise version in Dostoevsky's notebook:

Observation about disbelief until the seance at Vagner's, the table went 5 times, why B., and sufficient for disbelief. I began to think about this, although ½ came true […] And why didn't the other cases come true. *Law of a different belief in religion.* If only in miracles, but so as not to believe. Christ fulfils the moral state of the soul. Thomas, fakirs, miracles, tricks, the bird has flown – tricks! *The guarantee of morality – there's something to believe in.* One can't base miracles on anything. *The law of belief and disbelief.* (XXIII:234–5)[61]

Religious firmness, based on moral conviction (later the theme of Alyosha Karamazov) and not on miracles (Ivan's and the Grand Inquisitor's criterion), acts here as a means against temptation by spiritualist evidence.[62] It is not without reason that the image of the doubting apostle Thomas[63] repeatedly appears in Dostoevsky's notes about Modern Spiritualism, from which, in turn, he develops his quintessential discussion of realism and idealism in *The Brothers Karamazov*. Note, for instance, the following arguments from the writer's notebooks: 'Mathematical belief is the hardest to convince someone of. Thomas believed because he wanted to believe. I didn't want to believe and did not believe. The raps [...] did not act on my heart, just as the sound under the table did not [...] and so on (I must test it again). But if only I would want to believe, it would be a different matter. I, however, did not see supreme mysteries. The fakir is not solemnity and childishness of miracles' (XXIV:161).[64]

It is notable, however, that Dostoevsky did not deny the phenomena themselves. Though he wrote of how the rapping 'did not act' on his heart, he emphasized that he 'must test it again,' and he allowed that, perhaps, he had not yet seen the major wonders (that is, he had not tested himself 'completely').

Dostoevsky's friend, the writer and spiritualist Varvara Ivanovna Pribytkova, had every reason to say that 'something drew him to that unloved question, to which he undoubtedly attached a very serious significance.' In spiritualist 'events he did not believe, although he wanted to believe,' and Modern Spiritualism 'provoked, and at the same time attracted him.'[65] Pribytkova explained the ambivalence of Dostoevsky's attitude towards spiritualist phenomena as 'an involuntary awareness of their important significance for mankind in its present state, when materialism reigns everywhere.'[66]

If this is the case, then Dostoevsky evidently understood Modern Spiritualism's 'significance for mankind' differently than Pribytkova. The ontological question that he tried to resolve with the help of his personal experience was the infamous one about devils – that is, about the physical reality of evil. The spiritualist seance was the best place in the modern civilized world for one to verify this hypothesis under experimental conditions.[67] It is remarkable that in his notebooks Dostoevsky constantly returned to the theme of demons, which was so important for his novel (e.g., Father Ferapont's demons, the nightmares of Liza and Ivan). A few examples include 'Apropos of Modern Spiritualism. The seance of February 13. *Disgust for devils*. Fakirs. A miracle, a secret. The Masons'; '*I least of all believe in devils*'; '*But I don't want to believe in devils*: that would be too stupid and too crude. (The bells, a fact, as if nonexistent)'; and 'I could never imagine Satan' (XXIV:96, 97; emphasis added).

Whatever Dostoevsky wrote about the universal law of disbelief that he discovered at the seance, his imagination and mystical sense oscillated between acknowledgment and denial of the phenomenon – that is, between the existence and non-existence of spirits hostile to man. (At the same time, he completely rejected the 'mystical doctrine' of the spiritualists.) In order to escape from the paralyzing doubt and fear, he found it necessary to be rude to the medium (and through her, to the 'devil') and to 'disrupt the séance.' And that is just what he did.

It is notable that the writer later compared this spiritualist collision with the poetics of Alexander Pushkin's 'Queen of Spades' (1833). Thus, in his letter to Yu.F. Abaza of 15 June 1880, he wrote: 'And you believe that Germann really had a vision, one specifically conforming to his worldview, and meanwhile at the end of the story, that is when you have read it through, you do not know what to think: whether the vision came from Germann's nature or whether he really was one of those who are in contact with another world, one of evil spirits hostile to humanity. (N.B. Spiritualism and its doctrine). That's art for you!'[68]

The structuralist Tsvetan Todorov classified such oscillation in a literary work between natural and mystical motivations as 'fantastic.'[69] Meanwhile Dostoevsky did not confine his interpretation of 'The Queen of Spades' to the artistic sphere. Based on his experience, he compared the 'fantastic' poetics of the Pushkin tale with real social practice, literary conflict with metaphysical conflict, and aesthetic experience with mystical experience. The choice of the Pushkin tale for such a comparison was more than successful. The issue was not simply that the latter, like the spiritualist seance, was constructed like a hermeneutic trap:[70] is it a fairy tale? a deceit? a joke? mysticism? I propose that the author of *The Brothers Karamazov* read this tale precisely as a depiction of insoluble spiritual doubt and dreaded what he himself would experience (i.e., wanted to experience) at the seance. One can say that for Dostoevsky, the seance table was a modern analogue of the card table of the Romantic era: a place for testing oneself in the presence of unknown and hostile forces.[71]

It is notable that, as early as the day after his letter to Abaza, Dostoevsky turned to work on the chapter 'The Devil. Ivan's Nightmare,' in which, I suggest, he synthesized his notions of Modern Spiritualism as a temptation, and which he structured on the principle of the seance, during which (borrowing Dostoevsky's words) the fantastic connected with reality so closely that the observer (here Ivan and the reader) *almost* believed in it.[72]

I will venture several conclusions. We can understand Dostoevsky's position better if we compare it with various conflicting attitudes towards spiritualist phenomena that were expressed in the 1870s. Characteristically, Dostoevsky neither agreed nor disagreed completely with any of the contemporary hypotheses. Instead, from a confusing spiritualist controversy of his time, he drew his paradoxical vision of seances as psychological, ideological, and religious tests. He certainly did not approach the seance in the spiritualists' way – that is, as a place of intersection with another (supra-material) world that made its physical presence known through 'intelligent' manifestations. Nevertheless, he was fascinated with the spiritualists' idea of psychological experiment and enthusiastically used scientific terminology to describe the spiritual and moral processes he observed. He ridiculed Mendeleev's rationalistic attitude towards spiritualist seances. Yet at the same time he agreed with the scientist that mediums like Mrs Claire were charlatans. He did not see the seance through Boborykin's lens as a mere social and psychological phenomenon that exposed contemporary manias in their strangest and most extreme forms. Nevertheless, Boborykin's social psychologism appealed to Dostoevsky's perception of the seance as the place where the contemporary man reveals his cultural and moral ills. Unlike Leskov, Dostoevsky did not see the seance as a symbolic drawing room in which we gather and wait for an invitation to another vast and radiant room. Even so, he felt that a profound spiritual mystery was hidden there. Like antispiritualist priests and mystics of his day, he called the 'unseen presences' devils rather than souls. Nevertheless, he never spoke of these devils as material agents of evil.

All in all, I contend that Dostoevsky perceived the seance as the quintessential staging ground for the ideological and spiritual battle that he repeatedly depicted in his works.[73] For him, these were not the external entities making their presence known, but the soul of man testing itself and uncovering its doubts, contradictions, and dark secrets. In other words, as a result of personal experience Dostoevsky concluded that the true seance (a modern scientific and mystical play) is *inside* us. In turn, the true medium turns out to be the author who, through the painful and spiritually dangerous act of writing, 'materializes' (objectifies, verbalizes) in his work the 'unknown forces' of man's inner world. In fact, it is the writing desk, rather than the levitating spiritualist's table, that serves as the true means of communication with the unknown. In a word, for Dostoevsky, the spiritualist seance became a metaphor for the writing process. The author's riposte to the spiritualist controversy of his day might thus be called *literary* rather than scientific or mystical *spiritualism*: 'That's art for you!'[74]

Epilogue

What happened after the February seance? Madame St Claire, outraged by the attitude of the members of the commission towards her, quickly left St Petersburg. She took over a little theatre in Camden Town and became an actress. She failed, since, as a chronicler of London theatrical history poignantly put it, she was 'more of a spiritualistic medium than an actress,' so if the spirits 'had advised her to try her luck on the stage, it was bad advice.'[75] In 1881 her theatre burned down and she resumed her mediumistic practice. She died in 1884 at the age of forty-two.

Mendeleev published a report on the work of the commission in the newspaper *Golos* (Voice) that declared Modern Spiritualism to be superstition and deception. Vagner and Butlerov, naturally, did not agree with this verdict,[76] and Aksakov proudly noted that the twelve 'apostles of science' were unable to discredit the doctrine of 'the eternal existence of the spirit' and 'the infiniteness of forms of existence in the visible world and the world that is invisible to us.'[77] Boborykin sarcastically noted that 'the commission has not at all convinced us [...] that spiritualist doctrine is superstition,' for 'we knew this even without it.'[78] Leskov signed a collective protest against Mendeleev's hasty conclusions, which was published in *St Petersburg Gazette* and other papers.[79] Dostoevsky ridiculed the work of Mendeleev's commission in *A Writer's Diary*[80] and continued his strained relationship with the spiritualists. Finally, in 1881, after the death of Dostoevsky, Vagner requested of his widow permission to summon the soul of the deceased and learn whether he had changed his attitude towards spiritualism:

> For me it is quite important to know whether his views have changed there, in the other world, where the thirst for truth is quenched. I urgently would like to know if he looks upon the business of Modern Spiritualism the same way as he did here. Does he see in it only one, negative side, or does he acknowledge its beneficial value and its divine origin? [...] That is why I would like to hear the response of Fyodor Mikhailovich from

that world. – If a man who so harshly condemned Modern Spiritualism during his life can take away that condemnation, it would remove doubt from my soul and my acts – what more could I want?![81]

Thus the posthumous opinion of the author, who during his life condemned the mystical doctrine of the spiritualists, became essential for the enthusiastic spiritualist in order to put to rest his doubts concerning the benign character of spiritualist contact.[82] However, Anna Grigor'evna did not give Vagner permission to summon the spirit that was so dear to her.[83]

To quote Karamzin, perhaps by now they have become reconciled.

2 Russian Glubbdubdrib: The Shade of False Dimitry and Russian Historical Imagination in the Age of Realism

A mask was placed on the dead Dimitry's chest, and a pipe [*dudka*] stuffed in his mouth. For two days Muscovites swore over his body, pricked it and sullied it with all sorts of filth, then on Monday they took it the poor house (a cemetery for the poor and for those without family) and threw it into a pit where those who had frozen or drunk themselves to death were piled up. But suddenly a rumour spread through Moscow that the dead man was walking; then they dug up the body again, carried it beyond the Serpukhov gates, burnt it, poured the ashes into a cannon and shot them out in the direction from which self-proclaimed Dimitry had arrived in Moscow.

N.I. Kostomarov, 'The Self-Proclaimed Dimitry'

They summoned the Tsarevich Dmitry,
The so-called Pretender.
They asked him whose son he was.
He answered: That's my business.
They objected: No, not just yours!
Then he confessed honestly and simply:
I don't know!

E. Shvarts, 'One More Spiritualist Seance'

Introduction

At the very peak of the 'spiritualist season' of 1875–6, the ultraconservative publicist Prince Vladimir Petrovich Meshchersky (1839–1914), grandson of the historian N.M. Karamzin, published a fresh chapter of his satirical novel *Tainy sovremennogo Peterburga* (Secrets of Today's St Petersburg) in his own journal, *The Citizen*. The chapter was titled 'A Contemporary Historian' and described a discovery of 'historical Spiritualism.' In it, the historian Lyubomirov, who lives on the St Petersburg Side, tells the narrator that he has established contact with the souls of various historical figures and, on the basis of their testimony, can now affirm the correctness of his own hypotheses. '"Come to me at night some time," he all but whispered to me […], "that's when I talk to the spirits."' Lyubomirov reveals that he had been visited the previous night by a certain 'old man of the Godunov age.' They had spent three hours together, during which Lyubomirov read to him his most recent article on *Boris Godunov*:

> The Tsarevich Dimitry was never killed – I'm right; he, *he* told me this, do you see? It's the live testimony of a contemporary, not some dead servile chronicle. Now that's history, eh? *Genuine history!* – a historical medium, a speaking spirit, the triumphant critique of the historian's pure reason. Before, it was historians who wrote. But I, I write by intuition, by the intuition of spirits […] You know, I get all sorts of spirits, there was even one from the time of the Ryurik. Come by at night, come, I'll enlighten you, I feel sorry for you. But just read what I've written first, or you won't understand my conversation with the spirits![1]

Such, the storyteller summarizes, is the 'contemporary Russian historian,' trusting in direct facts and not calcified opinions.

Taking my cue from Meshchersky's parody, I will devote this chapter to the seemingly paradoxical juxtaposition of historian and spiritualist in the context of Russian culture of the Age of Realism. I will address the attempts of Russian historians, writers, and above all dramatists of the 1860s to 'materialize' the shades of the past, who were called on to provide answers to the most troubling questions of the time. My focus will be on the shade of the False Dimitry, which deeply affected the Russian historical imagination in the 1860s and 1870s.

Historical Spiritualism

The figure of the historical medium, who revealed the secrets of the past by interrogating great historical individuals and their contemporaries in the presence of witnesses (seance participants), was not

Meshchersky's invention. In America since the early 1850s, and later in Europe, contact had been sought with historical figures, who often disclosed the secrets of their time and the dark corners of their biographies. Each country had its cherished shades: in America – Washington and Franklin; in France – Charlemagne, Louis XIV, and Napoleon; in England – Cromwell. The shades summoned most often in Russia were those of Peter the Great and Ivan the Terrible. The latter, according to a contemporary witness, would appear in various drawing rooms simultaneously in the late 1860s, 'announcing his presence through table-rapping or the medium's empty chatter.'[2]

Stepping back, one sees that contacts with great historical figures of the past were especially popular at times of historical crisis. Victor Hugo, during his exile on the island of Jersey, appealed repeatedly to the spirits of Robespierre, Marat, Chenier, and Napoleon. During the Crimean War, Fyodor Tyutchev turned to spirits for answers to the historiosophical questions that troubled him. Ordinary people of past ages also made themselves known; from the 1870s onwards, they were believed to make actual physical appearances at seances. Among them was the famous spirit Katie King, daughter of the seventeenth-century Caribbean pirate Henry Morgan.[3] Historical spiritualism knew no geographical borders. Thus, American mediums made contact with historical personalities from distant Russia: the strangled Tsar, Paul I, gave a striking description of his death to the American 'musical medium' Jesse Shepard (Francis Grierson), while Sofia Perovsky, executed as a terrorist for assassinating Tsar Alexander II in 1881, spoke about her lofty spiritual mission.[4]

'Historical' spiritualism parodied some essential features of realist interpretations of history in the second half of the nineteenth century: trust in the historian as a professional medium who receives 'signals' from the past; the desire to employ positive science to solve the riddles of history; empiricism; and the secularization and democratization of the past, which should be accessible to all. Historians of those times called to mind Lemuel Gulliver, who, on the proto-spiritualist island of sorcerers, Glubbdubdrib, entered into direct contact with illustrious historical figures and learned from them that the past was not as it had been described in the classic accounts. In eliding spiritualism with the new historical method that was founded on a critical reinterpretation of old theories by an appeal to concrete facts (above all, to the data of archaeology and ethnography), Meshchersky was making an astute polemical move.

A Contemporary Russian Historian

Meshchersky's 'spiritualist' historian Lyubomirov is an obvious parody of the populist historian Nikolai Ivanovich Kostomarov (1817–85), who dedicated many years of research to the Time of Troubles and to the riddle of the identity of the first pretender.[5] Kostomarov was renowned for his critical attitude towards official historiography, wich idealized figures 'sacred to the heart of every Russian.'[6] In the words of the influential critic Nikolai Dobrolyubov, his revisionist studies shook 'the entire historical edifice erected by Mr [Mikhail] Pogodin with the help of Slavic-Russian mysticism.'[7]

Kostomarov waged a polemical battle with the Slavophile Pogodin throughout the 1860s and 1870s. Pogodin was especially riled by Kostomarov's demythologization of such national heroes as the Grand Prince Dimitry Donskoy, victor over the Mongol khan Mamai; the merchant Kozma Minin, leader of a people's militia during the Times of Troubles; and the peasant Ivan Susanin, saviour of the first Romanov.[8]

The caricature of Kostomarov by the monarchist Meshchersky appears to have been linked to a particular episode in this dispute. In his article 'On the Personality [*lichnost'*] of the Time of Troubles,' published in 1871 in the July issue of *Herald of Europe*, Kostomarov critiqued the well-known story of Kozma Minin's dream vision of St Sergius of Radonezh, in which the saint summoned the Russian people to fight against the Poles. Minin, in Kostomarov's view, was a 'subtle and cunning' man, not averse to playing the part of 'theatrical prophet' to achieve his aims. It was in order to galvanize the people in the great task of saving the Russian land that Minin, according to Kostomarov, thought up his wondrous vision. The historian based his conclusion on a reference in the chronicles of one of Minin's rivals, the scrivener Birkin, who accused the visionary of lying. 'Be silent!' Minin told him, and then threatened to tell the Orthodox world all he knew about Birkin. This appeal to the voice of an ordinary contemporary drew the fury of Pogodin, who published his reply in Meshchersky's *Citizen* in January 1873:

> If Mr Kostomarov himself [...] had seen St Sergius in his sleep, then I would not have hesitated to believe him. But were he to have claimed that St Sergius had patted him on the head on that occasion, then I, a sinner, must admit that I would have had my doubts, as Birkin did. *But Mr Kostomarov's dreams, if they happened, are of no concern to us. What matters is the*

fact that he sees the protagonists of Russian history in reality, then judges of them as if in a dream – and that is something I feel duty-bound to demonstrate before his obedient readers.[9]

Pogodin is clearly alluding here to Kostomarov's biographies of historical personalities, published in the 1860s and 1870s. In 1873, Kostomarov began publication of his collections, *Russian History through the Lives of Its Major Figures*,[10] in which he depicted an entire gallery of historical individuals. According to A. Markevich, 'delving deeply into the past with his intellect, and almost becoming part of it, he recreated it in his work in such vivid colours, in such pellucid images, that it drew the reader in and etched its features indelibly on his mind.'[11] The third collection of *Lives*, published in 1874, included articles on Boris Godunov and the first False Dimitry that drew a significant response in society.[12] Meshchersky undoubtedly had these articles in mind when he wrote his caricature of Kostomarov.

The official version of the history of the Pretender ran as follows. In 1601, during the reign of Boris Godunov, a young man appeared in Poland claiming to be the miraculously preserved tsarevich Dimitry, son of Ivan the Terrible. The 'Tsarevich' accused Godunov of usurping power and led a Polish and Cossack army on Moscow. Godunov's government declared him a pretender, and the Church excommunicated him and identified him as the fugitive monk Grigory (Grishka) Otrep'ev. In 1605, Godunov unexpectedly died. The False Dimitry overthrew Godunov's son and became Tsar. He plotted (according to the official version) the conversion of Moscow to Catholicism. In 1606 he fell victim to the popular revolt led by Prince Vasily Shuisky and his ashes were scattered on the wind. On becoming Tsar, Shuisky canonized the Tsarevich Dimitry, murdered in 1591, and reverted to Godunov's version of the identity of the Pretender as the fugitive monk Otrep'ev. The anathema on Grishka would not be lifted until the reign of Alexander II.

Kostomarov's position marked a fundamental break with this official version. In his opinion, the man who destroyed the House of Boris and governed for a whole year in Moscow was not the fugitive monk Otrep'ev. 'The question of the identity of this mysterious man has occupied many minds and has remained unresolved to this day,' the historian wrote.[13] Though 'his behaviour was such that he could be taken for the real Dimitry,' weighty arguments existed to suggest that he was not. Kostomarov examined various hypotheses to explain who the man was and whose interests he served, but then concluded that his identity could not be established with any scholarly certainty.[14]

In the context of Kostomarov's historical 'portraits,' Dimitry stands in obvious contrast to the tyrant Tsars – to his 'father' Ivan the Terrible and to his 'murderer' Boris Godunov (to whom Kostomarov felt a deep antipathy). Kostomarov's Dimitry is democratic, sincere, kind, chivalrous, enlightened, and thoroughly well intentioned. He strives to overcome Muscovy's cultural and economic isolation, encourages freedom of trade, defends freedom of conscience in his state, and – despite widespread assumptions to the contrary – has no plans at all to convert his people to Catholicism. Dimitry transforms the boyar Duma into a senate and attends it himself, keeping abreast of all the issues. He explains to the boyars the need to provide education for the people, and he tries to convince them to travel around Europe and read books. Being an active man, he is ill disposed to monks and promises to transfer part of their property to the people. He dreams about a great war with Turkey and the liberation of Constantinople. He participates in military preparations and willingly engages in simple work. In other words, Kostomarov's Dimitry recalls Peter the Great. At the same time, the historian notes, various failings brought Dimitry to his tragic end: his arrogance, his lack of respect for the customs and superstitions of his contemporaries, and his inability to restrain his passions.

'In the person of Kostomarov,' wrote his biographer, 'intellectual historian and artist were happily combined – and this guaranteed him not only a place in the first rank of Russian historians, but also the greatest popularity among the reading public.'[15] Kostomarov had created an artistic portrait of a historical figure that was based on a critical, scholarly analysis of diverse sources and that drew on a wide range of ethnographic material.[16] It was precisely this method that Meshchersky parodied with his spiritualist analogy: the historian ended up resembling a visionary spiritualist, one who finds his conjectures affirmed in the 'living testimony' of corpses. This parody can lead us towards more general considerations suggested by this parody regarding the correspondences between spiritualism and the historical imagination in the 1860s and 1870s.

'Real History'

The reformist 1860s witnessed the flowering of historical scholarship in Russia.[17] The trend towards Romantic historiography, which had been heavily influenced by idealist philosophy, was being replaced by a 'positive' science of the past that sought to adapt scientific methodology and that responded to the social problems of the day. The historian–scholar began to be viewed by society as a figure of authority – a professional connoisseur and interpreter of the past, which contained the 'key' to understanding the present. As Lionel Gossman writes: 'In the course of the 19th century historians withdrew more and more to the university, to be followed by historians of literature and literary critics; and thus history, like literary scholarship, passed from the hands of the poet and man of letters into those of the professor.'[18] Andrew Baruch Wachtel, who cites these words in his book *An Obsession with History: Russian Writers Confront the Past*, rightly notes that this process developed more slowly in Russia and, most important, that Russian writers never abandoned their claims to be competing with historians in the depiction and interpretation of history.[19] Tolstoy's *War and Peace* is perhaps the most vivid illustration of this pattern.[20]

Historians, for their part, constantly encroached on the territory of literature. Thus, in addition to his historical works, which were often structured like artistic texts, Kostomarov wrote literary works in various genres, basing them on his scholarly research.[21]

Historian–littérateurs and writer–historians of the 1860s all shared a zeal for the scientific reconstruction, materialization, and 'visualization' of the past. The idiosyncratic transferral of people and events from the past into the present served a dual purpose: (1) to establish historical truth through the painstaking collection and thorough analysis of 'facts' (i.e., what had actually happened before being obscured by Romantic myth) and (2) to provide scholarly explanations of the true state of affairs and historical predictions on the basis of a precise knowledge of the past, an understanding of the spirit of the people, and the laws of history.[22] The historian of the 1860s was not (yet) an ivory-tower specialist, but a sort of social medium who used his science to summon both the shades of eminent ancestors and the spirits of the ordinary people of the past. This new role differed fundamentally from Romantic notions of the historian (from Novalis to Gogol) as a poet and visionary who holds up entire historical epochs to the light of his imagination.[23]

If the phantasmagoria may serve as a metaphor for the Romantic imagination (the 'spectral drama' of Thomas Carlyle, in Terry Castle's interpretation),[24] then a metaphor for the realist imagination is provided by the spiritualist seance, which materializes the authentic 'spirit of the past' in the presence of an interested public.[25]

Dimitry's Shade

Thanks to the avalanche of historical publications in journals, Russia's past seemed close and accessible to the readers of the 1860s. As one might expect in a post-reform period, the public's attention was drawn to periods of violent change. Historians and critics portrayed the study of these moments as critical to an understanding of the present day. The reigns of Ivan the Terrible and Boris Godunov, and the Time of Troubles that resulted in the founding of the House of Romanov, attracted particular interest. A host of historical and ideological causes explained the appeal of the Time of Troubles: the death of a 'tyrant' Tsar and the post-reform ferment; the January Rising in Poland and the peasant revolts; the populist movement of the 1860s and 1870s and the quest for 'the Russian idea'; and ideological debates about the role of personality in history, about the role of the common people, and about progress and the cycles of history. The end of Ivan's reign and the Time of Troubles struck people of the 1860s as an almost ideal, iconic image of transition, when the old dies and the new is only just taking shape.[26] This period of historical disintegration *and* creativity, in which the most diverse forms and ideas were mixed together, proved a hermeneutic magnet, or trap, for contemporary society.

The protagonists of the Time of Troubles haunted the 1860s: Ivan the Terrible, Boris Godunov, Vasily Shuisky, (False) Dimitry. The Russian historical imagination has always been most attracted to the figure of Boris Godunov, 'a bridge figure' who was 'caught between the two great mythic forces of Ivan the Terrible and Peter the Great, between oriental despot and westernizing monarch.'[27] But it is no exaggeration to say that the 'mystical centre' of the Russian historical imagination was precisely the 'mysterious' figure of the 'self-proclaimed Dimitry': the embodiment of chance and unrealized possibility, a historical mirage, who undermined, if he did not destroy, the binary perception of Russian history as balancing between Ivan and Peter.

Ivan Kireevsky once described Dimitry as the shade who reigns in Pushkin's tragedy, *Boris Godunov*, from beginning to end.[28] In the 1860s he became the shade haunting all of Russian society,[29] connecting the present to the past. An interesting example of this mystical–historical link can be found in Leskov's antinihilist novel *At Daggers Drawn*, which is dedicated to the ideological discord of the 1860s. In one of his mystical speeches, the visionary and spiritualist Svetozar Vodopianov, who professes the reincarnationalism of Allan Kardec, asserts that

Dimitry was a gifted young man and certainly not a False Dimitry: 'the poor spirit is still troubled by such slander.' But when pressed further about Dimitry's identity, Vodopianov can only answer vaguely: 'When he was a spirit, he didn't want to state this clearly; and now he has once again been reincarnated.'[30]

The paradox is that the historians of the realist era chose as their object of research nothing other than a ghost. And they didn't just choose him: they strove to 'resurrect,' interrogate, and identify him through all the methods available to them. The historical (False) Dimitry proved the ideal candidate for the role of national spectre. He appeared as if from nowhere; he reigned in Moscow for a year; he was killed and burned (the rumour spread among the people, writes Kostomarov, that the tormented Tsar 'walks around at night,' hence the decision to burn his corpse) and scattered on the wind (his ashes were stuffed into the muzzle of a cannon and shot out in the direction from which he had arrived). Who was Dimitry? The runaway monk Grishka (the official version, dating from the time of Boris Godunov)? The Tsarevich, saved by a miracle? A nobleman from Kostroma? A non-Russian (a representative of the Polish *szlachta*, or a Belorussian, or a Ukrainian, or even a Jew)? Was he a Catholic agent ('a Polish spy')? A knight on the throne (prototype of Paul I)? A failed reformer (precursor of Peter the Great)? Saviour? Antichrist? Kostomarov, we recall, decided regretfully that such questions could not be answered: Dimitry remained unknown to history, 'Mr. X.'

In other words, the enigma of Dimitry became the insoluble equation of Russia's Age of Realism. The constant revisiting by historians of the figure of Dimitry may be viewed as the result of society's subconscious dissatisfaction with the capacity of strictly scientific methods to respond to a disturbing problem.[31] Where history ends, the historical imagination takes off. Kostomarov's compromised attempt to 'resuscitate' Dimitry in a scholarly, literary essay was no solution. Literature possessed far greater potential in this respect – above all, in historical drama.[32] It was precisely the latter that undertook the mission in the 1860s of bringing about the metaphorical materialization of the 'spirit of the past.' It is indicative that the theatrical 'reproduction' of history should have received the sanction of the historians of the new school. Thus, Kostomarov wrote in 1867: 'One has to allow the dramatist who deals with historical personages to invent whatever he likes, but only on the condition that the historian should say: "although history says nothing about this, the progress of events, the nature of the characters, the spirit of the era and the customs of the time are all presented by the poet just as they must have been." That, in our view, is what one must demand of a historical drama.'[33]

The Reality of Illusion

In the 1860s, Russian historical drama flourished as never before. In those years, wrote a historian of the Russian theatre, 'nearly all the most significant works of Russian historical drama, including Pushkin's *Boris Godunov*, were staged for the first time.'[34] Theatrical interest in Russian history peaked in the middle of the decade: of the forty new historical plays put on in the 1860s, more than half were staged between 1865 and 1868. This blossoming of historical drama was a vivid manifestation of the distinctive panhistoricism of Russian culture of the time – a tendency also represented by the rapid development of the historical novel (L.N. Tolstoy, A.K. Tolstoy),[35] historical painting (Surikov, Repin),[36] and historical opera (Tchaikovsky, Rimsky-Korsakov, Musorgsky, and, a little later, Borodin).[37]

The historical drama of the realist era was opposed to that of Romantic tradition. The new school was founded on a rejection of established patriotic schemata (represented with particular clarity in the work of Nestor Kukolnik). It was also defined by its pursuit of scientific truth; by a precise correspondence between what was depicted on stage and the data of historiography and ethnography (the reproduction of popular life and psychology); by its preference, in the wake of contemporary historical theory, for everyday, 'popular' (*narodnyi*) aspects of the historical process over a limiting emphasis on the state; and by its efforts to approach, through art, an understanding of the popular 'spirit' of the past.[38] In the words of the critic Pavel Annenkov, Russian historical drama became 'something akin to the new historical science.'[39] Alexander Ostrovsky, the most influential Russian playwright of the time, held that 'the historical writer, like the scholarly historian [...] should disclose the truth of past events and give the people material by which to judge the life of the nation – past and present.'[40] Indeed, Ostrovsky drew material for his historical dramas from numerous historical and ethnographic sources, and he consulted with leading historians. Meanwhile, the playwright N.A. Chaev furnished his plays with archaeological commentary and even tried to replicate the Russian language of the seventeenth century in his protagonists' dialogue.

Lastly, drama of the second half of the century unveiled the possibility of the universal reconstruction of the past: 'the decorations, costumes, and props were made after the painstaking study of museum material and historical research.'[41] Prominent historians attended performances and wrote reviews in which they drew attention to the precision (or otherwise) of the portrayals of the past. Thus, Kostomarov wrote of the first staging of Pushkin's tragedy in 1870: 'In its appearance, the arrival of *Boris Godunov* represents a true phenomenon. Never before have the external aspects of a production been treated with such painstaking care, such fidelity to archaeological truth.'[42] In his review of Ostrovsky's dramatic chronicle, *Dimitry the Pretender and Vasily Shuiskii* (1866), A.S. Suvorin wrote that the scene in which the crowd clashes with the invaders was staged with such force and realistic persuasiveness 'that all [the viewers] were ready to believe that the scene was occurring in reality.'[43]

Ostrovsky also spoke about drama's power to create the illusion that the past was being materialized on stage: 'The historian describes *what* happened; the dramatic poet shows *how* it happened. He transfers the spectator to the very scene of the action and makes him a participant in the event.' 'This effect of co-participation,' wrote a contemporary scholar of the Russian theatre, 'is founded not simply on the force of dramatic illusion, but on the real historical links which exist between the past and the present.'[44] What is actually occurring, however, is quite the opposite: it is the hero whom the dramatist transfers to the theatre, making him a participant in the contemporary ideological process. A hero, moreover, who must be of real interest and importance to society. Like Dimitry.[45]

'Dead, but Alive!'

Dimitry features in several plays of the 1860s and 1870s: in addition to *Boris Godunov* and the chronicles of Ostrovsky (1866) and Chaev (1866), he appears in Mikhail Pogodin's *History in Characters about Dimitry the Pretender* (published 1868), in an unstaged play by Nikolai Polozov, and, finally, in Musorgsky's opera *Boris Godunov* (1874). I have already discussed the paradox suggested by the Russian interest in Dimitry in these decades: realists (historians and writers) were turning to the 'shade.'[46] In an article on historical drama of this period, Lidia Lotman observed that the playwrights were motivated by the desire to disclose through art the 'dark' regions of their country's history.[47] This was true. But the result of this literary–historical detective investigation was still greater confusion. It was as if, in these works of the 1860s and 1870s, Dimitry had fragmented into ideologically conflicting shades: Pogodin's Dimitry differed from Ostrovsky's, while Chaev's resembled neither. Moreover, even in the work of a single author, the figure of Dimitry resisted straightforward interpretation. (Thus, Alexander Suvorin reproached Ostrovsky for the fact that his interpretation of Dimitry did not adhere to one or another historical version.)[48]

It is not my purpose here to analyse dramatic works about Dimitry,[49] but I will pause to consider one of their motifs, which reveals the mode in which this mysterious figure existed in the Russian historical imagination. I have in mind the motif of the shade of the tsarevich, first introduced in Pushkin's *Boris Godunov*. The most interesting example in this regard was supplied by A.K. Tolstoy in the third part of his historical trilogy, *Tsar Boris* (1870). Tolstoy, an idealist, had a distinctive attitude towards the realist agenda of historical drama of the 1860s: he set psychological truth (namely, deep insight into the mental experiences of historical figures) above historical accuracy, from which he occasionally allowed himself to deviate. Art, according to Tolstoy, 'should not contradict the truth' but should borrow from every phenomenon 'only its typical features' and cast aside the inessential: 'This is how painting differs from photography, poetry from history and, in particular, drama from the dramatic chronicle.'[50] This position allowed him not only to achieve his own artistic aims, but also to defamiliarize the contemporary realist model, highlighting its conditional, limited, and contradictory nature. A.K. Tolstoy may be viewed, in this respect, as a mystic penetrating the spiritual mystery of the past, and not as a scholarly spiritualist seeking the precise reproduction of historical facts (appearances).[51]

Initially, Tolstoy wanted to portray the Pretender on stage (on the whole, the writer shared Kostomarov's view that Dimitry and Grishka Otrep'ev were separate people). But in the end, he rejected this plan. In contrast to other plays of the time, Tolstoy's Dimitry is present not 'in the flesh' but as an immaterial shade ('Dead, but alive!'). Thus, in the fifth act of the tragedy, Boris is haunted by a vision of the tsarevich. Boris knows that the latter died long ago. He understands that the shade he sees is an optical illusion, a moonbeam reflected on his throne. He feels that he is losing his mind. But he cannot rid himself of the spectre. Caryl Emerson has shown exactly how the vision of Tolstoy's Boris differs from the 'bloody boys' of Pushkin's Tsar. It is not conscience that torments Boris, but an awareness of the senselessness of history. He returns to where he started.[52]

My interest here lies less in the symbolism of Dimitry's shade in Tolstoy's play (i.e., what it means for Boris and for the dramatic plot),[53] than in its significance in Russia's public and literary consciousness of the time. The shade of Tolstoy's Dimitry can be interpreted as the spectre that haunted Russian historical drama of the 1860s – a spectre that could not be dispelled even by scholarly and realistic attempts to embody it on stage. Following the example of scholars, realist playwrights sought to 'clarify' the shade, to materialize it as an unambiguous image (historical truth). But the outcome of this struggle with the shade proved quite different: the defeat of the realist, the destruction of 'the entire edifice of his life,' the spectralization of reality, and the gradual transition to symbolist drama with its new apprehension of reality.

Conclusion

Ostrovsky concluded his historical chronicles[54] about the Time of Troubles with the short and unsuccessful play *A Comedian of the Seventeenth Century* (1872). It was written to mark two hundred years of Russian theatre: the anniversary of the first performance of the comedy *The Play of Artaxerxes* in the court theatre of Tsar Alexei Mikhailovich in 1672.[55] Ostrovsky, in other words, sought to link the earliest manifestation of Russian drama to the highest point of its development.

A Comedian of the Seventeenth Century supplies a curious postscript to Ostrovsky's historical opus. This play is concerned not so much with history as with the theatre and its fate. Yet it is also a strictly historical drama. Drawing on contemporary historical works (Tikhonravov, Zabelin) for information about the period and the events he was portraying, Ostrovsky aimed – in accordance with his artistic principles – for the precise reconstruction of the psychology of a Russian of the late seventeenth century. The choice of historical moment was crucial. More than half a century had passed since the Times of Troubles. The storms had settled. A new dynasty was ruling the country with great confidence and carefully preparing for rapprochement with the West. The theatre was the harbinger of the cultural reforms of the future (the play emphasized the coincidence of the appearance of the first theatre with the birth of the great reformer, Peter). Russia was entering European culture, within which the playwright–comedian was accorded the role of moral arbiter of people and history.[56]

However, there was a certain irony in the realist's appeal to Russia's first experience of the theatre. In a chapter devoted to the theatre of Alexei Mikhailovich, Dmitry Likhachev offered a brilliant description of the unique encounter between the culturally ignorant Russian spectators (the Tsar and the boyars) and theatre's chief illusion – the resurrection of the past:

> This was a showing, a visual portrayal, a kind of resurrection of the past. Artaxerxes, who, to quote the play, 'had been confined in his grave for more than two thousand years,' utters the word 'today' three times in his monologue. Like the other personages 'confined in the grave' he comes to life on the stage, speaks and moves, punishes and pardons, weeps and rejoices. For a modern audience there would be nothing remarkable about 'bringing to life' a long dead potentate: this is an accepted dramatic convention. But for Tsar Alexis and his boyars, who had not received a West European theatrical education, the 'resurrection of the past' in the 'comedy chamber' was a real revolution in their ideas about art. It turned out that one could not only narrate the past, but also bring it to life, portray it as the present. *The theater created an artistic illusion of reality, divorcing the spectator, as it were, from reality and carrying him into a special world, the world of art, the world of history come to life.*[57]

If in the seventeenth century the earliest spectators learned how to accept the illusions of the theatre, then in the mythological consciousness of the realist epoch this metaphor was realized. It was as if the past had been materialized on the stage and was coming to meet the viewer via the writer–medium (but not the visionary!) and destroying the boundaries between what was and what is. And all of this was happening not as the result of miracles – the magical incantations of Prospero[58] or Romantic revelations – but quite naturally as the product of the scientific–artistic imagination, which was controlled by specialist historians and a public steeped in historical literature.

To a certain extent, the serious playwright and the (somewhat ludicrous) devotee of spiritualism were trying to do the same thing: to summon, interrogate, and tame the shades of the past. Like the spiritualist, the dramatist says, 'Come by at night [i.e., during the evening performance], come, I'll enlighten you, I feel sorry for you. But just read what I've written first, or you won't understand my conversation with the spirits!'

3 Dead Poets' Society: Pushkin's Shade in Russian Cultural Mythology of the Second Half of the Nineteenth Century

Pushkin died at the very height of his powers and, indisputably, carried some great riddle with him to his grave. And now we must solve this riddle without him.

Fyodor Dostoevsky

The other hand, thin and handsome, appeared on the round table. It grabbed the pencil, tore a sheet out of the album that lay near the lamp, wrote several lines on it in a light hand, added a flourish, and brought the piece of paper to Bukashkin, under his very nose. Then the lines were read out, repeated and passed around all those present:
'To Bukashkin, a brother in poetry
  I congratulate you, friend, with all my heart
  On the day of your enlightening:
  I glorify you all in heaven
  With the motion of my pen.
  Accept this composition,
  Beyond the grave all poets are friends,
  We live here without grief,
  But your lyre is dear to us.
    Alexander Pushkin, The Planet Saturn, October 18**'

A.V. Druzhinin, 'A Story Before Which All Inventions
Are Dust and Emptiness'

Introduction

In this chapter I seek to 'listen to' and interpret another famous ghost of the realist period. In doing so, I will turn to a group of texts that it might seem hazardous and difficult to take too seriously. These are the 'literary works' received at spiritualist seances in the second half of the nineteenth century and attributed by mediums to the spirits of dead writers. Ridiculed in the humorous press, this mediumistic opus enjoyed considerable popularity among those who were well disposed to spiritualism. Spiritualist poetry may be viewed not just as a literary curiosity, but as a particular genre that reveals the mechanisms by which the 'dead author' lived on in Russian culture of the second half of the nineteenth century. This culture found itself in the constant, even overbearing, shadow of the dominant intellectual and spiritual influences of past epochs. It was constantly exercised by the problem that may justifiably be called the latent 'eternal question' of the Russian intelligentsia – 'To whom should we listen? Whom should we believe?' – and it looked for answers to the great shades of the past, who responded to their summons like soldiers on parade.

My attention will focus on the 'poems from beyond' (*zagrobnye stikhotvoreniia*) received at spiritualist seances from Alexander Sergeevich Pushkin (1799–1837). These peculiar works show how the myth was formed of Pushkin as a shade that responded to the calls of the living.[1] This myth took shape in Russian mass culture of the realist epoch and to this day retains its relevance to the Russian cultural consciousness.[2]

'Posthumous Authorship' as a Cultural Phenomenon

As I have discussed, the invention of the planchette (a little table with three legs and a pencil in place of the fourth) opened a new world for those seeking contact with spirits. This world was populated by 'unknown presences' who could listen and communicate with the living by means of 'intelligent rappings.' They spoke in various languages, from the ancient to the extra-planetary; they informed spiritualists about the mysteries of the universe and the affairs of bygone days; they foretold the future; they gave private advice; they prescribed medicines to the sick; and they dictated entire religio-mystical doctrines.[3] Particular value was attached to missives from great sages of the past – from church fathers, philosophers, historical figures, and writers. From the 1850s to the 1900s, literary works received from the 'spirits' of famous authors with the help of tables, planchettes, small plates, and mediumistic trances, or directly from the deceased, were published in books and periodicals and were a topic of lively debate in society.[4] The West abounded in 'classics from the other side,' which included works transmitted by the spirits of Homer, Virgil, Dante, Petrarch, Boccaccio, Milton, Shakespeare, Dryden, Byron, Corneille, Chateaubriand, Goethe, Edgar Allan Poe, Saadi, and other coryphaei of world literature.

In the practice of spiritualism, the role of these texts was primarily functional: in an era of unbelief and materialism, they offered authoritative empirical proof of the existence of the world beyond the grave. At the same time, the persuasiveness of these communications depended (from the spiritualists' point of view) on the accuracy with which they responded to readers' perceptions of the 'spirit and style' of the works produced by the authors in question during their mortal span. As a rule, the choice of authors was determined by their significance for national (and world) literature, by the presence of the 'spiritual' theme in their opus, and by those aspects of their biographical myths that bore directly on spiritualist concerns, among them these: an early death, an unjust reputation among contemporaries, an unfinished task, and mysterious circumstances of death. All that was needed was a highly sensitive instrument to receive these literary communications – that is, a powerful medium. The ordinary participants of the seance, in their turn, acted as witnesses to the authenticity of the work transmitted 'from beyond.' They formed a type of scholarly council that ascertained, on the basis of empirical observations, the veracity of the phenomenon.[5] 'Spiritualism is a religion and also a philosophy, founded on facts,' American spiritualists wrote in an appeal 'to all the peoples of the Earth.'[6] From a historical and cultural perspective, spiritualist writing was a paradoxical phenomenon of the positivist epoch, which was possessed by innumerable spectres.[7]

Spiritualists gave the following theoretical explanation for the transmission of artistic works from the other world: as the product of the mental (psychic) activity of the individual, these works might quite reasonably be produced by the soul of a writer (or by his 'posthumous energy') even after his physical death.[8] The existence of poetry in the afterlife had already been written about by Emanuel Swedenborg, who had stressed, however, that this was poetry in a special, higher tongue, inaccessible to people's understanding and even perception. At the same time, Swedenborg allowed for the possibility of spirits communicating with the living in the language of mortals: in this case, spiritual language would be refracted in the consciousness of the living being, as if materialized ('clothed') in 'physical' form. The spiritualists, heirs of Swedenborg, made a regular practice of this exception and replaced esoteric experience with mass production. The result was that spirits dictated their works in 'our' imperfect tongue (indirectly, this thesis provided justification for the artistic mediocrity of the overwhelming majority of the messages); yet these works also reflected the new, higher, more spiritual status of the deceased writers. Mediumistic texts offered a distillation of the spirit, free from the materialistic 'blemishes' and 'errors' that marked the work of the given author in his lifetime. Every such text was presented as the author's final, recapitulative judgment about himself and the world he had left behind.[9]

A direct consequence of this was that, while Shakespeare's writing from beyond continued to sound 'Shakespearean,' and Byron's 'Byronic,' the mediumistic interrogations of writers merged into a kind of collective psychological (or pneumatological) portrait of the happy dead author, whose defining characteristics were tranquillity, forgiveness of past offences, estrangement from all mundane things, sympathy towards those yet to cross the boundary separating the terrestrial world from the spiritual, and praise of the beauty of the world beyond the grave. Consider, for example, these 'posthumous' verses of Edgar Allan Poe, transmitted through the famous American medium Lizzie Doten (the poem, which 'replaces' the famous 'Raven,' is called 'Resurrexi'):

From the throne of Life Eternal
From the home of love supernal,
Where the angel feet make music over all the starry floor –
    Mortals, I have come to meet you,
    Come with words of peace to greet you,
And to tell you of the glory that is mine forevermore.[10]

In spiritualist mythology, the dead author played the part of the happy émigré, writing ecstatic epistles to summon his slowcoach countrymen:

I too can tell the world
Of the bliss in store
For earthly souls
In other worlds.[11]

By way of illustration of this 'otherworldly poetology,' let us consider the message received by the French spiritualist Olympe Audouard (her book was translated into Russian in 1875). Audouard established firm mediumistic contact with the spirit of Alexandre Dumas (an author much taken with spiritualism), which, in its turn, put her in touch with William Shakespeare himself. The latter, in reply to her inquiry about the existence in his days of a spiritualist sect (an ancient debate among Shakespeareans), sent the following gallant letter:

> Madame, I am quite overjoyed to return to the earth to provide confirmation of the belief which was the chief consolation of my so troubled life. Yes, I was a spiritualist [...] The hope that my works might endow spiritualists with some moral support aroused my greatest delight. If you had summoned me before, I would have deemed it my duty to appear at your bidding, for every spiritualist is my brother [...] Should you tell me that you are insufficiently famous to dare summon such a great writer, I will reply, Madame, that you offend me by thinking that I take pride in my works. They are merely human works, and here their value is very low. In our parts genius, which we call the grandeur of the spirit, can be the property only of purified souls; to us, their greater or lesser fame on earth holds no significance. There are so many scholars and people of great note with whom I would find it unpleasant to engage in contact! And yet there are so many simple and uncelebrated mortals to whom I would appear with great joy, in order to relate truths about real life – that which you call the life *beyond the grave.*

The spirit of Shakespeare goes on to say that a sect of spiritualists, to which he belonged, did indeed exist in the England of his time. Spiritualists did not use tables then, but they had 'their inspirations' and were able 'to make spirits appear.' Describing his inspirations and visions, the spirit concluded:

> Please believe me, my sister in spiritualism, that it is with joy that I will appear, offering my support to spiritualism. My brain is no longer clouded with the mists of earthly glory, and I often say to myself with sorrow: 'Shakespeare is exalted as a genius, but nobody thinks of praying for his soul!' My self-love has ceased to exist, but my soul – it lives and suffers.[12]

Where were these dead writers located? From where did they arrive? Why were they so democratically disposed to curious mortals? The

'Elysium of the poets' favoured by neoclassical and Romantic poetry became, in the hands of the spiritualists, an idiosyncratic call-out service in which it lost its autonomy: harnessed to the life of the world, it served the latter's interests. Spiritualist texts were, as has been noted, feeble, boring, and predictable; but they were also ideological and acutely social. They manifested the ambition – so characteristic of the presumptions of the nineteenth century – to arrive at the final and definitive confirmation of the ideology being asserted, and they attempted to do so from a position of absolute authority, such as might be found in an epistemological paradise where all mysteries are solved and all earthly tendencies brought to fulfilment. These patterns might explain why so many Western reformers practised spiritualism: abolitionists and suffragettes, socialists and religious innovators.

The Spiritualist Poem as a Genre

In generic terms, mediumistic compositions are clearly unique: they exist somewhere between literature and mysticism, faith (or superstition) and science, hoax and myth, epistle and epitaph. In contrast to the conversations in the land of the dead and the allegorical monologues of dead geniuses, which were popular in the Classical and Romantic traditions ('The Shade of Molière,' 'The Shade of Byron,' etc.), mediumistic texts claim to be authentic communications from the dead. These 'posthumous' works also differ from the visions and revelations described by mystics down the ages in that they are neither esoteric nor supernatural. Rather, they are produced during seances in the presence of witnesses, using 'scientific,' empirical methods. They do not, as a rule, reveal a mystery, but merely confirm what the seance goers believe – or want to believe. Receiving a mediumistic work is always a minor performance with its own libretto and decorations and, of course, the invariable appearance of a dramatic spectre. It is a (pseudo-)scientific miracle play during which the spectators are also actors and the action takes place on the cusp of the physical and spiritual worlds.

  This is not a conventional hoax – that is, it does not construct the image of a counterfeit author within the boundaries of what is possible, in the hope of misleading the public. Rather, 'mediumistic' compositions cross a genuine boundary in that they construct a *posthumous* image of the counterfeit author, transforming the particular question of attribution into an ontological and existential issue.

Unquestionably, there is a genetic link between the phenomenon I have described and the categories of 'sham poetry' (*mnimaia poeziia*) and 'sham poets' (*mnimye poety*) that once drew the attention of Yury Tynianov. Thus, in his draft preface to *Mnimaia poeziia* (Sham Poetry, 1931), Tynianov unconsciously borrows spiritualist terminology: 'the apparition of a sham poet'; 'mock poetry as the reflection or shadow of language'; 'there are poets in whom our conception [*predstavlenie*] is materialized'; and last, 'fictitious, reflected [*otrazhennye*] poets become reality.'[13] What the scholar was describing had *already* happened in spiritualist practice, which gave material form to contemporary literary notions (I am interested here in the mechanism rather than the content of such materialization). 'Least of all,' Tynianov acknowledged in that same draft, 'am I able to deny the importance of the imaginary numbers [*mnimye velichiny*] in literature.'[14] Spiritualist literature belongs to this category and thus can illuminate our understanding of the deeper strata of the social reception of literature.

It goes without saying (unless we are spiritualists) that the messages received from the other world testified neither to life beyond the grave nor to the opinions of their 'authors,' but rather to how the participants of the seances (the sympathetically minded readers) perceived their authors or wished to perceive them.[15] If this process were taken to its logical extreme – that is, if every remotely significant author were to be called up and questioned – we would have a kind of mythological duplicate of 'real' literature, a particular type of *shadow literature* responding to readers' demands and expectations. From a utopian (or rather, dystopian) perspective, this shadow literature would entirely replace 'real' literature (both past and present), revealing its incompleteness (as in popular tales of the shadow replacing its bearer). 'On a more terrestrial level,' Helen Sword correctly observes, 'otherworldly narratives undermine the very institutions of authorship – copyright law, bibliographical conventions, the cult of the Great Writer – with which literate mediums have so eagerly sought to ally themselves.' The reading of these otherworldly compositions one after another would lead to 'a kind of metaphysical vertigo.'[16]

The success of literary table writing was linked, it seems, to the fact that it offered readers a unique opportunity to become not only authors of their favourite authors but also even masters of their souls. The spirit, Dmitry Mendeleev wrote, 'can only say what is familiar or conceivable to the mediums, and so, according to the spiritualists' hypothesis, the spirit becomes the medium's slave.'[17] The spiritualists, of course, could hardly have concurred,[18] but be that as it may, there is little doubt that the apparent modesty of the mediums and the scientific (positivist) propriety of the seance-goers concealed considerable egoism and pride. Spiritualist circles were perceived by their participants, to a greater or lesser extent, as gatherings of the chosen few.

Remarkable, also, is the extent to which the phenomenon of 'posthumous' authorship derives from the specific nature of the commonplace reception of literary texts, in which the 'lyrical hero' of the work, identified with the author, presents himself as a kind of speaking ghost: physically he is absent to the reader, yet he communicates with him on a spiritual level through his work (it is a formula for immortality – or, at least, a formula for the poet's spiritual existence for as long as, to adapt Pushkin's line, there is one last reader alive in the sublunar world).[19] The mediumistic poem may thus be described as a realized metaphor for naive reading, or – in the terms of ancient rhetoric – realized prosopopeia: 'the making of what is absent to speak [...] the rhetorical device that lies behind all haunting.'[20] Spiritualist practice of the second half of the nineteenth century can be compared with the exercises in prosopopeia demanded of schoolboys in the classical world: the writing of a literary text in the voice of a dead historical figure or mythological hero that reconstructs the character of the person being imitated.[21]

These considerations may help explain why the rise and spread of mediumistic literature coincided with a boom in publishing, the flourishing of literary criticism, and mass interest in archival research. The past was pouring into the present. This was a time of innumerable editions of 'posthumous' collected works, new biographical research, facsimiles of manuscripts, debates on the attribution of newly found texts, and accounts of diverse literary forgeries.

Spiritualist poetry, in other words, was both a consequence and a vivid manifestation of the radical reconfiguring of the relations between author and reading public in the middle of the century. It testified to the fact that the literary process was becoming secular, democratic, and commercial. The Romantic author as God, or as a medium whose lips God moves, had died, to be replaced by a spirit depending entirely on a new medium – whether reader, literary critic, or scholar – who would ask the deceased about matters related to actual social problems and expectations before informing society of his 'authentic' answers. It seemed to the spiritualists that the soul of the dead poet had a duty to work for the good of society both day and night. The dead authors' transcendental civic consciousness and universal responsiveness (*vseotzyvchivost'*) were well expressed by the literary phantom Kozma Prutkov in his letter to his homeland from the other world:

Пером я ревностно служил родному краю,
Когда на свете жил… И кажется, давно ль?!
И вот, мертвец, я вновь в ее судьбах играю –
    Роль

I served my native land fervently with my pen,
When I lived on the earth … And was it so long ago?
And now, a corpse, I once again play a part
    In its fate.[22]

Russian Spirit Mail

Russian 'spirit mail' is an extreme expression of the quasi-religious cult of literature and its masters (especially the great dead) that established itself in Russia in the second half of the nineteenth century. From the early 1850s, the summoning of the spirits of famous writers and the receipt of their letters, poems, and even novels became a favoured activity of Russian spiritualists. Most of these texts remained within the manuscript 'offices' of spiritualist circles; but some works were published and even acquired popularity. The spiritualist journal *Rebus*, which first came out in 1881, published the mediumistic verse of V.K. Tredyakovsky, V.A. Zhukovsky, D.V. Venevitinov, A.S. Pushkin, M.Yu. Lermontov, A.N. Apukhtin, P.I. Veinberg, M.A. Lokhvitskaya, and other writers. In the mid-1870s (the peak of the spiritualist movement in Russia), word spread of a manuscript version of the second volume of *Dead Souls*, which Gogol had supposedly dictated from the other world (Dostoevsky referred to it in his *Writer's Diary* of 1876 [XXII:32]).[23] Nearly every spiritualist circle that met on a more or less regular basis had its patron spirits (or spirit controls), among whom were many famous writers. Literary dilettantes also engaged in dictation from the other side; they included a legion of hacks, impostors, and poseurs.

The literature generated by the tables of the Russian spiritualists has yet to attract the scholarly attention it deserves. The analysis of spiritualist missives – texts that are manifestly apocryphal from the literary scholar's perspective – could prove to be, as Yury Lotman wrote of literary hoaxes and forgeries, 'an important source of valuable information'[24] about Russian literary mythology and mass-cultural consciousness of the second half of the nineteenth century. Some of the most informative missives of this type were attributed by the spiritualists to Pushkin – the chief national spectre of Russian culture.[25]

Pushkin From the Other Side

In 1899 the Russian spiritualist organ *Rebus* marked the centenary of Pushkin's birth with the publication of 'Zagrobnoe stikhotvorenie Pushkina' (A Poem by Pushkin from the Other Side) which had been received by the poet's sister Olga Pavlishcheva 'at a domestic spiritualist seance' in the early 1850s:

Входя в небесные селенья,
Печалилась душа моя,
Что средь земного треволненья
Вас оставлял надолго я.

По-прежнему вы сердцу милы,
Но не земное я люблю.
И у престола Высшей Силы
За вас, друзья мои молю.

А. Пушкин.

Entering the heavenly realms
My soul was saddened
To be leaving you so long
Amid the earth's disquiet.

You are as dear to my heart as before,
But I love not the things of the Earth
And I pray for you, my friends,
At the throne of the Almighty.

A. Pushkin[26]

Other such Pushkinian texts were also well known. In the autumn of 1883, for example, *Rebus* published the reminiscences of Mrs Zhelikhovsky about her sister, the celebrated theosophist Helene Blavatsky. They included an account of the appearance of Pushkin's shade to spiritualists in Nizhny Novgorod in the late 1850s. Zhelikhovsky, a witness of the event, recalled that Pushkin's spectre, which had been summoned through the mediumship of Blavatsky, was 'in a melancholic and gloomy spiritual state and in answer to our questions – why was he so sad? what was the cause of his suffering? What did he desire?' Pushkin replied with the following improvisation:

> Зачем, друзья мои, вам знать,
> Что я могу теперь желать?
> Покоиться на лоне смерти…
> Мне не достичь небесной тверди.
> Грешил я много на земле.
> И ныне мучусь в страшной мгле.

> Why, my friends, should you seek to know
> What I may desire now?
> To rest in the bosom of death …
> I shall not attain the heavenly firmament.
> I sinned too much on Earth.
> And now I suffer in the terrible dark.

'Poor Alexander Sergeevich!' said Blavatsky's father, after this poem was read to him.[27]

These poems stand out among comparable compositions by other authors from beyond the grave. In contrast to his less ambivalent fellow spectres, Pushkin's shade has a split personality, offering diametrically opposed information about its own condition in the afterworld. The poet comes to his relatives and friends from his heavenly abode and to Blavatsky from the infernal abyss. In the first case, Pushkin is in a state of perfect bliss; in the second, of deepest melancholy.

The texts I have cited demand to be seen as realizations of metaphorical 'views' of Pushkin, among which, in the words of the poet's very first biographer, P.V. Annenkov, 'one [view] presents him as the prototype of a demonic nature that recognizes nothing sacred on earth […] while another, by contrast, invests in him all the tenderness, freshness and intimacy of his lyrical works, reckoning the poet and man to be a single spiritual entity.'[28] The spiritualists, then, sought to solve the debate about Pushkin by summoning the deceased poet himself – evidence not only of their ambition to find authoritative confirmation of the existence of the spiritual world, but also of a specific cultural

Figure 1 Portrait of Pushkin from the anniversary edition of Strekoza.
(Russian State Library, Moscow)

demand characteristic of Russian self-perception: the need to be in constant 'contact' with Pushkin. It could be argued that Pushkin's mediumistic poems are located at the intersection of two mythologies that developed at roughly the same time (1850s to 1880s): a spiritualist mythology (about the souls of the dead, who come at our bidding with news of the world beyond), and a literary mythology (about the poetic immortality of Pushkin – the theme of *Exegi monumentum* – and his essential presence in Russian culture).

The reversibility of these mythologies[29] in the same period is also attested by the comic epigrams that accompanied a letter by Pushkin 'from the other world' in the humorous journal *Strekoza* (Dragonfly) in 1880. Here is one:

Смерть для меня (таков, знать, русский быт)
Двойной свой наложила отпечаток!
Я пулею Дантеса был убит,
А Исаковым - массой опечаток

Death (such is our Russian way of life)
Has left its double seal on me!
D'Anthès killed me with a bullet
And Isakov – with a heap of errata.[30]

These pseudo-spiritualist missives share an exclusively worldly, literary tendency. Hence the mockery of the 1880 'Isakov' edition of Pushkin's collected works (edited by P.A. Efremov).[31] The epigrams were the concluding item in the 8 July issue of *Dragonfly*, which was dedicated to the festivities surrounding the unveiling of the Pushkin statue in Moscow and which include a selection of his poems. This issue had opened with a large portrait of the poet in a black frame, above a romantic vignette and the caption 'A.S. Pushkin. Born 26 May 1799, died ... Has not died to this day.'[32]

History of a Hoax

I will now consider in greater detail Pushkin's first poem from beyond, 'Entering the Heavenly Realms,' which offers a good illustration of the process of spiritualist myth making.

The poem first appeared in the 'military, literary, and political' newspaper *Russkii Invalid* (Russian Veteran) of 11 January 1859, under the heading 'A Bibliographical Rarity.'[33] An editorial note accompanying the publication informed readers: 'We have had the good fortune to hear poems found among the papers of the late P.V.N., written by his friend Alexander Sergeevich Pushkin. It may be said that they come from beyond the grave. In them the poet, having migrated in faith and vision to the region where the sun never sets, communicates to his friends feelings that soar over those of the earth.'[34] 'P.V.N.' was Pavel Voinovich Nashchokin, Pushkin's closest friend, who died in 1854.

The poem was immediately reprinted in several publications, forcing the Pushkin scholar P.A. Efremov to try to puncture the myth with the following comment: 'It is with astonishment that we came upon this worthless poem in the press. It ought never to have seen the light of day: such a step merely displays a lack of respect for the poet's memory and for the public itself.'[35]

There are three stories about the origins of this poem. The most elaborate and colourful one was introduced by the littérateur N. Berg, who heard it from Nashchokin himself:

In the course of the winter of 1853 we conversed with the spirits by means of the little tables with pencils fastened to them. Pushkin and Bryullov wrote quite often [...] Once on Good Friday, we asked Pushkin whether he could appear before us, or at least give us a fleeting glimpse of his shade. He answered, 'I can. Gather again tomorrow, on Thursday, and I will come!' We notified all our acquaintances. You can imagine what kind of a crowd that was! Our small hall was packed with guests. The other rooms of the house were also filled with people we recognized – all awaiting Pushkin!

All were pale. However, nothing happened. No one came [...] When the guests had dispersed, I heard the sound of a bell ... I dressed and went off to church. The street was deserted. There was only some little figure of a man walking towards me along the sidewalk, apparently a drunkard, who bumped against my shoulder quite hard. I stopped and looked at him. He also stopped and looked. There was something very familiar in his features. Then we continued on our separate ways. Leaving the church, I promised myself that I would burn all that had been written by the spirits and put an end to such sinful gatherings. My wife supported me in this decision, but she asked me not to cancel the seance already scheduled for the following day, a Saturday. They gathered in the evening and began to write. The first spirit to be asked 'who's writing?'

answered, 'Pushkin!' 'Why didn't you come yesterday?' we asked him. 'You were all so frightened,' answered Pushkin's spirit, 'but I bumped into Nashchokin on the sidewalk as he made his way to the church services, and I looked him straight in the eye. Why didn't he recognize me?' On Saturday Nashchokin burned everything that had been received from the spirits, not saving even a single page. *He even burned the verses* ['Entering the Heavenly Realms'] *written by Pushkin's spirit.* [36]

Pushkin's nephew, L.N. Pavlishchev (1834–1916), a memoirist with a very lively imagination, recorded that the poem had been received 'in the autumn of 1853, shortly, as I recall, after the Battle of Sinop' (18 to 30 November):

It happened at the start of the Eastern War, when many were seized by ideas of a new crusade against the infidels, amid fear of the end of the world and horrors of other kinds ... At that very same time, in the autumn of 1853, [...] friends of the late Alexander Sergeevich, adherents of spiritualism through 'table turning,' gathered in Moscow at the home of the Nashchokins. These gentlemen summoned his ghost, and the ghost, as if directed by the hand of a young girl understanding nothing of verse, wrote on paper by means of a small table, one leg of which was replaced with a pencil, the following ditty in answer to the curious question, 'Tell us, Pushkin, where are you now?'[37] This was the poem 'Entering the Heavenly Realms.'

The famous actor and vaudevillist P.A. Karatygin (1805–79) presents the history of this poem quite differently. In his account, the poem appeared in January 1853 at a spiritualist seance at the home of Alexander Andreevich Katenin. Late in the evening conversation turned to the fashionable subject of table turning. Karatygin confessed that he did not believe in the possibility of the participation of spirits in the turning of tables and other phenomena. The guests decided to organize a seance. One of the advocates of table writing 'brought a tiny table [...] with a pencil stuck through the upper board' (i.e., a planchette). Events took the following course:

Our spiritualist suggested that we summon the spirit of some great person by means of the table [...] The consensus of the guests was for A.S. Pushkin was chosen by common consent. The question put to his ghost was regarding the location of his soul. This reminder of the great poet in the circle of people who had known him personally cast a shadow of sadness over our merry group. I did not approve of the choice of Pushkin for these childish experiments and mystification. Why call in vain upon the name of the immortal poet in order to ask him where his soul is located, when his entire soul has gone into his creative work? Meanwhile, the table was writing and, finally, upon the sheet of paper placed underneath it, the following verses appeared [...] I immediately wrote down this poem [Karatygin cites the poem, 'Entering the Heavenly Realms']. That it was a forgery, albeit quite skillful, that the ghost of Pushkin could never have written these verses, of this there was not a shadow of a doubt [...] Nevertheless, there was an idea in this poetry, and a sonority ... One could not call the verses wooden (although they were written with a wooden table). Probably, one could say that there was something Pushkinesque about them. Similarly, an actor can make himself up to resemble some well-known person, and imitate his voice. But the person being imitated is nevertheless not created. The transcript of these verses, undoubtedly, has passed through many hands and was perhaps preserved by many of my contemporaries.[38]

The concluding words of this account betray a hint that the composer of this poem 'from beyond' was Karatygin himself. In the words of Nabokov's Godunov-Cherdyntsev (in *The Gift*), spoken in a similar context, 'a prank, as often happens, did not work out in the way intended, and the frivolously summoned spirit' did not wish to disappear.[39]

The question arises: Why was this hoax destined for such a long life? I will consider three reasons. First, because it represented a quite successful imitation of Pushkin's style. Second, because it told the poet's admirers what they wanted and expected to hear from the deceased. Third, and last, because it presented in a pure, naively realistic, 'unclothed' form the mechanism of Russian society's relationship with its dead poet.

Sham Pushkin

E. Lann wrote that 'hoaxes should be classified not by genre, but by the individuals invented by the hoaxer – those sham authors to whom the forgery is attributed.'[40] As early as 1903, P.A. Efremov numbered the 'posthumous' poem among the texts that corresponded to the phenomenon (which he condemned) of 'sham Pushkin.'[41] That 'Entering the Heavenly Realms' is a forgery no one can doubt. But the word *mnimyi* (sham) may be interpreted here to mean not just the falsified Pushkin, but also the notional, imaginary, and legendary Pushkin – the image that those closest to the poet had canonized by the early 1850s and that later became the object of mythological conjectures in mass culture.

Indeed, 'Entering the Heavenly Realms' offers a generic picture of the notions of a 'purified,' 'transformed,' 'saved' Pushkin that formed in the circle of the poet's friends and family after his death. In particular I would name the letters of Sergei Pushkin and Olga Pavlishcheva, Pyotr Pletnev's account of the benevolence and 'deeply religious mood' he had witnessed in Pushkin on the eve of the latter's death,[42] and the canonical description of the poet's beautiful death in Vasily Zhukovsky's letter to Sergei Pushkin of 15 February 1837.[43] The poet's father, Sergei Lvovich, addressed the theme of the presence of the deceased in the life of the family. In a poem of 1837, addressed to P.A. Osipova's daughter, he wrote:

Склоняяся главою в прах,
Я слышу гения... Парит он над тобою
И блещет яркою звездою,
И молит он о том же в небесах.[44]

Bowing my head to the dust,
I hear the angel ... He hovers above you
And shines like a bright star,
And he prays [for you] in the heavens.

All of these motifs – benevolence, religious enlightenment, intercession for those closest to the poet – were later reflected in the image of Pushkin in 'Entering the Heavenly Realms.'

The image of Pushkin beyond the grave matched the spiritualist model perfectly (i.e. that same *collective portrait* of the dead author discussed at the beginning of this chapter) and could thus easily be reconstructed in the corresponding idiom. But, as I have said, the mediumistic persuasiveness of 'posthumous' epistles depends directly on the extent to which they evoke the 'style and spirit' of the deceased who is being interrogated. In terms of style, 'Entering the Heavenly Realms' is transparent enough. The universally familiar Pushkinian trademarks are on display: the four-foot iamb; the characteristic rhymes on *en'ia* and *iu*; the manner in which the poet addresses 'my friends'; the use of words and expressions often encountered in Pushkin's verse ('my soul,' 'as before,' 'dear to my heart,' 'I pray'; the word 'disquiet,' reminding the reader of the melancholic 'Elegy' of 1830); and the 'Pushkinian' mood of luminous sadness.

The 'spirit' of the poem is a more complicated issue, given the ambivalence of Pushkin's attitude towards the afterlife and personal immortality. In his great summarizing poem, 'I Have Raised a Monument to Myself Not Made by Hands,' posthumous being is linked to the existence of poetry in general: the soul will remain 'in the sacred lyre' and will survive 'as long as there is one last poet alive in the sublunar world.' However, there are no 'heavenly realms' in Pushkin's work,[45] and the image of the throne of the Almighty is a rarity in Pushkin's opus, eliciting an involuntary association with the mention of the 'throne of the Everlasting' in a work entirely incompatible 'in spirit' with spiritualist messages – the erotic and blasphemous 'Gabrieliad' (1821):

Пред нею вдруг открылся небосклон
Во глубине своей необозримой;
В сиянии и славе нестерпимой
Тьмы ангелов волнуются, кипят [...]
И, яркими одеян облаками,
Предвечного стоит пред ними трон

The heavenly vault abruptly draws asunder,
And, its unfathomed inner depth unsealed,
In dazzling burst of glory are revealed
Great clouds of angels, here and thither pouring
[...] Caparisoned in racks of shining cloud,
There stands before them the Eternal's throne.[46]   (IV:122)

Does it follow, then, that the author of 'Entering the Heavenly Realms' (whoever he may have been), while reproducing Pushkin's style with a certain success, also ascribed to the poet convictions entirely alien to him during his life, but essential for his spiritualist persona? I believe not. Elaborating Karatygin's thought, there *is* 'something Pushkinian' in the 'posthumous' poem, in substance as well as style.

The theme of life beyond the grave ('the fate of the soul') was among those most favoured by Pushkin throughout his artistic career: from the 'Elegy' written at the lycee ('I have seen death ...') to the final 'Monument.'[47] Thus, the 'throne' may allude not to the 'Gabrieliad,' but to the lesser known yet deeply religious 'Epitafiya mladentsu' (Epitaph to an Infant, 1828):

В сиянии и в радостном покое,
У трона вечного творца,
С улыбкой он глядит в изгнание земное,
Благословляет мать и молит за отца.   (III.1: 95)

In radiance and in joyful repose
At the throne of the eternal creator,
He gazes with a smile on earthly exile,
Blesses his mother, and prays for his father.

In this poem, seemingly uncharacteristic of the poet's work,[48] we find 'repose,' sympathy for the 'earthly exile,' and the infant's blessing and prayer for his parents. These parallels (even if they occurred unintentionally – the hoaxer's text was, by all appearances, an improvisation)[49] permit a better understanding of the specific genre of 'Entering the Heavenly Realms.' That poem represents a curious attempt to 'cross' the epitaph[50] – a rare but occasional genre in Pushkin's opus – with the traditional Pushkinian genre of the epistle to friends.

This generic duality is emphasized by the actual content of Pushkin's alleged reply to the question of his spiritualist friends: on the one hand, the poet says that he has entirely renounced the mundane ('But I love not the things of the Earth'); on the other, he still grieves for his friends left in the world and his soul is bound to them 'as before.' This ambivalence relates to a dilemma formulated by the poet during his own lifetime.

I have in mind above all the poem 'I Love Your Unknown Twilight' (published in 1826) and its earlier version 'But, Flying Off to Other Worlds' (1822). The former represents a polemical reworking of the latter. The central tension that these two texts resolve in different ways relates to the question of what will happen to the poet's soul after his death: Will it lose all its earthly feelings in the other world, or will it remain bound to the mortal world? Will it forget our vale of sorrow or will it pine for it? In the earlier version, the question is posed as follows:

Но, улетев в миры иные,
Ужели с ризой гробовой
Все чувства брошу я земные,
И чужд мне будет мир земной?
Ужели там, где все блистает
Нетленной славой и красой,
Где чистый пламень пожирает
Несовершенство бытия,
Минутной жизни впечатлений
Не сохранит душа моя,
Не буду ведать сожалений,
Тоску любви забуду я? [51]

But, flying off to other worlds,
Will I truly cast off all mundane thoughts
Together with the funeral shroud
And will the earth be alien to me?
In the place where everything dazzles
With imperishable glory and beauty,
Where the pure flame consumes
The imperfection of existence,
Will my soul really not preserve
The impressions of transient life,
Shall I not know regrets,
Shall I forget love's sorrow?   (II.1: 702–3)

The poet tries to convince himself that no, he will not lose his feelings, and no, he will not forget the world. However, in the final version, he leans towards a more sceptical reply:

Но, может быть, мечты пустые -
Быть может с ризой гробовой
Все чувства брошу я земные,
И чужд мне будет мир земной;
Быть может, там, где все блистает
Нетленной славой и красой,
Где чистый пламень пожирает
Несовершенство бытия […]
Тоску любви забуду ль я?… [52]

But perhaps the dreams are empty –
Perhaps with the funeral shroud
I will cast off all mundane thoughts,
And the earth will be alien to me;
In the place where everything dazzles
With imperishable glory and beauty
Where the pure flame consumes
The imperfection of existence [...]
Shall I forget love's sorrow?   (II.1: 227)

It could be argued that 'Entering the Heavenly Realms' traces the general design of these lines (in terms of meter, syntax, vocabulary, and ideas).[53] It appears to continue the poet's 'internal conversation' and becomes a kind of final verdict on the part of Pushkin, who has solved the mystery of death and is continuing – in a new, higher capacity, and of course on a different, higher level – that task of which he was so proud during his life: interceding and praying for his friends and kin. This ultimate testimony is the result of the conscious selection of those poetic statements in Pushkin's work deemed most consonant with spiritualism. It represents a focal point for the spiritualist themes and motifs of Russian Pushkiniana of the second half of the nineteenth century.

History of a Shade

The theme of Pushkin's posthumous life emerged in Russian literature about the poet almost immediately after his death and, in the second half of the century, developed into the myth of a shade that regularly appeared to the poet's countrymen. The deceased Pushkin was expected, summoned, seen, heard; he was the source of tidings and compositions from the other world. At the base of this myth lay various literary models, prominently represented in Pushkin's opus.[54]

In itself, the image of the poet's shade is a thoroughly traditional one. In the Classical and Romantic eras it was applied to deceased geniuses who live, according to Horace, in a happy land of poets, delight the gods with their singing, and sometimes visit their fellow writers on earth to encourage or bless them.[55] In Russian literature the allegorical image of the poet's shade began to appear in the Classical age (the shades of Anacreon, Homer, Virgil, etc.). In the 1810s and

1820s these were joined by the 'Romantic' spectres of Ovid, Tasso, Shakespeare, and the 'new' shade, Byron. Moreover, the Elysium of the great European poets was gradually adding Russian authors to its number: the shades of Lomonosov and Derzhavin.

At this time, furthermore, the theme of the poet's shade coincided with another popular theme – mystical visions of a dead friend or beloved in works by Zhukovsky, Batiushkov, and Pushkin. In the mythopoetical narrative that emerged, the kind shade of the deceased poet, living among his fellow greats in happy Elysium, remembers the friends he has left behind and occasionally visits them in dreams or visions. Thus the literary and mental bond with the poet–friend remains unbroken even after his death. This idea underpins the myth of the shade of Pushkin in Russian culture.

In Pushkin's circle, the Romantic myth of the shade of the poet–friend, which had previously existed only in the form of elegant poetic allegory,[56] was first projected onto reality after the premature death (in January 1831) of one of its creators, Baron A.A. Delvig.[57] But the influence of the myth of Delvig was limited to a few literary friends and sympathetic readers. Moreover, the myth was curtailed by the death of Delvig's friends. The myth of Pushkin's shade was another matter entirely, since it drew an entire nation into its sphere.

Why was the image of the dead Pushkin so easily spiritualized in Russian culture, and why was it interpreted as a shade? Answers must surely be sought in the reception of the poet's works and personality as both mundane and celestial. The shade (i.e., the material image of the soul) became a kind of *mediator*, uniting (and reconciling) in the mythopoetic consciousness the two hypostases of Pushkin, and also the two worlds: the heavenly, from which Pushkin arrived and to which he returned, and the earthly, to which he was inextricably bound.[58]

A further reason lies in the very structure of Pushkin's texts. As I have already noted, the author of a literary work may easily be mythologized through a 'naive' reading as a speaking ghost: he is absent, yet he speaks to us. This mythologized reception of the implied author becomes especially prominent when the actual author constructs his narrative strategy as a dialogue with the imagined reader. This, of course, was Pushkin's favoured literary strategy (*Ruslan and Lyudmila*, *Eugene Onegin*, *Count Nulin*, the epistles to friends). The poet's speaking shade can thus be seen as the mythological derivative of his narrative technique, which was aimed at creating the illusion of direct conversation with the reader.

The myth of Pushkin's shade, as an entity capable of responding to the requests of contemporaries, was further nurtured in the second half of the nineteenth century by numerous publications of unknown works by Pushkin and by biographical studies. These encouraged the illusion of the 'return' of the deceased and the continuation of his creative activity (the poet's death turned out to be not an end but a boundary, separating one period of his existence and activity from another). The mythological potential of these publications was inherent in their very titles: *Posthumous Collected Works* (1838–41), *New Letters of Pushkin, A New Chapter of 'A Captain's Daughter,'* 'Pushkin's Voice from Beyond the Grave Once More' (a publication of an unknown poem).

The memorials to Pushkin that appeared during this period also generated mythological associations: the estates, houses, and apartments where Pushkin had once lived became home to his shade. [59] To visit them was to put oneself in contact with the poet's spirit. The latter part of the nineteenth century also witnessed the development of a certain notion of the connoisseur, interpreter, and scholar of Pushkin, who was seen to be in constant contact with the dead poet and who strove, in Annenkov's words, 'to catch Pushkin's thoughts.'[60] The competition between these experts in the 1850s and 1860s (as between Annenkov and P.I. Bartenev) drew widespread public interest: Which of them stood closer to Pushkin? In spiritualist terms, the *scholar of Pushkin* gradually displaced the *friend of Pushkin* in the role of the poet's medium.

An important index of mythological notions about the poet's shade was supplied by the assiduous efforts to recreate in great detail an authentic material image of the dead genius.[61] The starting point for the curious history of Pushkin's 'materialization' was his death mask, taken by the sculptor S.I. Galberg in 1837. It provided, in the words of a contemporary scholar, the 'only documentary evidence of the structure of Pushkin's face.' [62] Plaster copies of this mask, with added hairs, were followed by busts and sculptures of the poet, and, finally, by monuments – the ultimate 'compressions' and materializations of his shade. [63]

Characteristically, Pushkin was known to Russians not just by his features but also by his handwriting. Facsimiles of the latter were invariably included in the poet's collected works (see, for example, the full title of Annenkov's edition of 1855–7: *The Works of Pushkin, Supplemented with Biographical Materials, a Portrait, and Photographs of his Handwriting and Drawings*).

Figure 2 Pushkin's Death Mask. A drawing by Eleonora Zhukovskaya
(Russian State Library, Moscow)

Figure 3 'Faith. Hope. Love.' Pushkin's missive from the beyond received by
Baron Güldenstubbe in the presence of Baron de Brewern. (New York Public
Library)

These publications created the illusion of being 'posthumous auto-graphs' of the poet, resembling the ones produced in spiritualist seances. Thus, for example, in 1856, the prominent German spiritualist Ludwig von Güldenstubbe published in Paris a facsimile of a pious note by Pushkin from beyond – 'Faith. Hope. Love' – which he claimed to have received in the presence of the author himself (and of Baron Brewern, a Russian national who assisted him) (see Figure 3).[64] It must be admitted, though, that the script in question does not resemble that of Pushkin.

Pushkin On Call

As I have discussed, the continued participation of Pushkin in contem-porary life was facilitated by heated literary and political debates: the poet was appealed to as the highest authority, and answers (often con-tradictory) were sought and found in his works to the most pressing issues of the day. The manner in which Pushkin was drawn into con-temporary debates was mythologized in the motif of the interrogation of Pushkin's shade, which was widely represented in Russian Pushkin-iana. In the Romantic 1830s and 1840s the poet's shade appeared to his friends and admirers, in secret and by individual invitation; by the 1850s and 1860s it had begun to receive the collective requests of con-temporaries. Consider this poem by the Slavophile poet Stepan Shevyryov, occasioned by the beginning of the Crimean War:

> Пушкин! встань, проснись из гробу!
> Где твой голос и язык?
> Поражай вражду и злобу,
> Зачинай победный клик!

> Pushkin! Arise, awaken from the grave!
> Where is your voice and tongue?
> Defeat enmity and malice,
> Release the triumphant cry![65]

From the 1870s onwards, the appearance of Pushkin's shade was depicted as a collective vision – as empirical, material proof of the poet's participation in the life of his native land. This vision was repre-sented especially vividly in the literature devoted to the celebrations of 1880. Note the striking parallel between Nashchokin's story of how Pushkin's friends and admirers gathered to see their dear poet in 1854 and the 1880 festivities in Moscow. However, in the latter case the scene of action was 'the entire square' rather than a drawing room, and the participants included 'the entire intelligentsia,' rather than a narrow circle of the poet's friends and kin:

> The entire square fell still in anticipation. And then a shroud fell at first at the feet of the poet's statue, and then fell completely away from the monument ... *As one of the living* there appeared before us *the one so familiar to us from portraits and busts,* the dear and familiar image of the poet. It is difficult to communicate the impression that took hold of everyone then. The sound of the bells, the strict singing of the national hymn, the square covered with masses of the most varied kinds of people ranging from pupils of educational institutions, banners, wreaths interwoven with ribbons, and finally that marvelous statue, it all created an indescribably wonderful sight [...] After a minute of general paralysis, a loud hurrah rose up from the square. One of the poet's sons who was present during the celebration shed tears that streamed along three paths down his face. Indeed, rarely is one fated to experience such moments.[66]

But this festive materialization was far from marking the end of the Russian love affair with Pushkin's ghost. The statue, it turned out, could come to life: it observed the poet's compatriots, appraised them, delivered judgments on contemporary affairs. Finally, the poet could even abandon his pedestal. This mythological narrative was presented particularly clearly in A. Gangelin's poem 'To the memory of A.S. Pushkin' (1887):

> Вот оживает он, увидя ликованье
> Собравшейся толпы к подножию его.
> Уста певца гласят: 'средь вас я для чего?
> Как только мертвое для взора изваянье?!'
> ... И он поник челом в глубоком размышленьи...
> Вдруг в ночь безмолвную с гранитной высоты
> Он сходит царственно в порыве вдохновенья,
> И песнь его гремит в честь вечной красоты.

> Now he comes alive, seeing the rejoicing
> Of the crowd gathered at his feet.
> The poet's voice sounds: 'why am I among you?
> As a graven image, to all appearances dead?'

… And he lowered his brow in deep thought …
And in the silent night from the granite heights
He descends grandly in a moment of inspiration,
And his song thunders in honor of eternal beauty …[67]

The noisy celebrations of 1899 marked the beginning of a new chapter in the history of the myth of Pushkin's shade. During this period, the poet's shade became *the collective property* of Russian society, with all the ensuing consequences. A characteristic feature of the 1899 festivities that has been regularly noted and mocked by critics was the mass production of tasteless images of the poet: from gorgeous pictures to cheap prints; from formal portraits to others created by less conventional means (such as a portrait made of flowers that was 'grown' in a large flowerbed on the Sokolniki Circle in Moscow). Depictions of Pushkin could be discovered in the most unlikely contexts – on sweet wrappers, medals, cigarette packets, labels on bottles of spirits, and so forth. Moreover, Pushkin appeared as an animate being in so-called tableaux vivants. Finally, it was in this period that, with the invention of cinematography, it became possible to see a living, moving, and (wordlessly) speaking Pushkin. Tellingly, the first piece of cinematic Pushkiniana related to the poet's duel and death – Vasily Goncharov's *Life and Death of Pushkin*.[68]

The subsequent fate of Pushkin's shade falls outside the scope of the present study, which is limited to the history of the poet's 'posthumous' appearances from spiritualist seances of the 1850s to cinema seances of the early 1900s. But it must be noted that 'Pushkin's shade' remained a living and active force in the twentieth century, as a focus of the 'spiritualist' motifs of native Pushkiniana. Moreover, the national myth became the backdrop or subject both of individual artistic myths about Pushkin (A. Blok, V. Khlebnikov, V. Mayakovsky, V. Nabokov, M. Tsvetaeva, A. Sinyavsky, A. Bitov)[69] and of various parascientific myths (such as the story of a sect of female radio operators who received signals from Pushkin from the cosmos[70] – in this sense, the new era of technological revolution was merely a case of old wine in new bottles). But that is a separate subject.[71]

Twentieth-century authors turned on more than one occasion to the 'spiritualist' motif of the summoning of Pushkin's shade. In this respect, Sasha Cherny's story (published in 1926) about the appearance of Pushkin's shade in the émigré community during the year of the worldwide Spiritualist Congress represents a kind of 'baring of the device.'[72] Summoned by Sir Arthur Conan Doyle, a passionate researcher of spiritualism, Pushkin's shade makes an unexpected appearance in Paris. It is visited by representatives of various competing émigré circles and newspapers, each of whom considers Pushkin a like-minded soul and suggests that the poet make a speech that has been specially prepared for him.

In that same year, 1926, Mark Aldanov published his article 'Unpublished Works by Pushkin. (In Connection with the Spiritualist Congress),' which informed readers of two 'entirely unknown works by Pushkin' that the poet's shade had dictated in French to the spiritualist Charles Dorino. Pushkin also gave Dorino a political interview during which, in Aldanov's words, 'he complained bitterly about the characterlessness of the Russian people with its eternal "Nitchego" [literally, 'Nothing'], and cursed landowners, the tsar, and the clergy, while also showering abuse on a sect of Russian nihilists and on German social democracy. In conclusion, he expressed his warmest sympathies towards spiritualism.'[73] Here we see Pushkin's speaking shade emerging onto the world stage and expressing typically Western preconceptions about the Russian people.

Curiously, this was also the year in which criminal proceedings were brought in Soviet Russia against adepts of a cult who claimed to have witnessed the appearance of the bloody shade of Pushkin by a well in Pikanskoe village, in the district of Barnaul. A severe punishment was meted out to the perpetrators of this superstition: the Bishop of Barnaul Nikodim and Archpriest Smirnov were sentenced to six years in prison 'in strict isolation,' and Priest Pogorzhinsky to four. But this merciless clampdown on superstition did not prevent Soviet ideologues and poets from exploiting the cultural myth of Pushkin's shade to their own ends.[74] Pushkin, like Lenin, made constant appearances in Soviet life: he was seen by Red Army men at Perekop; he was materialized in monuments; and he was constantly interrogated about present-day affairs. In short,

И на площади Красной,
На трибунах, под марш боевой,
Он являлся, приветливый, страстный,
С непокрытой, как мы, головой.

And on our beauteous Red Square
On the orator's stand, accompanied by a military march,

He appeared, friendly, passionate,
With his head, like ours, uncovered.[75]

Or, another vivid example:

Из столетия в столетья
Лучезарный гений слова
Ты в своем великолепьи
Появляешься нам снова.
Всей советскою страною
Ты вождем поэтов признан
И могучею волною
Входишь в мир социализма.
Пушкин, Пушкин, будь же славен
Славой родины чудесной.
Да здравствует Сталин!
Да здравствуют песни!

From one century to another,
Oh radiant genius of the word,
You appear again to us
In all your magnificence.
The entire Soviet country
Names you the leader of poets
And as a mighty wave
You enter the socialist world.
Pushkin, oh Pushkin, be glorious
With the glory of your native land.
Long live Stalin!
Long live songs![76]

Finally, the most recent festivities (1999) showed that this popular myth has retained its vigour. One illustrative example of this was the 'Pushkin questionnaire' that *Literaturnaia Gazeta* (Literary Gazette) asked ten contemporary writers to complete. It included such questions as the following: '3. What, in your opinion, is the essence of Pushkin's presence in our life? [...] 5. What would you have wanted to ask him? 6. On what topic would you have challenged him?' Some replies: '[I would ask] why great figures from among the deceased do not yet have the right to descend from the heavens to the still living popularizers and various "experts" and hold them to the strictest standards ... or, even better, simply beat their brains out' (Viktor Konetsky); 'How he, being an earthly creature in life, managed to become so ethereal in poetry' (Rygor Borodulin); 'I would turn to him with all kinds of questions: about the people, about Russia, about Chechnya, about history, about prose, about literature' (Mikhail Roshchin). [77]

Conclusion

According to Boris Gasparov, the image of Pushkin in Russian culture 'is perceived as an all-embracing expression of the Russian spiritual world – a kind of entelechy which is present in the sphere of Russian spirituality, whatever the latter's manifestations and whatever the vagaries of its historical fate.'[78] This is, of course, true for poets and intellectuals ('high' spiritualism) but not for the collective reception of Pushkin in Russian culture. Here, the ideal image of the poet is perceived in crudely materialist terms. The popular myth of Pushkin has required to this day empirical facts that confirm the continued presence of Pushkin in Russian culture. These include the publication of newly found texts and manuscripts; the discovery of biographical data or relics linked to his name; the appearance of new portraits, monuments, and films about Pushkin; and so forth.

   In sum, the cult of Pushkin that appeared in the realist era was not a cultural (quasi)religion, such as the cult of Shakespeare's shade described by Marjorie Garber,[79] but a cultural superstition exposing the ideological and psychological conflicts of the time. Its main features were these: (1) the reluctance of society to accept the death of the poet; (2) the formation of a 'purified,' idealized image of 'posthumous' Pushkin, who responded to the interests of one or another ideological group; (3) the presumption of the latter's interest in affairs of the present; (4) the constant summoning of his 'material' image with the help of competent intermediaries (at first, friends of the poet, then poets, Pushkinists, critics, artists, cinematographers, etc.) and the attempt to learn his opinion on vexing contemporary issues; and (5) the attribution to Pushkin of judgments reflecting the opinions and world view of the person who had summoned him. In the words used in Vladimir Mayakovsky's poem to describe how the author chatted with Pushkin's statue, we might say that we are faced with a 'sort of spiritualism' in the form of a non-stop national seance.[80]

PART TWO

Realist Exorcism: Spiritualism and the Russian Literary Imagination of the 1860s to 1880s

Realism, to my mind, implies, besides truth to detail, the truthful reproduction of typical circumstances.

Friedrich Engels, 'Über Kunst und Literatur'

Exorcism conducted through sober analysis makes only phantoms disappear; existing objects, when subjected to this test, prove the reality of their
existence.

D.I. Pisarev, 'Realists'

I fully understand that phantoms should vanish with the first ray of sun,
but, alas, I do not know when this ray will appear. That is what
oppresses me, that is what makes me fear for the future.

M.E. Saltykov-Shchedrin, 'Modern Phantoms'

4 Flickering Hands: The Spiritualist Realism of Nikolai Vagner

A luminous hand came down from the upper part of the room, and after hovering near me for a few seconds, took the pencil from my hand, rapidly wrote on a sheet of paper, threw the pencil down, and then rose up over our heads, gradually fading into darkness.

> William Crookes, 'Notes of an Inquiry into
> the Phenomena Called Spiritual
> During the Years 1870–1873'

If you have dreamt of a hand detached from the body, take it as a sign of solitude. You will find it difficult to attain a good understanding with others.

> *Modern Book of Dream Interpretations*

Introduction

Let us take a few steps back. In a letter from Staraia Russa dated 27 June 1875, A.G. Dostoevskaya informed her husband of her acquaintance with Nikolai Petrovich Vagner, the initiator of the debate over Modern Spiritualism that overwhelmed educated Russian society in the spring of that year.[1] Dostoevskaya's description of Vagner is ironic and vivid: 'A funny small man with a shrill feminine voice, a huge straw hat and a huge rug in his arms.' Dostoevskaya encountered him 'on a park bench reading letters (probably from somebody in the other world), so thoroughly absorbed in his reading that he noticed no one.' All of a sudden he 'jumped up, ran up and down the long path three times, and vanished.' 'He had,' Dostoevskaya concludes, 'the appearance of a half-crazed man (as befits a spiritualist).'[2]

This 'half-crazed spiritualist,' who in Dostoevskaya's portrait recalls the eccentric professors of Jules Verne, was one of the most colourful and little studied participants in the 'psycho-physical' controversies of the last third of the nineteenth century.[3] In this chapter I consider Vagner's spiritualist imagination (his vision of 'posthumous humanity') as an extreme instance of scientific millenarianism typical of positivist thinking in a period marked by the rapid development of the experimental sciences and religious ferment in high society.[4] My focus will be the image of the materialized hand – flying, waving, writing, vanishing – that is constantly encountered in Vagner's articles. I examine this dynamic anthropological image as the symbolic embodiment of the experimental method and teleology of spiritualism, a doctrine that propounds the gradual physical appropriation of the non-material world and that anticipates a definitive solution to the ancient debate about body and soul. I will also be concerned here with the relation this image bears to the metonymical principle of realistic representation[5] and to the metaphorical discourse of authorship that was characteristic of Russian literature of the 1860s and 1870s.

Materializations

As has been noted, Vagner's infamous letter on spiritualism was published on 1 April 1875 in the *Herald of Europe*.[6] A dispute about the essence of the soul and the tasks of psychology had been simmering for several years in this journal between the philosopher K.D. Kavelin, who hoped to reconcile positivism with speculative philosophy (through the concept of the 'organism of the soul'), and the materialist physiologist I.M. Sechenov, who viewed the soul as 'an organ of the brain.'[7] The introduction of the hitherto marginal spiritualist position into this serious epistemological and philosophical dispute proved highly explosive, with some readers concluding that they were faced with an April Fool's prank. Vagner, a famous St Petersburg naturalist, was calling on Russian society to take mediumistic phenomena seriously; to construct, through spiritualist seances, a solid scientific bridge between the material and spiritual worlds; and to resolve, through the summoning of souls and their scientific investigation, the long-standing debate between materialism and spiritualism.

Vagner's letter bore a peculiarly 'hagiographical' character. It related how its author, a materialist and sceptic, gradually came to believe in Modern Spiritualism (i.e., in the existence of life beyond the grave) under the influence of the seances conducted in St Petersburg by the French medium Camille Brédif. This public confession of a Russian scientist accorded with the pattern, already established in the West, of famous naturalists being converted to spiritualism (other included the American professor Robert Hare and the British scholars William Crookes and Alfred Russel Wallace). This set the pattern for the neophytes of the Russian movement.

The spiritualist phenomenon that struck Vagner above all others was the materialization of spirits under the influence of the medium's psychic energy. This was 'the crowning achievement of later spiritualism'[8] and the burning concern of the spiritualist literature of the late 1870s, and was closely tied to apocalyptic expectations of a 'positive' epoch.[9] The Western spiritualist press described – in meticulous detail – instances of materialization: the manifestations of luminous hands at the seances of Daniel Dunglas Home; the materializations of the spirits of John and Katie King under the influence of the English medium Florence Cook; plaster casts of the hands and feet of spirits; and spiritualist photographs. Explanations of these phenomena were proffered by N.B. Wolfe, W. Crookes, A.R. Wallace, H.C. Olcott, and A.N. Aksakov.[10]

The spiritualists' theories essentially revolved around the following questions. Do the hands, faces, and fully materialized figures constitute a 'positive' fact (i.e., the 'forming of a temporary otherworldly, functioning body'[11] or body part), a collective hallucination on the part of the viewers, or the tricks of a skilful conjurer?[12] How and of what are the spirits formed, if indeed they are formed – that is, are they ethereal or luminous bodies, perisprit, ectoplasm? How does the visible image of the spirit correspond to the appearance of its medium? How and to where do the spirits 'return' afterwards, and why can the 'hair cut off from such figures' be preserved after the disappearance of the figures themselves?[13] How can the process of materialization be inscribed in our physical picture of the world, and how can it be reconciled with the law of the preservation of matter? Of what does our world really consist and where are its physical boundaries? Vagner's letter offered no explanations. Its aim was quite different – to describe sensational phenomena that opened to the viewer a 'new world' awaiting its scholarly observer. Vagner appealed not to the logic of his readers but to their curiosity and imagination.

The professor's greatest delight was reserved for Brédif's main stunt: the appearances of the hand of the deceased Chinese lady, Zheke, from behind a curtain. The medium himself would be located behind a special screen, since it was thought that in a closed space he (or she) could concentrate the psychic energy required for the forming of a spirit (his hands, moreover, were tied). According to Vagner's testimony, the Chinese lady's hand differed not at all 'from an ordinary human hand,' nor did it 'in any way resemble the hand of Brédif.' Those gathered at the seance, Vagner reports, not only saw Zheke's hand but also 'touched or pressed its fingers.' The hand, in its turn, grasped and squeezed theirs and 'tried to drag them into the dark room'; then, from behind the closed curtain, it 'flitted' over the head of the medium, from whom it was plainly detached. Vagner himself 'squeezed its fingers and felt the nails.' Moreover, this hand tried to pull the ring off Vagner's own hand 'and quite clearly hooked it with a nail.'[14] Other spiritualist hands would appear from behind the table and fly through the air, waving, pointing out objects, and writing messages.

Vagner's letter galvanized a heated debate about experimental spiritualism, which had long been familiar to Russian society but had yet to gain any authoritative advocates among scholars in the natural sciences (Russia in this respect lagged behind the West).[15] In essence, Vagner brought Modern Spiritualism from the intellectual periphery to the heart of public debate and raised the possibility of the seance being viewed as a scientific laboratory, whose role was to strip the observed phenomena of their mystical character: 'Seances must be transformed into a series of psycho-physical experiments and investigations.'

'My scientific authority and my firm conviction agitated the entire intelligentsia,' Vagner recalled years later. The initiators of the debate began to receive letters from all quarters requesting invitations to attend Brédif's seances. 'Meanwhile,' Vagner continued, 'the party of *a priori* sceptics was not slumbering and began to publish articles refuting facts they had not seen.'[16]

Indeed, nearly every periodical responded to Vagner's article with stern reproach or mockery. In the article 'Magic under the Wing of Science,'[17] the critic E.L. Markov derided Vagner's psychic phenomena as 'devilry' (*chertovshchina*) and saw in spiritualism the 'revival in our rational age of a primitive, Shamanic doctrine.' The botanist S.A. Rachinsky, friend of an influential member of the Council of the Empire, K.P. Pobedonostsev, wrote that 'Mr Vagner's advice [...] to pursue the investigation of mediumistic phenomena is harmful, since this research can be carried out safely and profitably only by specialists in the field of nervous diseases and psychiatry, subjects entirely alien to the great part of our public.' Rachinsky recommended that such research begin with the medium, 'and then with those under the medium's influence.'[18] At a meeting held by the Physics Society at St Petersburg University on 6 May 1875, Mendeleev spoke of the need for scientists to expose so-called mediumistic phenomena.[19]

But it was already too late. The spectre of Modern Spiritualism, which had long been quietly affirmed by theologians and a few authors of religious sensibility, had broken free, becoming an important element in the public consciousness. It could be argued that the furious invectives delivered by spiritualism's adversaries represented a particular form of ideological exorcism (a singular instance of the struggle, characteristic of the entire century, against religious and ideological superstition).[20] Spiritualism, I would suggest, proved so significant and so unacceptable to its opponents not only because it touched – in an improbably vulgar form – on the most contentious issues of the age,[21] but also because, in arising at the intersection of theology, the natural sciences, psychology, and literature (i.e., the institutions that laid claim at that time to the role of 'experts of the human soul'), it *parodied* the utopian practices that underpinned them: the acquisition of lost faith with the help of reason and science; humanity's liberation from the spectres left over from the past, and the meticulous investigation of newly discovered natural laws; the objectification of the spiritual world of man; and the 'metonymical' (Jakobson) representation of reality in the artistic text through the medium of the author. In other words, Modern Spiritualism in the 1870s held up a unique mirror to contemporary culture, as its comic double and impostor, and as a shadow declaring its right to an independent existence.

Spiritualist Realism

The opponents of spiritualism perceived Vagner's letter as an affront to common sense, the laws of nature, and scientific ethics, and as religious blasphemy, fetishism, superstition, or (partial) mental derangement. The most generous explanation they found for his spiritualist enthusiasms was childish naivety, according to the principle 'to each wise man a dose of folly.' The ridiculing of Vagner reached its height in the summer of 1875. It was precisely then that A.G. Dostoevskaya first encountered him. Her reaction to him was influenced to a significant degree by the professor's reputation in the press, and it is interesting that Anna Grigor'evna almost guessed what it was that Vagner was reading with such passion. These letters really were 'messages from beyond' – or rather, evidence of astonishing phenomena of spirit materialization.

By the spring of that year, A.N. Aksakov (1832–1903), the main theoretician and advocate of spiritualism in Russia, had received from Helene Blavatsky, future founder of the Theosophical Society, a translation of the letters of Colonel H. Olcott about the mediumistic data he had recorded in October 1874 at the homestead of the Eddy brothers in Chittenden, Vermont.[22] The letters, published in the *New York Daily Herald* with illustrations by A.R. Kappes and T.W. Williams, appeared in a single volume in March 1875 under the title *People from the Other World*. As Vagner recalled several years later, 'for the three of us – me, Butlerov, and Aksakov – these letters were of the greatest interest and we gathered two or three times at Butlerov's place, where he would read two or three letters to us in an evening. These letters gave me a wealth of facts, which I published in *The Russian Herald* (October, 1875).'[23]

The publication in question is the article 'Mediumship'[24] – Vagner's extensive reply to the sceptics who were seeking 'to guard our society against the invasion of spiritualism.' Vagner submitted his article to the publisher M.N. Katkov personally, being unsure that the latter would wish to print it. They talked at length about mediumistic phenomena; indeed, Katkov even cited a few facts from *The Primary Chronicle* (the twelfth-century history of Kievan Rus') about the manifestations of individuals from the other world.[25] In his editor's note, however, Katkov found it necessary to distance himself from Vagner's article: 'These strange arguments are published here out of regard for the author's professorial status and fame.'[26] Let us pause to consider the contents of this article, which is unique in Russian journalism of the 1870s.

Vagner begins with a short, theoretical preface that places experimental spiritualism in the context of the contemporary debate on psychology. Mediumship, he affirms, is 'a specific instance of that general phenomenon' that may be labelled 'psychism': 'the urge of a human being to define and examine the existence of his own soul.'[27] 'Psychology,' the professor continues, 'always was, is and will remain a focus of all society, since society seeks in its problems not physiological truths [a rebuke to the followers of I.M. Sechenov], but *the foundations of the worldview that it should take for its social order*. Does the other world exist, or does everything end with our senses? Is the soul immortal, or is it just the product of matter and [subject for] destruction together with the body after death? Now there's a simple, childish question.'[28]

Vagner argues that mediumistic phenomena (above all, the materialization of spirits) give 'a categorical, positive answer' to this 'childish' question. He firmly believes that all doubts will disappear when the phenomena are fully 'investigated and proved *with mathematical precision*.'[29] At that point a synthesis will occur, one for which generations have yearned: 'the moral world will merge with the truths of knowledge and the *correct path* will be revealed for the development of the human spirit' and society.[30] After this scientific–millenarian preamble, Vagner moves on to the article's most diverting theme: 'the process of the formation and disappearance of spirits' (in other words, the materialization and dematerialization of ghosts). The principal source of his examples was, as I have said, Olcott's letters, translated by Blavatsky.

Vagner opens his list of scientifically proven phenomena with the spectre of Katie King, the most celebrated spirit in the spiritualist pantheon of the 1870s. The charming Miss King, a contemporary of Oliver Cromwell who lived in distant Jamaica, appeared on numerous occasions in the presence of the 'strong' English medium Florence Cook. Katie's manifestations in the flesh were described and investigated in detail by the famous English chemist and advocate of spiritualism, William Crookes, who observed her in the half-dark and under electric light, measured her pulse, and, having put his ear to her chest, listened to the beating of her heart.[31]

From London, Vagner transports his readers to Vermont, to the farm of the medium brothers William and Horatio Eddy, where, in 1874, many materializations occurred, transforming Chittenden into the 'spiritualist capital of the world.' In Vagner's account, astonishing episodes followed one after another with kaleidoscopic speed: shawls materialized and hovered in the air, an angry spirit shaved off half a medium's moustache and beard in his sleep, the Indian ghost Honto let Olcott measure her height in the interests of science, and also left him, as mementos, a lock of hair and a piece of her dress, which miraculously repaired itself that same instant.[32] The wonders of Chittenden reached their apogee with the arrival of the Russian medium and traveller Mrs B* (Helene Blavatsky).[33]

From the moment of Blavatsky's arrival, Vagner notes, 'there began to appear to her the materialized spectres of people she had known in life or whom she had encountered in the course of her lengthy wanderings.'

Figure 4 The materialization of the Georgian Mikhalko (left). (Van Pelt Library, University of Pennsylvania)

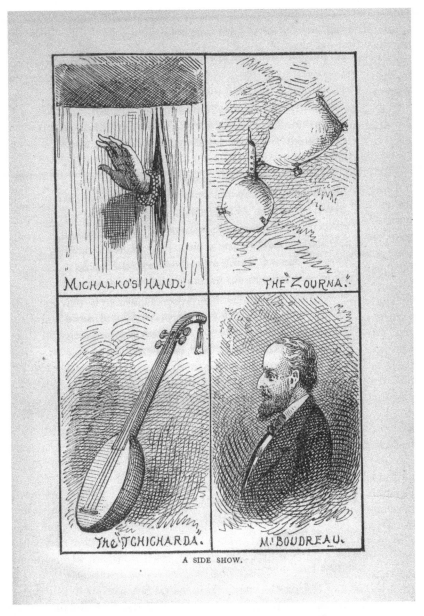

A SIDE SHOW.

Figure 5 Mikhalko's hand and beads (top left) appearing from behind the spiritualist Screen. (Van Pelt Library, University of Pennsylvania)

The reader is presented with a kind of spiritualist *défilé*, an exhibition of spirits of varied genders and ages dressed in the most exotic attire. On the very first evening, 'a ghost of average height' announced himself, 'smartly turned out in half-Turkish, half-Georgian dress.' When asked his name, the spirit replied, 'bowing and showing his teeth': 'Mikhalko Batono.'

Blavatsky instantly recognized him: she had known him as a serf working for a certain Gegidze in Imereti. As confirmation of his Georgian stock, Mikhalko performed, at Olcott's request, the folk song 'Tires, Tires, Berbere,' which Blavatsky immediately transcribed.[34]

Mikhalko also made subsequent appearances – whether full or partial – at the Chittenden seances. Thus, there once emerged from behind the curtain 'Mikhalko's tanned, soiled hand, covered with warts and wrapped round with beads of amber' (these, Blavatsky explained, reflected a local custom, thereby testifying to the authenticity of the Georgian apparition). Blavatsky asked the hand to play the Georgian Lezginka dance, 'and the hand strummed this lively *allegro* on a guitar for a good while.'[35]

'The appearance of Russian ghosts in an American backwater was a thing of interest,' continues Vagner, not, it seems, without patriotic zeal. Madame Blavatsky's nanny appeared to her, speaking in Russian and calling her by her childhood nickname, 'steeplejack.' Then there appeared a gentleman wearing the cross of St Anna. He turned out to be her uncle, the former President of the Criminal Court in Grodno. 'Yes, it's me, Yelena, your uncle Gustave,' he said, embracing her. Last, a Russian spirit gave Blavatsky the medal for bravery that had been awarded to her father for the 1828 campaign. The spirit confessed that the medal had been taken from the Stavropol grave of General Blavatsky, who died in 1873.[36] Representatives of other nations also appeared under the Russian medium's influence: a German, Frenchmen, an Indian, a young Kurd. Even a giant *djinn* appeared, 'wearing national dress.' A kind of otherworldly International was taking shape (or, one might say, a posthumous immigration from the Old World to the New).[37] Mysterious, invisible performers played 'various solos, duets, and, finally, a piece for an entire orchestra.'[38]

At the end of his article Vagner returns from Vermont to St Petersburg to report the mediumistic facts observed there under the influence of Brédif. Thus, Arthur Schopenhauer had made an appearance before one young philosopher (it was Vladimir Solovyov), adducing

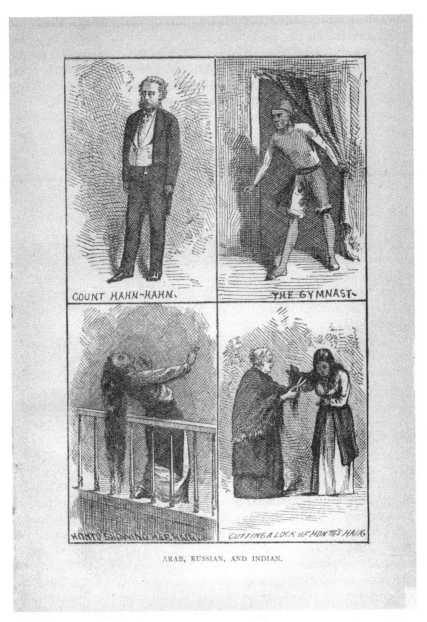

COUNT HAHN-HAHN.

THE GYMNAST.

HONTO SHOWING HER HAIR.

CUTTING A LOCK OF HONTO'S HAIR.

ARAB, RUSSIAN, AND INDIAN.

Figure 6 The materialization of Helene Blavatsky's uncle (top left). (Van Pelt Library, University of Pennsylvania) 'subtle biographical details' by which to prove his identity. The spirit of Goethe, in its turn, had taken a line from the poet's opus to refute the doctrine of reincarnation professed by some Russian 'sectarians' – that is, followers of Allan Kardec. In conclusion, Vagner turns once again to the phenomenon of the flying hand, rejecting the notion that Brédif had been caught out during one of his seances. It's not quite so easy, the professor remarks, to establish whose hand this was, given the well-known fact that 'doubles' of mediums' hands had appeared at other seances. Moreover, the ghostly hand had been seen and felt by other seance participants, and it bore no relation to the extremities of the medium Brédif. Vagner signs off with an appeal to the 'party of *a priori* sceptics': 'Renounce your pride of intellect and logic, and *there will unfold before you that world against which you are so harshly prejudiced.'*[39]

Let us try, then, to summarize the nature of the 'other world' as portrayed by the 'Columbus of Russian Spiritualism.' It is not a kingdom beyond the grave; not hell, heaven, or purgatory; not the cosmic communities of Swedenborg; not the planetary extravaganza of Kardec; not the 'Summer land' of the American spiritualist Andrew Jackson Davis; and not the astral world of the theosophists.[40] The 'other world' depicted in the article of the professor and naturalist is a world of palpable, colourful, and sonorous manifestations of a certain spiritual substance, which makes itself known in the hope of being studied further.[41] Under the influence of mediumistic force, the ghosts of dead Russians, Frenchmen, Germans, Indians, Georgians, and Persians freely traverse earthly space and may appear at any time. They are kind-hearted, playful, and complaisant, as ready to oblige ordinary human curiosity as to serve the interests of science. Among them are representatives of the fairer sex (Katie, Zheke, Honto), who lend to the spiritualist community its distinctively chivalrous and often playful character. At the request of the seance goers, the ghosts leave bits of clothing or locks of hair; they play musical instruments, gambol, dance, sing, and even smoke pipes. They can be touched, photographed under electric light, weighed, measured, embraced, and reproduced in plaster casts. A materialization offers seance goers the opportunity to make an anthropological investigation of otherworldly apparitions, who differ in no respect from living people (the same nails, hair roots, pulse, and heartbeat). This is no fantasy, hallucination, or mystical vision, but a scientifically verifiable incarnation of representative aspects of non-materiality; it is Spiritualist Realism.[42]

The Pursuit of the Hand

The adversaries of spiritualism immediately poured scorn on the 'kingdom of spirits' depicted by the professor of St Petersburg.[43] In a venomous feuilleton, the critic Gamma (G.K. Gradovsky) wrote that 'Mr Vagner is leading us into some kind of *fairyland*. All one hears at drawing-room soirees and in home study groups [*domashnie kruzhki*] are sundry idiocies derived from Mr Vagner's article [...] Thanks to his article, we find ourselves once again there, where marvels are, where the wood-spirit roams [Pushkin, *Ruslan and Lyudmila*].'[44]

The quotation from Pushkin's prologue to his 'magic' narrative poem *Ruslan and Lyudmila* was a merry play on Vagner's alias 'Kitty Cat,' under which he wrote popular fairy tales for children.[45] But the 'fairy tales' that Vagner was telling his adult readers were, in Gamma's opinion, nothing but a return to the infancy of humanity and to archaic times – in other words, a modern superstition.

In literary circles, Vagner's name soon became a derogatory term ('contemporary Vagners,' 'one of the local Vagners,' 'Wurst'),[46] and his image quickly acquired shades of parody, as a sort of comic spectre, often to be coupled with Professor Butlerov ('Butler'), and sometimes with the demonic 'father of Russian Spiritualism,' A.N. Aksakov.[47] Caricatures soon began to appear of the storytelling professor, the seer–professor, the mad professor, or the crank:

Странное явленье!
Человек науки
Верит в духов, в тени,
В неземные звуки.
[...] И читая бредни,
Думаешь невольно
«Для ученых наших
Простоты довольно!»

A most peculiar thing!
These men of science
Believing in spirits, shades
And unearthly sounds.
[...] Reading their ravings,
You can't help thinking:
All our wise men
Can be foolish as well.[48]

The author of the feuilleton 'In the World of Spirits (The Feelings, Confessions, Descriptions, and Observations of an Aksako-Butlero-Vagnero-Specialist)' wrote under the pseudonym Not-Vagner. In his satire, a patchwork of motifs of Vagnerian 'wonders,' we find spiritual-ists singing the anthem 'Tiris, Tiris, Barbare' and then falling amicably to the ground before the medium amid general shrieks of joy and ten-der emotion.[49] In another humorous sketch, Vagner and Butlerov appear at a masked ball dressed as madmen and singing couplets.[50]

It was Vagner's passion for materialized hands that elicited his crit-ics' greatest annoyance. 'What kind of chemistry, what kind of phys-ics, and what kind of philosophy can exist beside the hand of the dead Chinese woman, Zheke, which, in the words of the St Petersburg natu-ralist, "took form in our midst" (!),' demanded Evgeny Markov in response to Vagner's first letter.[51] 'In Vagner's world hands can emerge and do all sorts of things,' remarked another journalist, before offering an amusing sketch in which a spirit is being felt and which rephrases the words of Gogol's gallant devil in 'Christmas Eve': 'And what's this you have, beautiful Honto?'[52] 'If a hand should appear before me,' declared Mr Tsvet, one of Vagner's scholarly adversaries, 'then I will grab it; I'll grab it with my teeth ... I'll bite it; it upsets my common sense! I don't want to be mad. I want knowledge, reason.'[53] Professor A. Shkliarevsky noted that the materialization of a single detached human hand in St Petersburg 'would require the air of all European and Asiatic Russia.'[54] Ya.P. Polonsky (who, we recall, recom-mended Vagner to the Dostoevskys) wrote in his poem 'Old and New Spirits':[55]

Но никаких задач науки
Всех этих душ безличный рой,
Ни их сомнительные стуки,
Ни их *мелькающие руки*,
Своей таинственной игрой
Не разрешат...

No scientific problem
Will ever by solved
By the faceless swarm
Of all these souls,
Nor by their secret games
Of *flickering hands*
And suspicious taps.[56]

The 'flickering' hand became the sign, or synecdoche, of Modern Spiritualism: the morbid hallucination of the adherent, or the instrument of the charlatan–medium's 'sorcery.' As the debate on spiritualism raged, V.N. Egarev staged a parody of Vagner's 'world of wonders' in his St Petersburg puppet theatre: the conjurer exhibited hovering and grasping hands before explaining how such 'miracles' were performed. A journalist for *Dragonfly* titled his piece on the show 'The Death of Spiritualism at the Hand of Egarev.'[57]

This pursuit of the mediumistic hand, with its exorcist overtones, strikes one as deeply symptomatic: the hand is one of the crucial mediating symbols in the spiritualist eidology, an idiosyncratic key to the spiritualist imagination.[58]

Thing

The hand that appears detached from the body is a frequent image in the history of culture.[59] The Lord's hand came upon the prophet Elisha (2 Kings 3:15). A hand presaging the end of the kingdom of Belshazzar writes mysterious words on the wall, the meaning of which only Daniel can grasp (Dan. 5).

In medieval art and mystic iconography, a luminous hand emerging from a cloud symbolizes divine intervention. Hands and other human parts are present in Bosch's depiction of Hell. In the reign of King James I, a mysterious white hand appeared on three occasions to a certain functionary, forcing him to reverse his decision to deprive his son of his inheritance. In Walpole's Gothic novel *The Castle of Otranto* (1764), a gigantic hand forewarns the protagonist of his punishment. The author himself acknowledged that his idea was based on his vision of a frightening hand in armour. In V.A. Zhukovsky's ballad 'Adelstan' (1813), two enormous hands emerge from an abyss and the sinning hero dies between their claws.

Since the mid-twentieth century the 'disembodied hand' has been a fixture in horror films – an early example is *The Beast with Five Fingers* (1947). It has also featured in horror parodies, such as *The Addams Family* (1964–6) and *The Diamond Arm* (1968). The symbolism of self-propelled hands in nightmares was discussed by Sigmund Freud.[60]

It is absolutely clear, however, that the Vagnerian hand is quite different from these examples. Vagner's hand does not punish or strangle. It foretells nothing and threatens nobody (the terror of castration in Freud's interpretation). It elicits in Vagner neither sacred terror nor reverence, but rather surprise and the joy of possession. The appearance of the hand is material proof of the existence of the other world.[61] It is the symbol of the positivist's physical, tactile apprehension of the other world; it is also the materialization of the empirical epistemology of Modern Spiritualism, which seizes a part of the still inaccessible whole.[62] It is also a synecdoche for gifts (the hands of exotic aborigines from the other world leave talismans as presents); a guide leading one into the world of spirits (the hands beckon and disappear); and an instrument of music making and authorship beyond the grave (the message-writing hands in the accounts of Vagner and Olcott). For Vagner, therefore, the hand that appears in the flesh represents nothing other than the materialization of the soul. We have before us an idiosyncratic realization of Aristotelian anthropology: 'the soul is analogous to the hand; for as the hand is a tool of tools, so the mind is the form of forms.'[63] Last, the hand symbolizes friendly contact with the other side: the two worlds do not merely touch each other but seem to shake each other's hand.[64]

Indeed, Vagner's articles portrayed the spiritualist seance as a *special zone of amicable contact between the material and spiritual worlds*, a sort of 'meeting at the Elbe' of distant allies. The results of this encounter, Vagner hoped, would be an indestructible alliance of worlds that had been separated until then by death; the gradual realization of humanity's religious aspirations and scientific quests; and, ultimately, victory over death as the main 'phantom' of being. It was no less than the apocalyptic Utopia of an empirical positivist and evolutionary, a Utopia that posited the incremental development of humanity on the path to bodily immortality.[65]

Conclusion

What, in summary, are the principal differences between the spiritualist attitude towards supernatural phenomena and the pre-positivist approach? Spirits now are no longer transcendental guests in our world, nor are they 'marvellous visions,' or *das Unheimliche*; rather, they are 'scientific phenomena' attached to one or another medium as manifestations of a force (energy) that remains to be studied, as objects to be observed in the laboratory. They appear neither in castles nor in cemeteries, but in the presence of witnesses in a specially equipped room (the 'spiritualist cabinet,' or the 'hall of spirits and ghosts' at the farm of the Eddy brothers). They can be seen, interrogated, felt, drawn, and photographed. Pictures of them can be circulated through the press by the million and brought into literally every home. In other words, experimental spiritualism involves the total desacralization of the supernatural, rendering it segmented, anthropologized, scientistic, and vulgarized. In these respects the spiritualist seance, as a performance, may be contrasted with the phantasmagoria of the late eighteenth century. The latter, as Terry Castle has convincingly shown, staged the process of the interiorization of ghosts, the 'spectralization' of human consciousness, whereas the seance freed consciousness from ghosts, bringing them out into the open, materializing and taming them. 'The mystical and the supernatural,' wrote Vagner's like-minded friend, A.M. Butlerov, 'end at the point where knowledge reigns, and in this sphere ought not study and knowledge be our aim?'[66]

In essence, Modern Spiritualism succeeded in performing a kind of epistemological somersault, seeking to 'solve' at one stroke the main issue of the positivist program in the nineteenth century – ridding humanity, with the help of experimental science, of the spectres it had inherited from the past. Terror (hell, purgatory, 'the dark night of the soul,' fearful avengers from beyond) had vanished. But so, too, had its content:

Нет, эти духи, что стучат
Или ворочают столами,
Не те, которые грозят
Расстаться с нашими мечтами!
Они невежды, иль шуты,
Родные дети пустоты,
Тоски, неверья, увяданья,
Они – фантазия без крыл.
Они – не в силах дать нам знанья,
И дать нам веру нет в них сил.

These spirits that tap
And turn the tables –
It is not they who threaten
To surrender our dreams!
Ignoramuses and jesters,
The very children of emptiness,
Of sorrow, unbelief, and decline,
They are but a wingless fantasy,
In no state to bring us knowledge,
And with no strength to give us faith.[67]

Figure 7 The Persian-Caucasian song played by the spirit Mikhalko and written down by Mrs. Blavatsky. (Van Pelt Library, University of Pennsylvania)

In place of the awe-inspiring fingers, writing the enigmatic *Mene, Mene, Tekel, Peres* on the plaster of the king's palace, there flashes in the 'wingless' imagination of the spiritualist a lonely, wart-covered hand, strumming on his guitar the exotic and pointless 'Tiris, Tiris, Barbare.'

5 The Middle World: The Realist Spiritualism of Saltykov-Shchedrin

For as long as I remain aware that the images I have summoned up belong only to my imagination, I can toy with them and rule over them, being free to rid myself of them whenever I wish. But the moment I am blinded by the brilliance of the summoned images and forget my power over them, this power immediately disappears; the images become phantoms and live beyond my will, living their own life, oppressing me like a nightmare, influencing me, dominating me, instilling fear in me, and reducing me to a bag of nerves.

Dmitry Pisarev, 'Scholasticism of the Nineteenth Century'

Imaginary Reality

An opposite, yet no less paradoxical, attempt to rid the world of ghosts can be found in the works of the radical realist writer and satirist Mikhail Evgrafovich Saltykov-Shchedrin (1826–89). An ardent materialist, Shchedrin wholeheartedly despised spiritualists and attacked their idealist 'ravings' in a number of his works. In the present chapter I discuss the inner logic and consequences of his literary struggle with spiritualism, which he perceived as the most radical expression of Romantic idealism. I argue that, while Vagner's naive spiritualist realism rendered spiritual phenomena materialistic and scientific (rendering them devoid of any mystery and meaning), Shchedrin's realistic method led to the spectralization of reality, turning it into a phantom – one that frightened the writer himself. In this sense, Shchedrin's realism was indicative of the inner conflict of the Russian realist imagination of the

1860s to 1880s, which created an image of Russia as a house haunted by numerous apparitions: nihilists and afflicted peasants; great historical figures and humble little men; the superfluous man and the heroic revolutionary.

Let us turn to Shchedrin's major work – his novel *Gospoda Golovlyovy* (The Golovlyov Family, 1875–80). In its penultimate section, Shchedrin describes the 'frenzied, fantastical orgy' of his protagonist, the hypocrite Iudushka ('Little Judas'). The latter has lost all connection to the world of the living: his brothers, mother, and children have died; his mistress despises him; his servants are no longer afraid of him; there is no future, the present is empty, and the past is too terrifying to recall. Iudushka locks himself up in his study, where he yields to an endless 'bout of idle thought.' The protagonist's imagination, oiled by alcohol, brings him temporary release from reality and the fulfilment of his secret desires, offering him, for an instant or two, the illusion of happiness. In his dreams, he seizes untold new riches, defeats his rivals, avenges past insults, mocks his kin to his heart's content, and then subjects them to his sanctimonious preaching. In a state of ecstasy bordering on madness, he creates a world in his own image, populated by phantoms ready to serve his will and his words:

> Indulging his fancy in this way he gradually became as it were drunk; the ground slipped from under his feet, he felt as though he had wings. His eyes glittered, his trembling lips were covered with foam, his face turned pale and looked menacing. And as his imagination grew more active, the air around him became crowded with phantoms that engaged him in an imaginary struggle.
>
> His existence was now so full and self-sufficient that he had nothing more to desire. The whole world was at his feet – that is, the poor and limited world within his narrow field of vision. He could vary endlessly the simplest theme, taking it up again and again, and each time giving it a new form. *It was a kind of intoxication, clairvoyance, something similar to what happens at spiritualistic seances. Uncontrolled imagination creates an illusory reality, which, owing to perpetual mental excitement, becomes concrete, almost tangible. It is not faith, it is not conviction – it is intellectual debauchery, intoxication. Men cease to be human, their faces are distorted, their eyes glitter. Their tongues babble incoherently, their bodies make involuntary movements.* (XIII:217)[1]

The juxtaposition of Iudushka's crazed fantasies with the practice of spiritualism introduces a historical dimension to the psychological analysis of the protagonist: this is a modern sickness. The comparison between spiritualist practices and dreams, which are so far removed from reality as to paralyse a person's activity, can also be found in an early article, 'Modern Phantoms' (1863), which scholars have rightly viewed as one of Shchedrin's manifestos:

> There is no more effective means of undermining a principle and thoroughly exposing its falsity than the logical extension of this principle to the furthest consequences which it can force out of itself. *In this respect, the school of the so-called spiritualists has provided an unforgettable and invaluable service. They have shown that the path of idealism can lead to the most extreme absurdities* [...] What more could you ask for: light spirits, perfect spirits, rapping spirits ... and this entire *kabal* interferes in human fates and governs man. (VI:399)

In *Istoriia odnogo goroda* (The History of a Town), written in the same year (1863), the spiritualist analogy is once again employed – this time in relation to the historical process:

> The life of man, say the spiritualist philosophers, is a dream, and if they were to be entirely logical, they would add that history also is a dream. [...] One is inevitably conscious that at certain times in history there do seem to be gaps, before which the intellect pauses in bewilderment. The stream of life appears to break off its natural course to form a whirlpool, which twists and spumes until covered with a muddy scum, through which it is impossible to distinguish any clear characteristics or individual phenomena. Confusing, meaningless events succeed each other without connection, and people seem to pursue no other end than to survive the passing day. They tremble and triumph by turns, and the deeper their humiliation, the more vengeful and cruel is their triumph. The source of the disturbance is now clouded with mud; the principle in the name of which the struggle arose can longer be discerned; there remains only struggle for the sake of struggle, art for the sake of art, – that art which invented the rack, the gauntlet, and other such things (VIII:375–6)[2]

The same theme of 'broken time,' in its connection with the modern spiritualist craze, recurs in Shchedrin's late sketch 'Schastlivets' (The Lucky Fellow), from the cycle *Melochi zhizni* (Life's Trifles, 1887). The hero of this sketch, an eternal idealist, turns into a sanctimonious old prig at the end of his life, surrendering himself entirely to spiritualism and religious fantasy:

> *In eras of moral and mental decline, when real tasks slip through people's fingers, such phantasmagorias are far from rare.* Failing to find satisfaction in actual life, society rushes about at random and produces an abundance of individuals who throw themselves greedily on phantasmal fictions, finding in them their peace of mind. Neither arguments nor objections can help here, because, let me repeat, it is not the conscious intelligence, but illusoriness which lies at the very base of these new-fangled dogmas. Peace of mind is needed – and that's all [...] The rootless nature of life, the rattled condition of minds and the complete absence of real interests are probably the determining influences in such cases. (XVI.2:310–11; my italics)

Shchedrin found in spiritualism an important ideological metaphor: it represented the tragico-comic extreme (or self-exposure) of idealism, a symptom of the cowardice, inner poverty, and moral degeneracy of modern man, who lived in an age that was out of joint, confused, and teeming with phantoms.

Shchedrin had direct knowledge of spiritualism (above all, in its religious, French variety, as opposed to the experimental, Anglo-American movement). In a letter to V.P. Gaevsky of 19 June 1887, he recalled with disgust the spiritualist mobs (*sborishcha*) that gathered in the house of his father-in-law, Apollon Petrovich Boltin (XX:351). Boltin, as I have mentioned, was one of the most active advocates of spiritualism in Russia: the translator and interpreter of the works of the 'father of philosophical spiritualism,' Allan Kardec, and a participant in the debate about spirit and matter that unfolded in Russian journals in the 1860s.[3] Shchedrin's wife, Elizaveta Apollonovna, was also keen on spiritualism[4] (she communicated telepathically with her twin sister Anna, who later married the celebrated French spiritualist Tournier).

The 'light,' 'perfect,' and 'rapping' spirits mentioned ironically by Shchedrin represent the classes of spirits that Kardec described in detail in his *Livre des esprits*, translated by Boltin in 1862.[5] The preface to this spiritualist bible, which had allegedly been dictated by higher spirits, proclaimed that spiritualism 'is a *doctrine opposed to materialism*,' that 'the spiritualist world is the normal, primordial, eternal world,' while 'the physical world is a secondary world, which could have ceased to exist, or not have existed at all, without disturbing in the slightest the essence of the spiritualist world.'[6] In the practice of spiritualism, the summoned spirits readily answered the questions of seance attendees, sent them moral homilies, and disclosed the mysteries of the afterlife (above all, the mechanisms and teleology of reincarnation). The central postulates of Kardec's doctrine were the triune nature of man (the body, the soul, and the semimaterial envelope that links the first with the second), the absence of eternal punishment, the gradual perfection of souls, the multiplicity of worlds populated by spirits at various stages of their development, and the ultimate transformation of the earth. Material embodiments were perceived by the spiritualists as tests of the spirit, as a mode of gradual purification 'in the manner of a sieve.'[7]

In the radical *Otechestvennye zapiski* (Fatherland Notes), edited by Shchedrin and N.A. Nekrasov, spiritualist teaching was subjected to devastating criticism. In his article 'A Fashionable Superstition' (1871), the positivist V.V. Lesevich cited Proudhon: 'How great is the fall, and what terrible catastrophes does it portend [...] when people incapable of scientific work flee from nature and reason to summon spirits and miracles.'[8] Lesevich compared spiritualism to an 'unbroken dream,' 'as muddled as all other dreams.'[9] For the moralist Shchedrin, spiritualism was not merely comic, senseless and pathological (a collective hallucination), but deeply *immoral*. To his mind, this deterministic doctrine led not only to the clouding of consciousness and alienation from social life, but also to the loss of one's human countenance, mental degradation, the fatal waste of vital energy, and the destruction of the personality (entropy and death). For Shchedrin, it could be said, the phantasmal world of spirits represented an ideological and moral 'antiworld.'

Realist Exorcism

One of the fundamental (and most complicated) tasks of the realist program was the reconstruction in the work of art of an 'objective view' of 'reality,' in order to expose the innumerable illusions and spectres that tradition had imposed on humanity, obscuring real problems and impeding their solution. The words 'phantom,' 'spectre,' 'ghost,' 'hallucination,' and 'phantasmagoria,' all of which occupied a prominent place in the Romantic lexicon, did not vanish from the realist vocabulary, but acquired negative connotations: from V.G. Belinsky onwards, they served as signs of illusory relations, false doctrines, and obsolete institutions from which rational, mature individuals and societies had to free themselves. The philosophical sources of this realist exorcism are well known: they range from the empiricism of Francis Bacon, with his four 'idols,' to the materialism of Ludwig Feuerbach and Karl Marx. [10] 'Only what is rotten fears the touch of criticism and turns to dust, like an Egyptian mummy, from a breath of wind,' wrote D.I. Pisarev. 'Exorcism conducted through sober analysis makes only phantoms disappear; existing objects, when subjected to this test, prove the reality of their existence.' [11] Turgenev's nihilist Bazarov was of the same mind, seeing belief in ghosts as a symptom of archaic 'Romanticism.' [12]

The phantoms of the public consciousness (their essence, source, and effect) were one of Shchedrin's key concerns.[13] He devoted to the subject the above-mentioned article 'Modern Phantoms,' in which he proposed a 'theoretical definition' of the concept of the phantom (*prizrak*);[14] then, following in a European philosophical tradition, he provided a classification of the phantoms of modernity: honour, family, property, the State, monarchy, morality, religion. Like Pisarev, Shchedrin was convinced that phantoms had to be fought through the 'strict analysis of those concepts by which we move and live' and that 'if these concepts are robust in their own right, analysis will not kill them, but will merely cleanse them and give them greater force and strength' (VI:393).

Yet in contrast to the optimists of the early wave of realist exorcism, Shchedrin was aware of the deep-rootedness of 'phantoms' in life and, moreover, their indestructibility through history. The ideological odyssey of mankind presented itself to him as the replacement of certain phantoms by others. Great upheavals and social revolutions, sweeping away the spectres of the past, merely cleared the ground for new phantoms: 'The history of humanity, from its very cradle, proceeds through a succession of phantoms – the question is, when will humanity liberate itself from them, and will it ever do so? This question represents the dark, agonizingly tragic aspect of history' (VI:385).

From here, in turn, derives the 'agonizingly tragic' mission of the writer – to expose phantoms while remaining aware of their historical indestructibility: 'It is not easy to free oneself from phantoms, but it is essential *to remind the world* that it is under their sway, that it is mistaken in thinking that it lives the real, not illusory, life' (VI:388). The full liberation of humanity from the rule of phantoms is conceivable only in the very distant future: 'In the end, perhaps the time really will come when even the general consciousness will no longer perceive phantoms as ideals' (VI:388).

I repeat: the main aim (even mission) of the satirist, in Shchedrin's view, was to expose concretely historical phantoms, thus clearing the way for real, 'healthy, unconfused life.' But the unforeseen outcome of the satirist's repeated assault on the phantoms ruling society was his own subjugation to their power and the gloomy *spectralization* of the world he portrayed: the shadows born of mistaken principles became embodied in reality and *replaced* reality.

The most striking example of this pattern is undoubtedly *The Golovlyov Family*, which relates the disintegration of a family of provincial gentry. The protagonists in this novel become living ghosts inhabiting a real world, which thereby acquires the features of a gigantic phantom.[15] One could hardly explain this thoroughly spectral world solely through recourse to the author's satirical program, with its criticism of a (grotesquely depicted) way of life based on false foundations (the gentry family, the institution of inheritance, fetishism, unjustified hopes).[16] The author portrays the life of spectres as the only real life (not an imaginary reality, but the reality of the imaginary): the protagonists can escape it only in their morbid imaginations, which are deprived of ontological status, leading to torpor and spiritual death. Like the novel's heroine, Aninka, the reader is unable to imagine that in the world portrayed by the author 'any kind of future is possible, that a door exists, through which one could emerge elsewhere' (XIII:250).

What are the literary and ideological sources of Shchedrin's portrayal of phantasmagorical reality?

Realist Spiritualism

It would be accurate, but not sufficent, to interpret *The Golovlyov Family* as a social satire that describes the collapse of the institution of the family and the degradation of the way of life and consciousness of the landowning class. As recent studies have shown, *The Golovlyov Family* should be viewed in broader aesthetic and ideological contexts.[17] Of particular interest is the novel's genetic link with the Gothic genre: the terrifying closed estate, redolent of the burial vault; the castle-like house within whose walls an ancestor was once imprisoned; the hypocrisy and bloodthirstiness of the current master (the motif of Iudushka's vampirism), who entangles his poor victims in a web of words; the theme of ancestral inheritance; the shades of murdered relatives; 'filicide'; the allusion to incest in the novel's final chapter; and the final decline and ruin of the 'cursed' line.

But in contrast to the Gothic fiction of Horace Walpole, Matthew Lewis, or Gogol, Shchedrin's phantoms come from within, rather than outside, historical reality: the supernatural here has social, economic, psychological, and biological causes. It is this materialist interpretation that distinguishes Shchedrin's 'realist Gothic' from the mechanistic model of Anne Radcliffe, a model marked by scientific and rational explanations of miracles.[18]

Shchedrin's ideology also differs from that of the Gothic tradition. In *The Golovlyov Family*, the past (Iudushka's crimes, Aninka's sins) comes to light in the form of the undead (*umertviya*), or visions, but it demands nothing, portends nothing, and threatens nobody; it merely hovers dully before the protagonists like their own reflection and fate.[19] It is not the crime that instils horror, but the very existence of the sinner.

Different, too, is the treatment of the theme of the criminal's punishment. With Iudushka (a petty miscreant rather than a Gothic monster), the Golovlyov line dries up. A sense of horror at the crimes he has committed arrives too late; the mother's curse denotes a punishment in this life, not the next. The plight of insignificance and 'eternal' confinement in the burial vault of one's own house recalls not the divine punishment of the Gothic villain (of the sorcerer, say, in Gogol's *A Terrible Vengeance*, before whom there opens the infernal abyss), but the 'eternity' of Svidrigailov (the bathhouse with spiders in every corner). In *The Golovlyov Family*, though, the punishment occurs *within the limits of this world*.

Another source of the novel's ideology and imagery was graveyard poetry and, related to this, the theosophical allegorical novel (and narrative poems) of the late eighteenth century.[20] Shchedrin had been familiar with these genres since childhood (his father enjoyed literature of this kind). The gnostic and spiritual imagery that permeates *The Golovlyov Family* derives from them (mediated perhaps by Gogol's *Dead Souls* and *Selected Passages from Correspondence with Friends*): the world as a graveyard; gloomy 'shining emptiness' and 'sparkling nothingness'; empty, destructive speech; man as walking dust; life as prison; demonological images and motifs (deprived, however, of their supernatural character); metaphysical cold and solitude; the vileness of decay; and apocryphal interpretations of the history of Christ and Judas. The novel's passionate moralizing also derives from these traditions and bears a manifestly mystical and religious subtext: the belated awakening of Iudushka's conscience under the influence of the Easter Mass; his decision to abandon his home on a slushy Easter night; and his death from cold en route to his mother's grave. Undoubtedly, the novel suggests social and moral explanations for these themes and motifs: the spiritual degeneration of a gentry family; the fetishization of worldly goods; the absence of spiritual needs and moral values; aimless and empty existence.[21] In their totality, these elements create the symbolic image of a desolate, closed, and fundamentally rotten world in which the moral consciousness of the 'implied author' languishes.

Moreover, the originality of the novel's 'gnostic realism'[22] resides in the fact that the inhabitants of the estate – both the living and the dead – remain for all time (as if by gradual accumulation) in Golovlyovo. Thus, the end of the novel sees the resurfacing of the numerous *umertviya* of former victims of the house (not ghosts, but precisely 'deaths' [*smerti*], who come to life in the sick consciousness of the protagonists): Stepka, daddy, mummy, Iudushka's sons. Iudushka, in his turn, is compared to a spectre, even though he is still alive.[23] The boundary between life and death is erased, and reality turns into phantasmogoria – or rather, Golovlyovo turns out to be a closed space outside life or death. It is a kind of 'third state,' a spectral region, the reality of which Shchedrin describes in spiritualist terms. The narrator can try all he wants to convince the reader that life should not be so, that it is so because people are not living in the right way, but he himself, like the reader, is possessed by this phantom image, which cannot be driven out because it is derived from reality.

The spiritual concerns of this realist novel also include the important theme of the 'middle place' elaborated by Iudushka. Thus, at the wake for his brother Pavel Vladimirovich, Iudushka suddenly begins blathering away about the afterlife. He does so to rub salt in his mother's wounds, yet the subject really does preoccupy him (Iuduhska's verbosity does not preclude the possibility of something vital slipping through his words). '"Or take the Roman Catholics now," Iudushka continued [...], "they don't deny immortality, yet they say that the soul does not go straight to hell or to heaven but finds itself for a time in a kind of intermediate place"' (XIII:89).[24] The Orthodox priest, of course, rejects this 'groundless doctrine,' but Iudushka, for whatever reason, insists on it. In the draft ending of the novel (the fragment 'By the Jetty'), this theme is developed further. The 'idealist' neighbours, who are inclined to interpret Iudushka's behaviour in terms of the intervention of a Satanic force, suddenly remember that the master of Golovlyovo once 'spoke about the existence of some middle place' in which the souls of the dead allegedly abided until arrangements had been made for their billeting in heavenly abodes.

This rumour is immediately followed by mention of a book by the German theosophist Karl Eckhartshausen, *The Key to the Mysteries of Nature*, a mystical work that for many years enjoyed great popularity among Russian provincial idealists (XIII:601–2).[25]

I would suggest that in *The Golovlyov Family*, the 'middle place' is linked less to the idea of purgatory than to the image of the 'middle world' given in the works of J.H. Jung-Stilling, a German pietist writer whose name often appeared in Russian literature in the 1810s to 1830s alongside that of Karl Eckhartshausen.[26] After death, according to Stilling, the soul is transferred to Hades, the 'gaol of the dead' (*uzilishche mertvykh*) – a kind of pneumatological incubator in which it matures for eternal life. The souls of the righteous, already prepared for eternal life, immediately fly off to paradise; the souls of sinners are also not detained there for long and quickly fall, under the weight of their sins, into the infernal abyss; only the souls of those who failed to define their position in life languish in Hades, occasionally visiting the land of the living, to which they remain bound in spirit. It is possible that Iudushka, who has a fear of the devil, hopes to find himself in this intermediary state between earth and the afterlife; however, it is precisely this 'neutral' condition that, it seems to me, defines his ghostliness (neither dead nor alive) as a character.

In general, the phantasmagorical world of the novel resembles this 'middle' world of spirits. Except that, unlike Stilling's 'gaol,' there is no way out from it upwards or downwards, nor in self-oblivion, suicide, or the self-deception of the morbid imagination: there is 'night, eternal, unbroken night – and nothing else' (XIII:259) except loathsome phantoms.

Conclusion

Terry Castle, expanding on Freud's interpretation of the uncanny (*das Unheimliche*), has shown how belief in ghosts was transformed in the late eighteenth-century consciousness. The Enlightenment's efforts to free society from its naive belief in phantoms yielded an unexpected outcome: 'Ghosts were not exorcized – only internalized and reinterpreted as hallucinatory thoughts [...] By relocating the world of ghosts in the closed space of the imagination, one ended up by supernaturalizing the mind itself.'[27] Ghosts, in other words, became thoughts and idées fixes. The forming of the Romantic consciousness was directly linked to this process.

I would argue that the struggle of the materialist Saltykov-Shchedrin against modern ghosts of the mind may serve to illustrate the new, realist phase in the exorcist narrative of the nineteenth century. The realists' efforts to scatter the phantoms of the Romantic (ideal) imagination in the light of reason led not to the disappearance of spectres and to the discovery of reality as it is, but to the penetration (or ousting) of ghosts into that very 'reality' portrayed by the author. The material, 'commonplace' world, as perceived by the consistent materialist, becomes inevitably 'spectralized'; and since the author recognizes nothing outside this world, this spectralization proves deeply traumatic to him. The paradox of Shchedrin consists in the fact that reason generates nightmares when awake, not asleep.

'I fully understand that phantoms should vanish with the first ray of sun,' Shchedrin wrote in his cycle of sketches, *Kruglyi god* (The Whole Year Round, 1879), 'but, alas, I do not know when this ray will appear. That is what oppresses me.' And later: 'Our reality is so overcrowded, so filled with them, that we cannot see the contours of life for the hordes of phantoms. Not only that: we ourselves are partly becoming phantoms, taking on their image. Could there be a worse affliction than this? Alas! These phantoms are stronger than strength, more alive than life! *And I, who am writing these lines, I write them under the yoke of phantoms, and you, who are reading these lines, – you also read them under the yoke of phantoms*' (XII:424; my italics).

It is entirely logical that this oppressive contradiction could be resolved for Shchedrin only through the apocalyptic removal of human history. At the end of *History of a Town*, the awful *It* (an über-ghost, which signifies the flooding back of accumulated sins and mistakes) sets a boundary to the illusory life of the inhabitants of 'Stupidville' (Glupov): 'Full of fury, *it* rushed along, churning up the earth, roaring, droning and moaning, occasionally belching hollow, croaking sounds. Although *it* was not yet near, the air in the town stirred, the bells dinned of their own accord, the trees were ruffled and the cattle went wild, rushing about the fields in vain attempts to find their way into the town. *It* came nearer, and as it approached the course of time gradually slowed down' (VIII:427).[28]

Shchedrin's art exemplifies a striking feature of radical Russian realism, one that makes it so different from its moderate French and British counterparts: having been stripped of the Romantic veil, 'life as it truly is' becomes in Russian realist fiction (or, at least in its militantly materialist trend) not just filthy, unjust, scary, and boring, but meaningless, inert, degenerate, and revolting. The 'soul' (which the materialist realists denied) reappears in the text as the implied author's and reader's futile longing. So overwhelming is this revelatory vision that hallucinations are sure to follow.

6 The Underworld: Dostoevsky's Ontological Realism

'As we all know, Your Excellency, because of the new order down here.'
'What new order do you mean?' 'Well, you see, Your Excellency, we have,
so to say, died.' 'Ah, yes! But still, the order.'

Fyodor Dostoevsky, 'Bobok'

There are lots of people who say that I am mad. Look at my idea, not at
me. Is the idea a correct one? Isn't there a frightening correspondence?

Stavrogin to Shatov, *The Notebooks for The Possessed*

Introduction

Vagner and Shchedrin introduced two radical approaches to the
supernatural in the realist age: the positivist spiritualist (which ended
up with the materialization of the supernatural and the annihilation
of mystery) and the materialist (which led, in its turn, to the nightmarish spectralization of reality). In this context, Dostoevsky's 'fantastic'
realism,[1] with its emphasis on literary penetration into the deepest
realities of the human soul (or realism 'in a higher sense' [XXVII:65]),
represents an attempt to find a path between the Scylla of meaningless experimental spiritualism (parodied by Dostoevsky in his *Diary*)
and the Charybdis of self-destructive materialism. Though many
scholars have discussed this artistic practice,[2] I find it productive to
reconsider it in the context of the spiritualist quests of the 1860s
and 1870s. Here I will focus on the short story 'Bobok,' which Mikhail
Bakhtin called 'the quintessence of Dostoevsky's artistic ideology, if

not the "microcosm of his entire creative output."' Indeed, this short, programmatic story not only condenses 'in extreme and naked form' many central motifs of Dostoevsky's writing but may also serve as one of the best illustrations of Dostoevsky's depiction of 'moral (spiritual) realities' by means of the fantastic.[3]

Unbridled Fantasy

'Bobok (Notes of a Certain Person)' was first published on 5 February 1873 in Dostoevsky's *Writer's Diary* column in the newspaper–journal *Grazhdanin* (Citizen). The plot of the story is simple: an alcoholic journalist named Ivan Ivanovich, who is suffering from auditory hallucinations (always hearing the word *bobok* [a little bean]), attends the funeral of a distant relative. Lingering in the cemetery after the other mourners have departed, he unexpectedly 'overhears' the cynical, frivolous conversations of the dead. From these exchanges he learns that human consciousness goes on for some time after the death of the physical body, lasting until total decomposition, which the deceased characters associate with the awful, gurgling, onomatopoetic *bobok*. One of the dead, the 'scoundrel of pseudo-high society,' Baron Klinevich, realizing their complete freedom from earthly conditions, proposes to his fellow corpses that they entertain themselves by telling nasty tales of their existence 'on the top floor' – that is, during their lives. But Ivan Ivanovich suddenly sneezes, and the merry society of the departed falls silent (more, as the narrator suggests, from their reluctance to share such an important secret with a living man than from embarrassment or fear of the police). Appalled by what he has overheard, Ivan Ivanovich exclaims: 'Debauchery in a place like that, debauchery of one's final hopes, debauchery among sagging, decomposing bodies, debauchery that does not even spare the final moments of consciousness! These moments are given to them as a gift and ... And the main thing – in a place like that! No, this I cannot accept' (XXI:54).[4]

The nature of this 'strange Decameron of the dead' (as Robert L. Jackson has called 'Bobok') has long occupied critics and scholars of Dostoevsky.[5] Is it a morbid joke, a feuilleton, a social satire, a classical menippea, a parody on materialism, a parody on spiritualism, a parody on libertinage in the spirit of Marquis de Sade, a parable, or a prophecy?[6] What is the goal of the story? What is an actual interpretive context for this story? What is the 'metaphysical status' of the paradoxical afterlife–preannihilation existence that is described by the dead philosopher Platon Nikolaevich in this story?[7] Despite the wide range of interpretations, almost all critics agree that 'Bobok' is a 'test of an idea' story. The question is: which idea?

Indeed, the ideological implications of Dostoevsky's depiction of posthumous activity remain obscure. Obviously, the temporary after-life existence depicted in 'Bobok' does not coincide with Orthodox conceptions of hell or with the soul's tribulations (*mytarstva*), nor with the Platonic doctrine of the spirit, nor with Catholic Purgatory, nor with the spiritualists' 'scientific' notions of the next world, nor with Allan Kardec's theory of 'mischievous spirits,' the lower class in the French philosopher's hierarchy of the afterlife. Hence some critics' tendencies to attribute the 'heretic' narrative to the author's pathological imagination ('something is wrong with his *"top floor"'*),[8] moral corruption ('a kind of fusillade of the Eucharist'),[9] or mystical inclinations (a penetration into the 'secrets of the grave').[10] As Konstantin Mochulsky writes, 'the most unbridled fantasy could not create a shriller sensation of mystical horror.'[11]

Nevertheless, one should recognize that the history of ideas knows a similar terrible 'fantasy' – not 'unbridled,' but 'regulated' to the highest degree, inscribed in the 'strict order' of a certain cosmological doctrine. My discussion proposes a hypothesis that illuminates the ideological and artistic origins of Dostoevsky's portrayal of the underworld, as well as grounding the theosophical context of his 'fantastic realism.' In a word, I consider 'Bobok' a programmatic mystery play (a theosophic menippea)[12] that artistically 'voices' and 'tests' a certain spiritualist idea.[13] I also propose that the comic narrator of this story can be seen as a literary mask of Dostoevsky himself, who employs philosophical irony as a means of conveying a metaphysical message in the age of positivism and disbelief.

Infernal Society

The Enlightenment scientist and seer Emanuel Swedenborg (1688–1772) created a grandiose picture of the afterlife in his masterpiece *De coelo et ejus mirabilibus, et de inferno* (On heaven, the world of spirits and on hell, as they were seen and heard by Swedenborg, 1758; translated into Russian by A.N. Aksakov in 1863).[14] According to the theosophical doctrine of this Swedish seer (namely, the theory of correspondences [*correspondentiae*]), after death the human soul passes through several stages of purification of its internal content (good or evil) and as a result finds its deserved eternal reward: paradise or hell. More-over, according to Swedenborg, 'all who arrive from the spirit world are already connected with some *society of heaven or hell*' by their inter-nal nature (cf. the theme of 'one's society,' the 'good' society of corpse debauchees in 'Bobok'). After death, the two first states last 'for some several days, for others months or even an entire year.' The 'home-grown' philosopher Platon Nikolaevich, according to his fellow deceased, offers a similar description of their situation:

> Up above, while we were still alive, we were wrong in thinking that death up there was really death. Here the body more or less comes to life again; the remnants of life are concentrated, but only in the consciousness. This is – I don't quite know how to put it – a continuation of life as if by inertia. In his view, everything is concentrated somewhere in the consciousness and continues for two or three months ... sometimes even for half a year. (XXI:51)[15]

As a result of this 'purification' stage, Swedenborg believed, 'the exte-rior and interior of everyone must come together into one.' Of greatest interest for the interpreter of the theosophical background of Dosto-evsky's story is Swedenborg's description of the 'second state of man after death.' In this state 'the exterior' disappears, and the spirit is revealed as it truly was in life. Swedenborg proclaims:

> When in this second state spirits become visibly just what they had been in themselves while in the world, what they then did and said secretly being now made manifest; for they are now restrained by no outward considerations, and therefore what they have said and done secretly they now say and endeavor to do openly, having no longer any fear of loss of reputation, such as they had in the world. They are also brought into many states of their evils, that what they are may be evident to angels and good spirits. Thus are hidden things laid open and secret things uncov-ered, in accordance with the Lord's words ... (Luke 12:2–3)[16]

Thus, the law of eternal requital is manifested in the fact that the wicked spirits voluntarily expose their entire essence, choose the corre-sponding society of spirits, and after this self-sentence, fall into the abyss forever.

Swedenborg claims that initially, spirits act 'without *external restraints*, which are, as just said, fear of the law, of the loss of reputation, of honor, of gain, and of life, they act insanely, and *laugh at honesty and justice.'*[17] Recall Klinevich's proposal to 'cast aside all shame':[18]

'But never mind them! *We're getting a nice little group together and everything will take shape of itself. But meanwhile I don't want any lying.* That's the only demand I make, because it's the most important thing. It's impossible to live on earth without lying, for life and lies are synonymous; but down here, just for fun, let's not lie. The grave means something after all, damn it! *We'll each tell our stories to the others and be ashamed of nothing.* I'll tell you about myself first of all. I'm a carnivore in essence, you see. Up there, all such things were held together with rotten ropes. Down with ropes! Let's live these two months in the most shameless truth! Let us bare our bodies and our souls!'

'Let us bare ourselves!' cried all the voices. (XXI:52)[19]

The 'mystical ravings' of the half-decomposed philosopher also correspond to the Swedenborgian system. He speculates that 'the stench here is a moral one' and that it apparently originates 'from the soul, so that after two or three months it can reach a new awareness ... this being is, so to say, the final concession of mercy' (XXI:51).[20] Consider Swedenborg's revelation: 'For as everyone in the world has been delighted with his own evil, so after death he is delighted with the stench to which his evil corresponds [...] I heard a certain spirit crying out loudly as if from inward torture when struck by a breath flowing forth from heaven; but he became tranquil and glad as soon as a breath flowing forth from hell reached him.'[21]

It is significant that Klinevich rudely interrupts the speaker at the reference to the 'last mercy,' in direct correspondence to his internal nature and will: 'That's enough; I'm sure the rest is all nonsense. The main thing is that we have two or three months of life and then, finally, bobok! I propose to you that we spend these two months as pleasantly as possible and to do so, that we arrange things on an entirely new basis. Ladies and gentlemen! *I propose that we abandon all sense of shame!'* (XXI:51–2).[22]

It is Klinevich, rather than the narrator, who ascribes the meaning of the absolute end to the word *bobok*. Indeed, only in this way may a wicked person comprehend the mystery of the next world: his perspective on the afterlife is limited by himself, that is, by his evil self. In other words, *bobok* mirrors *the consciousness of sinners*. This reflection, as well as Svidrigailov's vulgar description of 'eternity,' is in fact the actualization of *divine justice* (otherwise, how can one interpret the words of the 'Swedenborgian' Platon Nikolaevich concerning the last mercy, which Klinevich immediately ridicules?). In accordance with Swedenborg's conception of the Master Plan, Dostoevsky's description of his heroes' situation represents not a final period in the life of the soul, but a decisive stage of self-evaluation and self-exposure – a stage that, as previously mentioned, precedes the soul's ascension into paradise or descent into hell.[23]

As Swedenborg notes, 'those that have not believed in the world in any life of the soul after the life of the body are greatly ashamed when they find themselves to be alive. But those that have confirmed themselves in that disbelief seek affiliation with their like, and are separated from those that have had faith. Such are for the most part attached to some infernal society.'[24] It is significant that among the decaying corpses in Dostoevsky's story there is one who is almost untouched by decomposition. A God-fearing Orthodox merchant (a 'simple man') who shies away from Klinevich's unholy orgy, he is the only one, as Bakhtin writes, who has kept his connection with traditional Christian beliefs 'and thus behaves properly even in the grave,' accepts death as a sacrament, interprets what is going on around him (among the debauched dead) as 'a visitation of tribulations upon their souls, [and] impatiently awaits the *sorokoviny.*'[25] He addresses his neighbours: 'It was my wife and little ones who put me here; it wasn't my wish. The mystery of death! I wouldn't have lain next to you for anything, not for gold of any color. I'm here because of my means – it's a matter of price, ma'am. Because that's something we can always manage, to pay for a third-class grave' (XXI:45).

The behaviour and words of the commoner reflect the Swedenborgian notion that good souls reject any communication with evil (and as a result achieve redemption).[26] As Ernst Benz comments on this thesis in his superb study of Swedenborg's life and work, 'the fruit of the human personality matures; the pull of the heart, which led the individual on earth, is completed there.'[27] This may well be the secret that Ivan Ivanovich misses, which the dead are so careful to conceal from mortals.

I suggest that the posthumous shamelessness of Dostoevsky's dead finds its ontological motivation in Swedenborgian doctrine. Moreover, the theosophical notion of the soul's *last internal self-exposure* completely corresponds to Dostoevsky's artistic psychologism, providing a metaphysical dimension to the very 'anacrisis, provoking the consciousness of the corpses to reveal themselves with *full*, absolutely unlimited freedom,' about which Bakhtin writes in his discussion of 'Bobok.'[28]

Of course, Dostoevsky's story does not boil down to the illustration of a Swedenborgian idea: the latter is projected (or translated) into a contemporary Russian context and 'developed' by the writer in his own aesthetic and philosophical terms. Thus, for example, the narrator's final words about 'these moments [of consciousness that] are given to them [i.e., the dead] as a gift' echo one of Dostoevsky's most important themes (both personal and philosophical) – the life that God miraculously grants to the convict and the moral responsibilities of the 'resurrected' – as can be seen in Dostoevsky's exultant letter to his brother Mikhail, written immediately after the mock execution of 22 December 1849 (XXVIII:164); or Prince Myshkin's words about the convict's last moments.[29]

But the dead in 'Bobok' are not able to perceive the hidden meaning of the granted life because their earthly existence predetermined their afterlife consciousness: after death, man's inner self and fate are revealed 'not by any court or jury but by himself.'[30] In this sense, this short story epitomizes the inner hell in Dostoevsky's moral philosophy.[31] The dead are, so to speak, 'locked in the bobok' without any desire for salvation.

It would certainly be a great mistake to suggest that Dostoevsky believed in Swedenborg's visions of the world beyond. Of course, for him, as an Orthodox believer, the literalist descriptions of the otherworld signified a dangerous materialization of the spiritual, a violation of the sacrament of death by a mortal, and a kind of positivism in faith. Recall Dostoevsky's critical attitude towards spiritualist seances as expressed in his notes,[32] *Diary* ('Spiritualism. Something about Devils. The Extraordinary Cleverness of Devils, If Only These Are Devils'), and *The Brothers Karamazov* (the devil in Ivan's nightmare). What I am trying to suggest is that Dostoevsky, while opposing Swedenborg on certain crucial matters, was interested in his spiritual psychologism as an epistemological method and in the seer's systematic theosophical imagination (a visualization of his idea). I also contend that Swedenborg's interpretation of devils as former humans, with their 'earthly' consciousness, inner sufferings, and memories, perfectly corresponded to Dostoevsky's symbolic anthropology.

Echoes and Correspondences

The idea of a Swedenborgian influence on Dostoevsky is by no means new. In 1919, Leonid Grossman observed that Dostoevsky had several books by and about Swedenborg in his library (including *De coelo et ejus mirabilibus, et de inferno* in A.N. Aksakov's translation). Grossman speculates that Swedenborg's views are reflected in Father Zosima's mystical contemplations concerning 'prayer, love, hell, and communication between worlds.'[33] Tunimanov, in his commentary on 'The Dream of a Ridiculous Man,' which appeared in *Writer's Diary* in 1877, demonstrates convincingly that story's dependence on Swedenborg.[34] Finally, in his profound essay 'Dostoevsky and Swedenborg,' Czesław Miłosz suggests a strong ideological connection between the Swedish seer and Dostoevsky's vision of evil in *Crime and Punishment*. Especially attractive for Dostoevsky's metaphysics, Miłosz argues, was Swedenborg's idea that 'every heaven or hell is a precise reproduction of the states of mind a given man experienced when on earth, and it appears accordingly – as beautiful gardens, groves, or the slums of a big city.'[35] Thus, for example, Svidrigailov's dreadful image of an eternity in a bathhouse infested with spiders resembles some versions of hell described by Swedenborg.[36]

But at what point did Dostoevsky become acquainted with the work of Swedenborg? It is known that in January 1877 the 'father of Russian spiritualism,' Aksakov, presented Dostoevsky with an inscribed copy of his translation of *De coelo et ejus mirabilibus, et de inferno*. But it seems that Dostoevsky was already familiar with Swedenborg's views by that time. In his preparatory notes for the January 1876 edition of his *Diary* (for an article on 'fashionable' spiritualism), Dostoevsky mentions Swedenborg and his conceptions about absolute evil: 'Are there devils? I could never imagine Satan. Job, Mephisto, Swedenborg: wicked people ... On Swedenborg [here!]' (XXIV:9). Obviously, Dostoevsky is refering here to Swedenborg's unorthodox interpretation of the devil in his *Heaven and Its Wonders:* 'It has been believed heretofore in the world that there is one devil that presides over the hells; that he was created an angel of light; but having become rebellious he was cast down with his crew into hell.' This belief, according to Swedenborg, is erroneous, for 'there is no one devil to whom the hells are subject' and '*all who are in the hells, like all who are in the heavens, are from the human race*' and 'those who have gone there from the beginning of creation to this time amount to myriads of myriads, and *every one of them is a devil in accord with his opposition to the Divine while he lived in the world.*'[37]

According to Miłosz's hypothesis, the writer was introduced to Swedenborg as early as the late 1860s – perhaps during his stay in Germany. Though we do not have any direct evidence of Dostoevsky's reading of Swedenborg at that time, there is much to support Miłosz's version. Thus, in his preparatory materials for *The Devils* ('For the Fantastic Page,' June 1870), Dostoevsky puts into Stavrogin's (here the Prince's) mouth a condensed summary of Swedenborgian doctrine. This condensed image of Swedenborg's idea reflects 'the inner self' of Dostoesvky's hero, as if he had exposed his own metaphysical depths in words:

> We are apparently transitional creatures, and our existence on Earth is apparently a (process) that of a chrysalis turning into a butterfly, made permanent [...] I believe that people become either devils [besy] or angels. You say that eternal punishment is an injustice, and that French philosophy which is so good for digestion has developed the notion that all will be forgiven. Yet life on Earth is the process of regeneration. Whose fault is it that you may be regenerated to become a devil? Naturally, everything will be taken into account. But it still remains a fact, a result – exactly as everything on Earth comes to something else. Note also that devils have knowledge. Consequently, even beings beyond the grave [zagrobnye natury] possess consciousness and memory, and not man alone; they may be, however, non-human. It is impossible to die. There is being, but no such a thing as non-being.[38]

Stavrogin's monologue – a kind of theosophical self-definition – reveals those aspects of Swedenborg's doctrine that Dostoevsky chose to characterize his Prince of Devils: the theory of correspondences between external and internal natures and the idea of the balance between the worlds; visions of the afterlife as a logical continuation of our earthly life and retribution as originating in humans' free choice (we judge and punish ourselves); the vision of devils [*besy*] as former humans; and, finally, the motif of devils' consciousness and memory. This final idea was especially important for Dostoevsky's elaboration of Stavrogin's character.[39] The following quote from chapter 4 of *Heaven and Its Wonders* may serve as the theosophical background for Stavrogin's wicked soul as depicted by Dostoevsky. Swedenborg discusses here 'the Memory, Thought, and Affection' in the world beyond and identifies the evil memory of the sinner with the latter's internal diary or confession ('a memorandum-book'): 'That *when a man leaves the world he takes with him all his memory* has been shown to me in many ways, and many of the things I have seen and heard are worthy of mention, some of which I will relate in order [...] *All their* [i.e., the sinners'] *deeds were disclosed and reviewed from their memory in order, from their earliest to their latest years; these were chiefly adulteries and whoredoms.'*

Swedenborg testifies that 'every detail in regard to what and how much they had received, as well as the time, and their state of mind and intention,' were brought to the sinners' recollection 'and made visibly clear to the number of many hundreds.' He also mentions that 'in some cases *their memorandum-books, in which they had recorded these things, were opened and read before them page by page.*' Those sinners 'who had *enticed maidens to shame or had violated chastity* were called to a like judgment; and the details of their crimes were *drawn forth from their memory* and reviewed.' Moreover, 'the *very faces of the maidens and women were also exhibited as if present,* with the places, words and intentions, and this as suddenly as when a scene is presented to the sight, the exhibitions continuing sometimes for hours.' Finally, Swedenborg claims that he learned 'from a man's memory, when it was seen and inspected by angels, what his thoughts had been for a month, one day after another, and this without mistake' and that 'from these examples it can be seen that *man carries with him all of his memory, and that nothing can be so concealed in the world as not to be disclosed after death.*'[40]

Recall Stavrogin's *written confession*, in which he tells about his inability to forget about the poor girl whom he seduced and destroyed: this image constantly haunts the great sinner's memory ('At Tikhon's'). Overall, I argue that Swedenborg's *Hell* should be considered one of the important sources for Dostoevsky's epistemology of the demonic.[41]

The story 'Bobok' was published in the February 1873 issue of *The Diary*. It is very likely that Dostoevsky, who had become familiar with Swedenborg's doctrine by then, found the direct impulse for his imagination in an article on the afterlife and resurrection published in the January 1873 issue of the Christian journal *Strannik* (Wanderer). The author of this article, Ivan Polkanov, discussed Swedenborg's visions of afterlife existence and shame, as well as the theme of the seed turning into a plant as a metaphor for the regeneration of the soul.[42]

In *Heaven and Its Wonders*, the revelations regarding the internal memory of devils precede the depiction of spirits' self-exposure and shamelessness in the afterlife, which, as I propose, Dostoevsky dramatized in 'Bobok.' One may contend that the fantastic cemetery story ideologically echoes the antinihilist novel that portrays the devils' realm on earth. In this respect, together with the 1877 'Dream of a Ridiculous Man,' which portrays the hero's sepulchral lamentations and his journey with an 'unknown being' from his grave to a happy star resembling Swedenborg's heavenly society, these works represent a kind of literary Swedenborgianism – a striking psycho-metaphysical analysis of the *zagrobnye natury* (beings beyond the grave).[43]

Homo Mysticus in the 1860s and 1870s

There is nothing surprising about Dostoesvky's interest in Swedenborg's doctrine in the 1860s and 1870s. Both a mystic and a scientist (a renowned military engineer, astronomer, physicist, and political economist), Swedenborg presented a psychological riddle for the positivistic age. 'Generally speaking, in our days Swedenborg's personality has begun to attract [public] attention once again,' we read in the article 'Swedenborg and His Religious Teaching' in the journal *Khristianskoe chtenie* (Christian Reading, 1866).[44] Indeed, the theosophist's personality and writings were actively discussed (from secular salons to religious academies) in the West and in Russia during these decades.[45]

In Russian perceptions of the seer during this period, two major tendencies predominated: Swedenborg as a mad dreamer and Swedenborg as a prophet, a forerunner of modern scientific spiritualism. Both visions were known to Dostoevsky and affected his own perceptions of Swedenborg.

In 1861 an extensive essay on Swedenborg's life by Matthias Schleiden, a well-known botanist, appeared in Russian translation.[46] Schleiden argued that the seer, who described his afterlife excursions in the minutest detail, was neither an impostor nor a liar but a noble, pious, and respectable man, albeit mentally deranged. Schleiden interprets Swedenborg's visions of the otherworld, fantastic conversations with the dead, and interplanetary journeys as hallucinations originating in his nervous system: 'strong rushes of blood to the head' led to 'a disturbance of the equilibrium of the nervous system.'[47] In 1862, Nikolai Chernyshevsky wrote a programmatic review of Schleiden's essay in which he interpreted the phenomenon of Swedenborg in the context of realists' struggles with idealism and 'Romantic superstitions.' He found that Schleiden's observations were applicable to 'all dreamers' who mistake their fantasies for the truth, and he speculated that 'if we knew the details of their lives with the same historical accuracy that we know of Swedenborg's life, then we could find an explanation and interpretation of their fantasies in different societies and living conditions, we could track how they progressively became more and more enthralled with their dreams.'[48] Chernyshevsky considered such mystical fantasies morbid and dangerous for society.

This medical approach to the *Homo mysticus* is characteristic of positivist discourse of the 1860s. In a number of contemporary 'psychographies,' Swedenborg's prophetic ecstasies were interpreted as messianic psychosis, a possible result of his epilepsy. The psychologist Pavel I. Kovalevsky summarized: 'Swedenborg's entire systematic teachings present certain elements of a systematic rave' and resemble epilepsy.[49] Needless to say, such interpretations were of a personal interest for Dostoevsky, himself an epileptic.

Another intellectual trend presented Swedenborg as the creator of a mystical system based on empirical foundations.[50] Vladimir Dal' attempted to reconcile Swedenborg's theosophy with Orthodox doctrine, though Orthodox theologians of the time harshly criticized Swedenborgian visions.[51] Finally, modern spiritualists praised the seer as a genius medium, a Columbus of the otherworld. Indeed, the 1860s and 1870s (the period of Russia's 'religious revival,' according to Georgy Florovsky) witnessed an interest in the question of posthumous existence and manifestations of the human soul, with special attention given to the notion of a world where souls await their final destiny.[52]

This mystical 'intermediate zone,' absent in Orthodox cosmology, served as a source for the literary imaginations of some of Dostoevsky's contemporaries: Dal', A.K. Tolstoy, Polonsky, Leskov, Maikov, Vagner, and later Sluchevsky. In Russian literature of this period there was a certain spiritualist (or 'pneumatological') trend that displayed strong antimaterialist sentiments, developed tense relationships with official church doctrine, and gravitated towards various mystical systems originating in or close to Swedenborgian theosophy. Though this trend was never as influential as the analogous 'occult revival' in French literature (de Nerval, Baudelaire, Rimbaud, Villiers de L'Isle-Adam), it provided continuity with the Russian Romantic tradition (Gogol, Odoevsky, Lermontov), challenged the dominant realist mode, and prefigured the mystical renaissance of Russian symbolism. Dostoevsky's defiant 'fantastic realism' is closely linked to this idealistic tradition.

Ontological Realism

Why did Dostoevsky the writer turn to Swedenborg's vision of the afterlife rather than to the Orthodox visions of ordeals of the soul (e.g., Feodora's posthumous wanderings) or any fashionable mystical teachings of his day? His artistic imagination could not have been attracted either to Jung-Stilling's idea of an 'incarceration of the dead,' a peculiar pneumatological incubator in which souls of imperfect people ripen prior to their future advancement;[53] or to Allan Kardec's world of spirits, in which the soul waits until it is reincarnated according to the moral level achieved during its previous physical manifestation; or to a 'borderline zone' of theorists of Anglo-American experimental spiritualism (Robert Owen); or to Andrew Jackson Davis's happy 'Summerland.'[54] Swedenborg's rationalization of humans' spiritual destiny was closer (but, of course, not identical) to Dostoevsky's beliefs, but only as an idea brought to its logical and descriptive end – as a 'meaningful hallucination' corresponding to Dostoevsky's insights about spirituality in the modern world.[55]

What distinguished Swedenborg's system from other pneumatological doctrines of the time were its profound psychological realism and its strong legalistic character: in the afterlife, the soul reveals itself completely and forever instead of progressing upwards from a lower to a higher level through a series of reincarnations.[56] There are two possible destinations for the soul – heaven or hell. For Swedenborg, hell was not a fiction or a temporary state, as some liberal theologians of that period argued, but a spiritual reality – a complete realization of the wicked one's self, an eternal 'inner abyss.' In Swedenborg's view, everything depended on humans' free will and ability to love.[57] As Benz has rendered this principle, 'it is people who make their life hell through their evil and people who make their life heaven through their love [...] The earth is the theater in which a way is prepared for the separation of souls according to the basic tendency of their nature [...] Heaven is the theater of elevated mankind, hell that of self-destructive humankind.'[58]

This cosmic spiritual drama (the theosophical *Divine Comedy* in which, unlike Dante Alighieri, the 'world of spirits' represents a crucial stage for humans' spiritual *self-revelation* rather than an 'intermediate zone' for *purification* and gradual renewal) undoubtedly appealed to Dostoevsky's creative mind and his 'binary' ethical beliefs, which focused on free will, non-negotiable personal responsibility, and the inner sufferings of a human being.[59]

Interestingly, in his article 'Vlas,' which preceded 'Bobok' in *Writer's Diary*, Dostoevsky ridiculed the expressive folkloric 'vision of hell' that Nikolai Nekrasov depicted in his poem 'Vlas':

Where nimble devils, unrelenting,
Attack the wrecked here within,

A restless witch, skilled in tormenting,
With Ethiops as black as sin ...
Some are impaled on rods of iron
While others lick the red-hot floor.[60]

The real hell, according to Dostoevsky, perhaps has nothing to do with this psychologically naive *lubok* picture presented by his fellow poet. Instead it lay within a man's soul, which was tormented and lured by 'the most colossal power over the human soul' – the 'mystical horror' of sin.[61] Needless to say, this concept of the inner hell was extremely important for Dostoevsky, as can be seen in *Crime and Punishment, The Devils,* and *The Brothers Karamazov.*

In addition to the 'psychological logic' and grandiose mystical panorama depicted in his major opus, Dostoevsky was fascinated with the seer's personality. In his unpublished fragment on clairvoyance and Swedenborg (May–June 1877), Dostoevsky speculated that the gift of prophecy is related to mental illness (this is one of Dostoevsky's favourite themes: from Svidrigailov's monologue on ghost seeing, to Prince Myshkin's morbid epiphanies, to Dostoevsky's own stories about his epileptic fits and prophetic visions). Though in this fragment he presents Swedenborg as an honest dreamer whose hallucinations speak volumes of his Protestant heart,[62] Dostoevsky aesthetically praises the product of Swedenborg's fantasies: 'He wrote several mystical works and *one beautiful book about heaven, paradise and hell, as a witness,* affirming that the world beyond the grave is open to him, that he is able to visit it as much as he wants and whenever he wants, that he can see all the dead, as well as all of its spirits, both lower and higher, and that he speaks with them' (XXV:262–3).

Of course, Swedenborg's illumination of and interactions with the spiritual world are no more real than the narrator's auditory hallucinations in 'Bobok,' the Ridiculous Man's interplanetary fantasies, or Raskolnikov's nightmarish apocalyptic microbes. Yet they *are* real in the sense that they reveal 'the heart and soul of the author himself' and, moreover, symbolically portray his deep understanding of the mysteries of human consciousness, which are not visible through a rationalistic (scientific) lens. It would not be an exaggeration to conclude that for Dostoevsky, Swedenborg was a spiritual or (better) *ontological* realist rather than a real seer, a psychologist 'in a higher sense'; one of those writers who were 'sent by God to proclaim to us the mystery of man, of the human soul.'[63]

The Laughing Swedenborg

Swedenborg's symbolic interpretation of humankind's internal drama finds its distinct voice in Dostoevsky's ideological choir. Characteristically, Dostoevsky's rationalistic opponents immediately denounced 'Bobok' as a shameful manifestation of the author's mysticism, obscurantism, and 'religious madness.' Thus in the March 1873 issue of the satirical periodical *Iskra* (Spark), Dmitry Minaev rudely described 'Bobok' as the apotheosis of the author's mental disease. In Minaev's satirical poem, the narrator describes his visit to an insane asylum inhabited by Russian writers. Here he runs into a patient who looks absolutely crazy. The latter roars at him:

Повсюду царство дьявола . . .
В отставку подал Бог . . .
Лишь я чертей всех выведу . . .
Бобок . . . бобок. . . бобок. . .
Пожары, революции . . .
Порок . . . вдоль-поперег . . .
Кто это? 'Бесы'? Стойте же . . .
Бобок . . . бобок. . . бобок. . .
И далее он бросился
Со всех безумных ног,
Крича, вопя, неистово:
Бобок . . . бобок. . . бобок!

Satan's kingdom is everywhere ...
God has retired ...
I will expose all the devils ...
Bobok ... bobok ... bobok...
Fires ... revolutions ...
Vice ... Here and everywhere ...
Who is this? The Devils? Wait!
Bobok ... bobok ... bobok ...
And then he took off running,
Madly at full speed, Shouting furiously:
Bobok, bobok, bobok.[64]

Here the leftist satirist uses the meaningless word *bobok* to discredit Dostoevsky as the author of the antinihilist apocalyptic *Devils*. In the

6 February issue of *Iskra*, the author of another article used the same
device to portray *The Devils* as a product of Dostoevsky's ailing imagination and its characters as a group of insane people who, from time to
time, scream the ridiculous word *bobok*. It is interesting that the anonymous author of this critical essay compares Stavrogin to the drunken
narrator of 'Bobok': 'This fellow had delirium tremens, or, in the people's vernacular, saw "little green devils," whom, truth be told, you
quite often encounter reading Dostoevsky's *The Devils* and his diary
excerpts in *The Citizen* ... It is somewhat difficult and awkward to read
this kind of novel in which all of the characters without exception are
capable only of repeating the meaningless words "bobok, bobok,
bobok."'[65]

In other words, Dostoevsky's critics interpreted (in accordance with
their realist epistemology) his literary visions and political mysticism
as manifestations of his own madness, summarized for them in the single word *bobok*. From this perspective, Dostoevsky was portraying
monstrous visions of his troubled mind, rather than real life. As is
known, eighteenth-century rationalists applied the same diagnosis to
Swedenborg.[66] In 'Bobok,' however, Dostoevsky seems to be deliber-
ately provoking his critics: they laugh at him as a crazy mystic, he
laughs at them as blockheaded realists who see nothing beyond material reality (beyond the *bobok*, so to speak) and who are therefore incapable of penetrating his message.

Yet 'Bobok' remains a humorous and polemical work in which
'some of Dostoevsky's favorite philosophical views' are placed 'in
the mouth of a distinctly unappealing' character.[67] As Tunimanov
demonstrates, this story begins as a response to the critic L.K. Paniutin's blatant personal attack on the 'troubled' writer: '*Writer's Diary*
recalls the well-known notes that end with the exclamation, "And
yet the Algerian bey has a bump on his nose!" It is enough to take a
look at the portrait of the author of *Writer's Diary*, at present exhibited at the Academy of Arts, to feel toward Dostoevsky that same
"pity" that he mocks so inopportunely in his journal. It is the portrait
of a man exhausted by severe illness.'[68] In 'Bobok,' the defiant author
of the *Diary* voluntarily dons the mask of the crazy literary man ('My
face may be very like that,' says the deranged narrator) and makes
his comic alter ego resemble both Gogol's poor madman and 'prophetic' Swedenborg.[69] 'I have begun to see and to hear some strange
things,' claims Ivan Ivanovich, who prepares to document what he
has heard in the cemetery (recall the complete title of the seer's book:

Heaven and Its Wonders and Hell: From Things Heard and Seen). Finally, Ivan Ivanovich proclaims that he plans to listen for voluble corpses at other 'grades' (he refers, of course, to the various prices of cemetery plots, but the idea of communities of the dead harks back to Swedenborg. Did Dostoevsky plan to write a 'comic' cycle of 'afterlife conversations'?).[70]

The form of the narrator's revelations is unquestionably eccentric. But, to paraphrase Stavrogin's rhetorical question, isn't the idea a correct one? Isn't there a frightening correspondence between this weird vision and spiritual reality? Indeed, Ivan Ivanovich is one of Dostoevsky's 'tragic clowns,' whose hallucinations, according to the writer, contain deep psycho-metaphysical insights.[71]

Conclusion

For Dostoevsky, in the educated, positivist society of the early 1870s, provocative irony seemed the only acceptable means for speaking of spiritual and theological issues that the dominant mode of thinking had displaced into the 'shadow world' of contemporary consciousness.[72] A 'modern Swedenborg,' who brings forth the inner truth, would have to be a ridiculous author or, rather, a holy fool.[73] In its turn, a 'modern prophetic vision' of the depths of the contemporary soul would have to be a provocative ontological menippea – a visible part of the universal spiritual drama that is concealed from the onlooker's gaze and revealed to the reader via the mediumship of the writer.

7 The (Dis)infection: Art and Hypnotism in Leo Tolstoy

Take the familiar instance of a hypnotic seance. The operateur wills that the receptive subject shall become possessed of certain feelings and emotions, or that he shall perform a definite act. The infection is carried to the subject by a few strokes or passes or through the agency of a brilliant fixed body held in his line of vision. Directly the subject becomes the tool of the operateur's will. The psychosis has passed from one to the other without any physical exertion on the part of either, and is known to us only by the expressions in the hypnotized subject. Even the analogy alluded to in the beginning of this article, namely, that which obtains between physical and psychical infection, still holds true, for in place of infected blood, tissues, or organs, we are now dealing with an infection of the will, of the intellect, or of the emotions. While in physical infection the channels for the entrance and transmission of the microbic element is either the blood or the lymphatics, in psychical infection the portal is either the reason or one or more of the special senses.

Henry S. Stark, 'Psychical Infection'

Tolstoy was a shrewd and unsentimental man. He surely felt that only the miraculous economy of art could hope to win over our flawed minds and bodies, turning brotherhood and love, that impossible ideal, into a 'habitual feeling, an instinct for everyone' ... Who would not wish to be drawn into its life-sustaining circle?

Caryl Emerson, 'Tolstoy's Aesthetics'[1]

Introduction

In the first half of 1886 (no later than spring), Leo Tolstoy attended a spiritualist seance at the home of one of his Moscow acquaintances, Nikolai Alexandrovich Lvov (XXVII:467–8). According to the memoirs of Tolstoy's friend N.V. Davydov, who had arranged the visit, the writer had wanted to attend a seance for some time, 'in order to convince himself of the fabrication of all that goes on at such things.' Unlike Dostoevsky, who, as we remember, had attended a seance to test himself and the strength of his belief (disbelief), Tolstoy visited the seance to see how educated people could possibly believe in such nonsense: 'After all, it would be the same as believing that, if I started to suck on my walking-stick, milk would begin to flow, something which has never happened and can never happen.'[2]

Nikolai Lvov was a suitable subject for such observations: a confirmed spiritualist, he believed (naturally, on the basis of his own observations) in the materialization of spirits; had sought, with the help of a medium, advice from representatives of past humanity; and was interested in occult doctrines (most likely the spiritualism of Kardec and Blavatsky) and the newest psychical experiments (first and foremost in the fields of hypnotism and telepathy). Tolstoy thought him half mad: 'Lvov,' he wrote in his diary on 19 April 1884, was talking 'about Blavatskaya, the transmigration of souls, the powers of the spirit, the white elephant and the oath of allegiance to the new faith. How can one keep sane when exposed to such impressions?' (XLIX:84).[3] There is an extremely unlikely, though colourful, anecdote about how Lvov, who did not believe in death, once 'told his friends that three days after his death he would be smoking an invisible cigar, and invisibly participating in all the activities of his household.' So he invited Tolstoy 'to come and see him pass into the beyond': 'Three days later he sent for the count, but when Tolstoy reached the house it was too late. However, he stood by the inanimate body and was greatly impressed by the incident. That was in 1886' (in fact, Lvov died in 1887).[4] It would have been fascinating to speculate on what the author of 'The Death of Ivan Ilich' (1886) would have thought standing by the body of the dead spiritualist.[5] However, in this discussion we are concerned with a different topic – Tolstoy's interest in the power of (self-)persuasion, rather than afterlife.

The medium at Lvov's seance was one Mr Mamchich.[6] Famous in spiritualist circles, he was capable – according to the testimony of an eyewitness – of making teacups jump around in a cupboard.[7] Besides Mamchich, Lvov, and Tolstoy, the seance was attended by P.F. Samarin, K.Yu. Milioti, and Davydov, who recorded what transpired. The participants, as was accepted, sat around a circular table in a dark room. The medium fell into a trance 'and then there were heard knockings against the table, and there began to appear small phosphorescent wisps of light, but very soon all movement ceased.' Samarin 'tried to catch the wisps and bumped into someone's hand; soon after this the medium awoke, and at this point the manifestations ended.'[8] The next day, Davydov recalls, Tolstoy 'confirmed to me his opinion that everything in spiritualism is either self-deception [*samoobman*] which is undergone both by the medium and the participants of the seance, or simply a fraud, created by a professional.'

Tolstoy's impressions of the seance at Lvov's became the inspiration for the comedy *The Fruits of Enlightenment* (1887–90). It would seem that Tolstoy worked out the general plan for the comedy immediately after the seance (the earliest sketch begins with the words 'Lvov sits, turning his saucer around the earth towards the peasants' [XXVII:433]). Originally intended for his own domestic theatre at Yasnaya Polyana, Tolstoy worked on the play continuously from 1889 to 1890. Almost all of the characters had real-life prototypes: the participants at Lvov's seance, members of Tolstoy's household, and other acquaintances. The plot was simple, in the spirit of the Neoclassical Enlightenment tradition. Tanya, a cheerful and clever servant (in earlier drafts an old nanny) manages to extract from her master, a spiritualist by the name of Zvezdintsev, an agreement to sell some land of vital importance to some peasants who had come to petition him. To this end, she convinces her fiancée Semyon to play the role of medium, while she herself hides behind a sofa and performs all sorts of 'spiritual phenomena': she makes noises, rings a little bell, touches one of the sitters with a thread, plays a guitar, and throws a pillow, a pencil, a lampshade, and, finally, a piece of paper with the contract needed by the peasants. All of the machinations of this 'mischievous spirit' find their 'theoretical' confirmation in the statements of a professor/spiritualist, who refuses to go back on his words even after Tanya admits to having created the 'spiritual phenomena.'

The description of the spiritualist seance in the fourth act serves as the focus of the comic action. It should be noted that the seance at Zvezdintsev's differs from the 'medium-oriented' seances I discussed earlier: here a hypnotist is included among the participants, whose function is to lull the medium into a trance. The practice of inviting a hypnotist (to be more precise, a 'magnetizer') to a seance was widespread throughout the 1880s.

The comedy is a biting satire of the false enlightenment of the privileged educated class, which had 'grown bloated from idleness' (the very title of the comedy alludes to the conclusion of Denis Fonvizin's 'Minor' (1783): 'There you have the deserved fruits of bad mores'). The moral truth, as one might expect, is on the side of the peasants. The comedy was received as a satire on spiritualism, which had once again become a topic of great social interest towards the end of the 1880s, as well as an attack on certain specific spiritualists. Thus, N.P. Vagner discerned both himself and fellow spiritualist Butlerov in the character of Professor Krugosvetlov. In a letter to Tolstoy he reproached the writer for having 'lowered himself to lampooning professors and scientists': 'It was difficult and painful for me to hear how you, with your typical artistic mastery, sneered at both me and my late friend' (Bulterov died in 1886) (XXVII:569). Tolstoy attempted to convince Vagner that he had neither him nor Butlerov in mind, but simply depicted in his characters the 'personification' of a 'comic contradiction which unceasingly appears: an avowal of strict scientific methods, and the most fanstastical formulations and assertions' (ibid.). (As an aside, in outlines and drafts of the comedy Krugosvetlov was called Kutler or Kutlerov, a comic combination of the names of two spiritualists, constantly linked in the periodicals of the 1870s and 1880s.) Another of Tolstoy's 'victims' was the fashionable 'healing hypnotist' Osip Feldman (in the comedy, Grosman), whom I discuss later. The trustful Lvov could not take offence, as he was already dead (or, as his beliefs would have had it, he had already been reborn).

Mediums and Hypnotists

Spiritualism both interested and revolted Tolstoy. His first encounter with the phenomenon of mediumship occurred in Paris in March 1857, when he attended (together with Ivan Turgenev) a seance held by the 'sorcerer' Daniel Dunglas Home. 'Hume [*sic*] both succeeded and did not succeed [*sdelal i ne sdelal*],' he recorded in his diary, concluding, 'I must try myself' (XVII:118).[9] In January 1876, at the peak of the 'spiritualist season,' Tolstoy admitted to his friend, the philosopher N.N. Strakhov, that Vagner and Butlerov's articles on mediumism disturbed him 'terribly' and that he had even decided to write a response in which he aimed to prove that 'peasant stories of "devils" are just as authentic as theirs, but neither Butler nor Wurst, sitting stupefied over their microscopes and converters, deserve any credit for this, but rather the fresh-faced peasant, who knows much less (their analysis, to use your terms, is less developed), but still has the foundation of all knowledge – belief, a religious outlook towards the world (a synthesis, if you will) which is incomparably more correct than that of Wurst.'[10]

Tolstoy agreed with Strakhov's criticism of spiritualism as a positivist superstition (a scientific cult), adding 'it is suspicious that these facts come from a group of people for whom science had been an obstacle in claiming that something existed in the human individual that did not submit to the laws of the physical world.'[11]

According to S.A. Behrs, it was during this time that Tolstoy visited Professor Butlerov, the ardent propagandist of psychical research. He was dumbfounded by Butlerov's spiritualist beliefs. 'In all likelihood,' Behrs notes, 'this visit served as the basis for the comedy *Fruits of Enlightenment*, while in *Anna Karenina*, Levin denounces spiritualism with literally the same expressions as Lev Nikolayevich himself.'[12] (We should note that Vronsky, however, demonstrates a decided interest in spiritual experiments.) In the novel, Tolstoy mocks not only the scientific and experimental dimensions of spiritualism, but also the 'philosophical' aspects of upper-class spiritualism, as seen in the sanctimonious Countess Lidia Ivanovna, whose interests are catered to by the famous medium Landau (a parody of D.D. Home). All in all, in the late 1870s Tolstoy perceived spiritualism as a disgusting (from both the moral and rational points of view) occupation characteristic of the parasitic educated elite and semimad naturalists.

It is evident that Tolstoy always mocked the spiritualists, their quasi-scientific doctrines and academic arrogance. Yet their theories are not completely alien to his world view, which had been shaped by the late 1870s.[13] Like the spiritualists, Tolstoy believed that there is a force that is present in all of us, that there are a few individuals who are more sensitive to the movements of this force than others, and that these individuals are capable of wielding it. This force is certainly not a magnetic, odic, psychic, or any other scientifically defined energy; it is 'simply' Truth, Love, Light, or Life 'as it truly is.' These chosen ones are not shamans, mediums, hypnotists, or (to use a modern expression) Jedi; rather, they are individuals who have a strong moral sense. They do not egoistically confront the good force but completely yield to it. There is no death or annihilation in Tolstoy's theodicy of Universal

Love. Instead, there is an inevitable merging with this force and a (possible) future transformation (L:192).[14] It could be said that Tolstoy hated Modern Spiritualism because for him it represented a poor caricature (or a profanation) of his own deeply held beliefs.

Tolstoy's major attack on spiritualism occurred in the second half of the 1880s (the comedy *Fruits of Enlightenment*) and was by no means arbitrary. This period was characterized by a new wave of popular interest in paranormal phenomena, now originating from rapid developments in experimental psychology. First and foremost this concerned the boisterous debates over hypnotism between the Paris and the Nancy schools of psychology.[15] Is hypnosis a paranormal (traditional mesmerism), physical (Jean-Martin Charcot), or psychical (Jean Liébault and Hippolyte Bernheim) phenomenon? Does hypnotism have certain consequent stages? Can healthy people be hypnotized? Could hypnosis be used for therapeutic ends? Could it be used in criminal investigation to obtain evidence? Is it safe to use for both the hypnotists and the hypnotized? These questions attracted physiologists, psychiatrists, sociologists, criminalists, and, of course, spiritualists (from the 'old guard' of investigators of 'psychism,' such as Vagner and Aksakov, to the newer occultists, such as Blavatsky) to the study of hypnotism. The spiritualists argued that recent discoveries in the field confirmed their claims regarding the immortality of the soul, nervous fluid and ether, and the possibility of spiritual communications.

In the 1880s, hypnotism was widely discussed in scholarly and popular journals. Hypnotic seances – which replaced or modified traditional spiritualist seances – took place in both scientific societies and private apartments. Professional healing-hypnotists would go on tour, and their performances were well attended by the public.[16]

Hypnomania reached its peak towards the end of the decade and was accompanied by widespread social mistrust as to its influence. 'Attracting a crowd predominantly by means of strange movements and psychic manifestations of hypnosis,' hypnotic seances in the 1880s produced a 'strong and sometimes staggering impression on viewers,' inducing nervous attacks among those who were distinguished by their elevated impressionability.[17] Doctors, priests, and even occultists talked of the dangers of hypnosis. Madame Blavatsky wrote about the 'vampirism of some healing-mediums' in her *Isis Unveiled*:

> But, what if the healer be morally diseased? The consequences may be infinitely more mischievous; for it is easier to cure a bodily disease than cleanse

a constitution infected with moral turpitude [...] If the gift of prophecy, as well as hysteria and convulsions, can be imparted by 'infection,' why not every vice? The healer, in such a case, conveys to his patient – who is now his victim – the moral poison that infects his own mind and heart. His magnetic touch is defilement; his glance, profanation. Against this insidious taint, there is no protection for the passively-receptive subject. The healer holds him under his power, spellbound and powerless, as the serpent holds a poor, weak bird. The evil that one such 'healing medium' can effect is incalculably great; and such healers there are by the hundred.[18]

In 1890, at the insistence of the Ministry of Health, public demonstrations of hypnotism and magnetism were outlawed, 'and any undertaking of hypnosis with a therapeutic goal was permitted to be done only by [certified] doctors in accordance with the requirements of the law (Article 115, Vol. XIII) concerning patient operations, i.e., in no way but in the presence of other doctors.'[19]

The 'victims' of Tolstoy's satire, Professors Butlerov and Vagner, were two of the most active participants in the contemporary debate on spiritualism and hypnotism. The former addressed these topics in his articles and speeches beginning in the first half of the 1880s. He was especially enthusiastic about the phenomena of thought transference and mind reading, which, he claimed, cleared the way for further psychical research.[20] From 1882 to 1886, his close friend Vagner gave a series of lectures on spiritualism and hypnotism and published several programmatic articles in *Rebus*. He would often include evidence of instances of somnambulism, clairvoyance, long-range transmission, divination of thoughts, and other psychic phenomena. In his articles, Vagner stated that 'these phenomena, based as they were on facts, belonged to the realm of "psychological hypnotism."' In ordinary hypnotic phenomena, he reminded his readers,

> the subject, owing to fatigue of attention or to an artificially produced tendency to sleep, fell into the hypnotic state *under the influence* of the hypnotist's will. The power to exercise his own will was removed and the will of the hypnotizer directed the whole of his neuron-muscular mechanism as if he were an automaton [...] What played the main role was the will of the hypnotizer.

Unlike *ordinary hypnosis*, Vagner argued, *psychological hypnosis* offered an entirely different picture:

Here, the hypnotizer acted on the will of the subject but did not put him to sleep, so that the subject became able to enter into communication with the minds of both the hypnotizer and other people and was able to read their thoughts more or less easily.[21]

(Running ahead, I will note that this communicative aspect of hypnosis, in all likelihood, disturbed Tolstoy the art theorist).

Vagner's lectures attracted throngs of listeners:

His audiences numbered about five to six hundred persons, the chief of whom were physicians, university students, or literary men. He had great difficulty in gaining permission to give lectures, as they approached a subject which has been condemned alike by clerical and scientific authorities, the former attributing all psychical phenomena outside of the church to Satan, and the latter to physiological disturbance, to be rectified by orthodox medication. To gain his hearing Professor Wagner called animal magnetism by the less disagreeable name of 'hypnotism.' He quoted facts of history from ancient times down to the present, noticing the discoveries of Van Helmont, Mesmer, Reichenbach, Dupotet, and others, not forgetting Braid, the introducer of the term hypnotism. Professor Wagner solved all the mysteries of the subject by introducing a *psychic principle*, not a resultant of the organism, but a force having individuality and consciousness, whose vehicle is the nerve fluid within the organism and the ether of space without. [22]

This thesis is parodied in a speech given by Professor Krugosvetlov in Tolstoy's comedy:

Phenomena seem to be supernatural only because the causes of the phenomena are ascribed to the medium himself. But this is incorrect. The phenomena are produced, not by the medium, but by a spiritual energy working in the medium, and that is a great difference. The whole matter lies in the law of equivalency [...] But the energy itself has not been acknowledged as such until recently, when, at last, we came to acknowledge the medium, the vibration of which produces the mediumistic phenomena. And just as the phenomena of light remained inexplicable until the existence of an imponderable substance, that of ether, was accepted, even so mediumistic phenomena seemed mysterious as long as there was another even more delicate and imponderable substance, which I not subject to the laws of the three dimensions.[23]

Strakhov, a zealous opponent of modern spiritualism, sarcastically called the naive professors 'very good examples of our modern enlightenment.' The professors, in turn, responded defiantly that such an appellation was a great honour for them. As Butlerov maintained: 'Time will show whose side scientific truth is on.'[24]

In the 1880s the figure of the hypnotist (or 'magnetizer,' in the traditional terminology of the period) occupied a central place in discussions of paranormal phenomena, which would manifest themselves while one was under hypnosis. Journals, in particular *Rebus*, were swamped with stories about performances of the famous touring hypnotists of the early to mid 1880s. The most famous hypnotist of that decade was Osip Feldman (1863–1912), who came to be known as 'the Modern Cagliostro.'[25]

In 1885–6, *Rebus* described numerous 'miracles of hypnosis' that Feldman had performed. For example, he had once read several strophes from the *Iliad* (in Greek hexameter) to a hypnotized subject and then had him repeat them back without a single mistake in words or meter even though the subject did not know Greek. On another occasion, a subject under Feldman's suggestion managed to solve a difficult trigonometric problem. One subject was told to see everything in green colour. A short-sighted subject became far-sighted; another subject's hallucinatory anger was 'changed into a feeling of pleasure, [from] laughter into crying … under the influence of the magnet.'[26] Among his other spectacular achievements: he cured a case of severe epilepsy; he successfully treated a woman with a chronic organic illness; and finally, he cured 'a case of persecution mania in which he used the method, later employed by Freud, of having the patient relive a traumatic experience.'[27]

There were many legends concerning 'Feldman's' feats. It was said that he would take seriously ill patients out of hospitals and command them to instantly become healthy, at which point they 'would rise and be cured.'[28] There was even a rumour that he had once saved the life of the Chief Procurator of the Holy Synod, Pobedonostsev, who, while swimming in the Black Sea, had been stranded far from shore when a storm hit and had begun to drown before the very eyes of a crowd that had gathered nearby: 'No one ran to help him [Pobedonotsev]. But among the crowd there appeared the famous hypnotist Feldman, who was able to suggest to him at a great distance that there was no storm, that he was full of strength and that he only had to make a few more strokes in order to reach the shore. The hypnosis was successful, and Pobedonostsev was saved.[29]

The hypnotist was compared to magicians and healers such as Cagliostro and John of Kronstadt, but his might was attributed to a natural as opposed to mystical power, the existence of which was ostensibly corroborated by scientific authorities. As one contemporary aptly noted, Feldman was considered to be a 'miracle of science.'[30] In response, the press (medical publications in particular) attempted to debunk these miracles. Feldman's opponents called him a braggart, a con man, and an impostor for giving medical consultations, which he was not licensed to do. Feldman's fame (or infamy) reached its peak in 1889, when the hypnotist gave a series of public performances in a dozen cities.[31]

It was this 'notorious Feldman' who requested a meeting with Tolstoy in April 1889 – the very time the author was hard at work on *The Fruits of Enlightenment*.

The Modern Cagliostro

Feldman himself described this meeting in his brief article, 'Tolstoy's Attitude towards Hypnosis,' published in 1909. The text is not well known, so we will allow ourselves a fairly detailed summary. One spring day in 1889 (17 April, to be precise), Feldman set off to meet Tolstoy at his house in Khamovniki. Tolstoy greeted his guest cordially (in particular, the hypnotist recalled the 'kind grey eyes' of the writer, affably looking out at him from under thick, overhanging eyebrows). Feldman had come to Tolstoy to put to rest the many doubts he [Feldman] had, but the writer, having discovered his guest's occupation, immediately began to ask him questions about hypnotism. Judging from the questions asked, the memoirist writes, Tolstoy was familiar with the literature on hypnotism, and was particularly interested in the problem of individual free will while under hypnosis. '"It is terrifying" he [Tolstoy] said, "that there are moments when an individual, even if he is in a hypnotic trance, completely loses control over himself and submits himself entirely to the power of the hypnotist!"'[32]

Tolstoy questioned the 'healing medium' in particular detail about those moments when subjects, under suggestion, would commit actions contrary to their own convictions or personal character. Tolstoy's interest was not coincidental: at this time he was working not only on *The Fruits of Enlightenment*, but also on 'The Kreutzer Sonata' and his articles on art, in which the question of the power of a foreign consciousness over the mind and will of an individual plays a central role. In 'The Kreutzer Sonata,' Pozdnyshev rhetorically asks: 'How can

one allow anyone who pleases to hypnotize another, or many others
and do what he likes with them. And especially that this hypnotist
should be the first immoral man who turns up?' (XXVII:61–2).[33]
Tolstoy immediately decided to acquaint Feldman with his friend
N.Ya. Grot, the president of the Russian Psychological Society, but Grot
was not at home. A few days later, Feldman visited Tolstoy once more.

We should note that the kind and well-wishing (according to Feldman) host entered the following note in his diary on the day of the first
meeting: 'Feldman arrived, a hypnotist. Charlatanism, and that which
isn't charlatanism, is completely useless.' He was even more laconic
about the second meeting: 'After breakfast, Feldman came. Rubbish
[pustiaki]' (L:68). The indirect result of Tolstoy's meetings with Feldman was the inclusion of the hypnotist Grosman into his *Fruits of
Enlightenment*, a character who would drop the names of famous theoreticians of hypnotism and brag of his own personal successes. It is
quite easy to see in this character the traits of Tolstoy's guest.[34]

As we see, Tolstoy's attitude towards hypnotism had two sides: it
was charlatanism (or rubbish), and it was a serious, terrible force, capable of subjugating the will of an individual (or, according to the theory
of hypnotism, an individual who is inwardly prepared to submit to the
will of the hypnotist).[35] This dual nature, I would suggest, is closely
tied to the thoughts Tolstoy was developing at the time as to the role of
art in contemporary society.

Artistic Hypnotism

On 18 April, the day after his meeting with Feldman, Tolstoy wrote in
his diary: 'I've begun to improve [my article] about art. It's going well.'
The article in question was 'On What Art Is and What It Isn't, and on
When Art Is an Important Occupation and When It Is an Empty One,'
which Tolstoy worked on during the spring of 1889 (this article was to
become the basis of his treatise *What Is Art?*). In it the author worked
through what has since become known as his trademark theory of art
as 'moral infection':

> The drive to make everything that is hazy and unclear for others clear and
> irrefutable for one's self – this is the source out of which scientific and
> artistic activity arise.
>   This comprises the activity of creating artistic objects, and this activity
> is connected to the emotions and sensations of the one who experiences

them. *These emotions and sensations have their own source in imitation, or even more likely – in the property of infection, in a certain hypnotism,* in the fact that the artist's spiritual tension, which comes from clarifying that which had first seemed doubtful to him, is conveyed through the artistic work to the recipient ...

Artistic ... work ... is then finished ... when it is carried out with such clarity that it imparts itself to people, and can evoke in them the very same emotion that the artist experienced during the creative process. It is infectious. (XXX:220–1; my italics).

Tolstoy's aesthetic theory has been well studied.[36] What interests me here is the genesis of its central concept of *infection.* I argue that Tolstoy adapted this concept from the discussion about psychic infection and mass hypnosis that was unfolding from the late 1870s to the early 1880s. As is known, this term entered the psychological lexicon from epidemiology of the 1860s and 1870s.[37] Mental contagion was first introduced in Prosper Lucas's *De l'imitation contagieuse ou de la propagation sympathique des névroses et des monomanies* (1833). The notion was also discussed in Prosper Despine's pamphlet *De la contagion morale: Faits démontrants son existence* (1870). From the late 1880s until the beginning of the First World War, as Daniel Beer indicates, 'paradigms of "mental contagion" came to inform theories of mass psychology.'[38] In Russia the term was presented by the eminent psychiatrist Viktor Khrisanfovich Kandinsky (1849–89) in his *Obshcheponiatnye psikhologicheskie etiudy* (Comprehensible Psychological Essays for the General Reader; the second part of this tract was titled 'Nervous-Mental Contagion and Mental Epidemics'). Kandinsky argued that there was an analogy between physical and mental epidemics: 'Like a contagion [*kontagiia*] of smallpox or typhus, a mental disease [*dushevnaia zaraza*] is transmitted from one person to another, to a third [...] spreading with ever more power, afflicting an ever greater mass of people, as long as it finds fertile soil. In the past, smallpox and the plague have carried off thousands and tens of thousands of victims and devastated entire countries. Mental epidemics are no less harmful.'[39]

It seems that Tolstoy found this analogy between physical and psychic infections useful.[40] Thus, Mrs Zvezdintsev in *The Fruits of Enlightenment* suffers from bacillophobia. However, according to Tolstoy, the entire Zvezdintsev household and all of its guests are (morally) infected: the idle son, the morally depraved daughter, the half-witted mother, even the doctor, who receives money for maintaining the mistress's delusions.[41]

In his tract, Kandinsky used yawning as an example of the simplest kind of psychic infection – that of involuntary imitation.[42] As we know, this example was consistently employed by Tolstoy in discussing the effects of art, both positive and negative, on the public.[43] See, for example, the famous passage from the twenty-third chapter of 'The Kreutzer Sonata,' with its description of the infectious effects of the first presto of Beethoven's sonata:

> What is music? What does it do? And why does it do what it does? They say music exalts the soul. Nonsense, it is not true! It has an effect, and awful effect – I am speaking of myself – but not of an exalting kind. It has neither an exalting nor a debasing effect but it produces agitation. How can I put it? Music makes me forget myself, my real position; it transports me to some other position not my own. Under the influence of music it seems to me that I feel what I do not really feel, that I understand what I do not understand, that I can do what I cannot do. *I explain it by the fact that music acts like yawning, like laughter: I am not sleepy, but I yawn when I see someone yawning; there is nothing for me to laugh at, but I laugh when I hear people laughing.* Music carries me immediately and directly into the mental condition in which the man was who composed it. My soul merges with his and together with him I pass from one condition into another, but why this happens I don't know. You see, he who wrote, let us say, the Kreutzer Sonata – Beethoven – knows of course why he was in that condition; that condition caused him to do certain actions and therefore that condition had a meaning for him, but for me – none at all. That is why music only agitates and doesn't lead to a conclusion. (XXVII:61; my italics)[44]

Or, another example from an early draft of Tolstoy's article on art:

> An artist, having reached his goal, feels pleasure from having satisfied this emotion of tension. The sensation of this very feeling of tension and its gratification, the submission to this feeling, its imitation, *its infection, like yawning, the experience in a few short minutes of everything that the artist experienced while creating his work is the same pleasure which is experienced by the recipient of the work of art.* This, in my opinion, is the one feature of art which distinguishes it from all other activity. (XXX:221; my italics).

One could add to the end of the last phrase, 'all activity, save hypnosis.' But such an addition would clearly be undesirable for Tolstoy, who was attempting to differentiate between psycho-hypnotic infection and ethical infection (or as Gustafson puts it, 'False art intoxicates, true art infects'[45]):

> And everything, according to this definition, which conveys to people something novel, something that has been extracted by means of this tension of an artist's sensations and thoughts, is a work of art. (ibid.)

In *What Is Art?* Tolstoy presents his famous definition of art as emotional infection:

> If a man infects another or others directly, immediately, by his appearance or by the sounds he gives vent to at the very time he experiences the feeling; if he causes another man to yawn when he himself cannot help yawning, or to laugh or cry when he himself is obliged to laugh or cry, or to suffer when he himself is suffering – that does not amount to art ...
> To evoke in oneself a feeling one has once experienced, and having evoked it in oneself, then, by means of movements, lines, colors, sounds, or forms expressed in words, so to transmit that feeling that others may experience the same feeling – this is the activity of art.
> Art is a human activity consisting in this, that one man consciously, by means of certain external signs, hands on to others feelings he has lived through, and that other people are infected by these feelings and also experience them. (XXX:64–5)[46]

The 29 January 1889 entry in Tolstoy's diary, which discusses the author's painstaking work on his light comedy about spirits, is of particular interest in this context:

> It's a strange thing, this concern about perfection of form. It's not coincidental. But nothing is easy, when the content is good. If Gogol had written a crude, weak comedy, not even one millionth of the people who read it now would have read it. You need to sharpen a work of art, so that it can penetrate. You need to sharpen it....which means you have to make it perfectly artistic. Then it will cut through indifference and repetition and have an effect. (XXVII:655)

The problem for Tolstoy is this: How is one to infect the reader (or all readers) with a work of art? How can the author 'achieve the (proper) effect'? Tolstoy succeeds in his exposure of the seance as charlatanism and frivolous entertainment of the educated class by means of effective comic art (infection by laughter); the viewer laughs at that which, from the point of view of Tolstoy the moralist, is deserving of mockery. It becomes completely clear to the viewer that the truth stands with the peasants, whereas the wealthy and educated characters are actually fools and ignoramuses. At the same time, this laughter hides what was a serious concern for Tolstoy – namely, that (alas!) educated people are inclined to give themselves over to moral hypnosis. Some of them (critics and theoreticians, considered to be social authorities) go even further and invent false explanations for such rubbish. (One might call such academic support of illusion the 'Krugosvetlov phenomenon'). Tolstoy discusses such critics at length in his treatise on art:

> These hypnotized people, being in an abnormal condition, were perfectly enraptured. Moreover, all the art critics, who lack the capacity to be infected by art and therefore always especially prize works like Wagner's opera where it is all an affair of the intellect, also, with much profundity, expressed their approval of a work affording such ample material for ratiocination. And following these two groups went that large city crowd (indifferent to art, with its capacity to be infected by it perverted and partly atrophied) headed by the princes, millionaires, and art patrons, who, like sorry harriers, keep close to those who most loudly and decidedly express their opinion [...] And thus, thanks to the masterly skill with which it counterfeits art while having nothing in common with it, a meaningless, coarse, spurious production finds acceptance all over the world, costs million of rubles to produce, and assists more and more to pervert the taste of people of the upper classes and their conception of the art. (XXX:140)[47]

Gustafson justly states that 'when Tolstoy the writer writes of art, he always thinks of a musical event. Tolstoy's art of infection is the art of a good performance.'[48] One may add that he also thinks of a hypnotic seance as a model for bad art. In *What Is Art?* Tolstoy famously compares listening to Wagner to a spiritualist seance:

> People say, 'You cannot judge without having seen Wagner performed at Bayreuth: in the dark, where the orchestra is out of sight concealed under the stage, and where the performance is brought to the highest perfection.' *And this just proves that we have here no question of art, but one of hypnotism.* It is just what the spiritualists say. To convince you of the reality of their apparitions they usually say, 'You cannot judge; you must try it, be

present at several seances'; i.e., come and sit silent in the dark for hours together in the same room with semi-sane people and repeat this some ten times over, and you shall see all that we see. (XXX:139; my italics).[49]

And later on:

Sit in the dark for four days in company with people who are not quite normal and through the auditory nerves subject your brain to the strongest action of the sounds best adapted to excite it, and you will no doubt be reduced to an abnormal condition and be enchanted by absurdities. (140)

The biographical 'key' to this fragment might very well be the seance at Lvov's, while the ideological 'key' is Tolstoy's reading of literature on hypnosis (first and foremost, as I propose, his familiarity with Vagner's psychic theories about 'waking hypnosis' and Kandinsky's discussion of mental infection), as well as his conversations with Feldman about the influence of hypnosis on individual free will.

It should be said that Tolstoy was not the only writer who attempted to draw a parallel between the artistic effect and hypnotic contagion. This idea 'hovered in the air' throughout the late nineteenth century. In 1894 *The Questions of Philosophy and Psychology,* the same journal in which Tolstoy had published his own writings on philosophy and aesthetics, published A. Giliarov's review of Étienne Souriau's *La suggestion dans l'art* (1893), 'one of the several testimonies of the current fascination with theories of hypnosis' (the very same issue included Tolstoy's 'On the Question of Free Will'). In Souriau's book, creative processes and artistic activity are linked with phenomena observed during hypnotism and suggestion:

Poets, musicians, and artists enchant us in a way similar to hypnotists and their subjects, music by its rhythm, poetry by its meter and rhyme, painting by its brilliant colors, all works of art with their 'artistic possession' act on us in the same way that hypnotists' 'hypnogenic devices' do: monotonous sounds, fixation of sight, suggestion. When we look at a painting or statue, listen to music, immerse ourselves in a work of poetry, we fall into a condition reminiscent of hypnotic lethargy, which then proceeds, similarly, to ecstasy. And just as in hypnotism, where hypnosis is significant only as a means to facilitate suggestion, 'artistic' hypnosis is but an expedient means by which to achieve the main goal of a work of art – to ingrain its message into our souls. As a result of the power of artistic suggestion we, just like subjects under hypnosis, experience illusions, hallucinations, deviant ideas, split consciousness and so on. Finally, poets, artists and composers have experiences that are comparable to those had by subjects who have undergone prolonged suggestion. As soon as the poet is possessed by a creative idea, he cannot rest until he carries it out, i.e., he expresses it in his work.[50]

Giliarov, however, considers the analogy between art and hypnosis to be illusory. Though it can not be denied that 'there exist such works of "artistry" which possess the ability to immerse one into a dream [*pogruzhat' v son*],' he notes that

> every truly artistic work acts in a way completely opposed to hypnosis: it does not narrow the 'field of consciousness' but rather broadens it, it does not impoverish the content, but enriches it, it does not reduce spiritual activity, but rather increases it, and moreover it does this without any kind of intermediate stage, like lethargy.[51]

This conclusion is completely in the spirit of Tolstoy, who likewise contended that true art broadens the spiritual horizon of the individual; that true art liberates, and does not subjugate, individual free will; and (which is most important for Tolstoy) that true art connects the author and his readers in a unified act of aesthetic and ethical infection. By contrast, bad art, according to Tolstoy, can and does act similarly to hypnosis, depriving the viewer or listener of reason and will.

Tolstoy's Seance

Hypnotic infection, which could force people to act against their own moral will, had been Tolstoy's idée fixe since the late 1880s. Infection, he argued, could be caused not just by art (poetry, drama, music), but also by newspapers, universities, medicine, the state, or the church:

> A minority of people, about 20%, is insane in its own right; these people are possessed by the mania of egotism, which leads to the concentration of all of their spiritual energies on themselves. The rest, the majority, of about 80% of all people are hypnotized by scientific, artistic, political, and, most importantly, religious hypnosis and thus also don't use their reason. That is why the insane always succeed in this

world, as they are possessed by the same sort of insanity that possesses the majority. (LIII:324)[52]

Once again, the direct source of Tolstoy's hypnophobia, we believe, can be found in the social psychology of the late 1880s and 1890s, from the already mentioned works of Kandinsky to the *Psychologie des foules* of Gustave Le Bon, translated into Russian in 1896 as *Psikhologiia narodov i mass* (Psychology of the People and Masses).[53]

Psychologists of this school examined 'ideological epidemics' of the past and present and derived laws of mass psychology. According to Le Bon, as a result of psychic infection there 'occurs an orientation of feelings and thoughts of the collective in one and the same direction' and the 'psychological law of mass unity' begins to take effect.[54]

Tolstoy differs from contemporary psychologists in that he does not *analyse* mass consciousness, but rather denounces the 'peddlers of infection,' contemporary social and governmental institutions, and decadent art. At the same time, he understands infection as a moral disease, not a psychological one. In other words, it is moral hypnosis.[55] The late Tolstoy presents civilization as a giant hypnotic seance that lulls weak-willed humanity into a condition of moral and spiritual paralysis and dependence. Those most prone to such infection are, to be sure, the members of the upper classes. The least susceptible are the peasants. Thus the role (more precisely, the mission) of the true (i.e., for Tolstoy, Christian) artist is to lead people (those who can still be saved) out of the hypnotic state, to force them to wake up from the lie and see the truth (which, for Tolstoy, consists of brotherly love and solidarity).

However, there arises a paradox in that this goal can only be achieved with the assistance of the very same weapon used by the enemies of truth (albeit with different goals in mind) – infection. The true Artist of Tolstoy's aesthetic theodicy is the antipode and nemesis of the Hypnotist – this modern sorcerer, 'endowed with the social capital to accomplish miraculous cures.'[56] Yet what if the 'truth' of the good artist is nothing more than a mirage and it turns out that he is not, in fact, a 'spiritual healer' but a usurper such as 'the great Feldman'? This is precisely how Tolstoy's numerous opponents viewed him, claiming that for decades the Russian public had been subjected to the insane count's own grandiose hypnotic seance. 'Tolstoy is a fanatic with his own mad views,' wrote Pobedonostsev (the same one who was supposedly saved by Feldman and who had told Dostoevsky not to write on spiritualism) 'and unfortunately, he seduces and leads into madness thousands of naive people … Mad people who believe in Tolstoy are obsessed, just like himself, by the spirit of untamed propaganda, and they want to transform his teaching into action and inspire the peasants […] One cannot hide the fact that in recent years mental unrest has increased drastically, and it threatens to disseminate bizarre, perverse ideas on faith, Church, government, and society. This negative direction of thoughts is alien not only to the Church, but also to the nation. It is as if an epidemic of madness was gripping people's minds.'[57]

Tolstoy's Walking-Stick (Conclusion)

Towards the end of his remarks on Tolstoy and hypnotism, Feldman recounts a story about a certain mentally disturbed girl. This girl, having concluded that all people were immoral and depraved, had locked herself in her room and refused to talk to anyone. She wouldn't let anyone touch her and refused to eat the food prepared for her by her family's cook. Instead, she cooked her own food on a kerosene stove, and, as Feldman notes, 'would stand in front of a portrait of Lev Tolstoy for several hours and share her thoughts with him out loud.' In order to cure her, her parents resorted to deception: they would write letters to her in Tolstoy's name, in which the writer ostensibly instructed her on what to do. 'The patient would read the letters and unquestioningly carry out all that they recommended.' The parents eventually decided to resort to hypnotic treatment, and summoned Feldman. The latter, in turn, realized that without the consent of the patient he would be unable hypnotize her (this was a principle of the school of hypnotism to which he belonged), and advised the parents to ask for Tolstoy's help, since the writer 'with his charm, could have a salutary effect on the patient.' Feldman wrote to Tolstoy and received the following response:

> I cannot respond to your letter in a definitive manner. I do not believe at all in insanity as a discrete condition; it seems to me that there exists a gradual scale that runs from the ideal, fully healthy individual (who does not exist) to the highest degree of psychological disturbance, and it is impossible to draw the line between the healthy and the ill. I've often met people considered to be insane, who, in my opinion, were no more insane than those who are considered to be healthy. Thus, I think that the girl, whom you mention in your letter, should not be cured.[58]

On the other hand, Tolstoy wrote, he could not possibly refuse meeting and talking with the girl, but at that very time he was going away for a month, perhaps longer. 'After such a response from Tolstoy, of course, one couldn't even think of sending the sick girl to him,' concluded Feldman.[59] It is tempting to view this finale as an ironic response from the healing hypnotist to the moralist writer, who had once mocked the former in a witty comedy. Indeed, the story sounds like a biting parody on the famous episode in Tolstoy's 'Father Sergius' (1898), in which the spiritual healer is seduced by an insane merchant's daughter.

Tolstoy's theory of true art was his response to the initial demands of realism, which I have called 'realist exorcism': a demand to banish the spirits and idols of the past and present from contemporary life and consciousness in order to demonstrate what true life is. The methods and results of such an exorcism, as I have attempted to demonstrate, have varied. The spiritualist Vagner strove for the 'scientific' objectification (materialization) of spirits. His antipode, the materialist Shchedrin, exposed the ghosts and illusions of contemporary society through satire (and in the end concluded that this exposure only cleared space for a new generation of phantoms to flourish).[60] Dostoevsky attempted to ontologize the inner world of the human soul ('realism in a higher sense'). Tolstoy offered an idiosyncratic *moral disinfection* of people's minds through salutary infection with his visions. He took the realists' utopian aim 'to lure readers into the realm of fiction and to maintain credence in the illusion' to its limit.[61] One more step (admitting the illusionism of the author as self-sufficient) and we are already within the magic realm of modernism.

No spiritualist hypnotist could convince the rational and moralizing Tolstoy that milk would flow from his walking stick, should he perchance suck on it: this would be stupid and there would be no reason for it to come from there. But Tolstoy the Realist, if we develop the metaphor a bit further, both believed and could make others believe that with this very same walking stick (or even better – pen) he could draw water from stone, part the Red Sea, and lead the people to the Promised Land.

Epilogue: The Spirit of Literature – Reflections on Leskov's Artistic Spiritualism

When I look at myself in mirrors
I see, it seems, Aesop.
However when Dembrovskii approaches the glass,
There immediately appears an ass.

A.S. Pushkin

It is, perhaps, a light and mischievous spirit making fun of you.

N.S. Leskov, At Daggers Drawn

[The artistic text] bears the marks of intellectual structure: it possesses a memory, in which it can concentrate its previous meanings, and at the same time it has the capacity, joining in a chain of communication, to create new meaningful messages. If we accept the definition of the intelligent soul which Heraclitus of Ephesus gave – the psyche as self-expanding Logos – then we may examine [the artistic text] as an object possessing this property.

Yu.M. Lotman, 'Brain – Text – Culture and the Artistic Intellect'

1.

I conclude this book with a discussion of Nikolai Leskov's brilliant Christmas story 'The Spirit of Mme Genlis: A Spiritualistic Event,' which not only unites many of the topics introduced in this study, but also – in its own way – 'plays out' its central argument: the ontological kinship and rivalry between realist literature and spiritualism, writers and mediums, as two agencies that claim their knowledge of the objective truth about the soul. This hilarious tale relates a 'strange incident' from the life of the author himself, is told in the first person, and consists of sixteen short sections (some of them only a quarter of a page), dynamically following one after another and repeatedly confounding the expectations of the reader.[1] This story is rightly considered a classic of the literary anecdote (*literaturnyi anekdot*) – a genre, according to Boris Eikhenbaum, at the foundation of Leskov's artistic method.[2] To retell the anecdote is a thankless task, but we are obliged to do so in order to be able to get to the heart of his 'pneumatological joke' (so different from Dostoevsky's metaphysical humour).

2.

In the winter of 186* the narrator (hereafter 'Leskov') meets a Russian princess recently arrived from abroad – a society lady, educated and highly moral. The princess is fascinated with the then fashionable spiritualism. She has her personal oracle – a late eighteenth–early nineteenth century French writer, Stéphanie Félicité Genlis, the author of numerous sentimental–didactic pieces, including an anthology of adages titled *The Spirit of Madame Genlis*, addressed to young women coming out in society.[3] The princess keeps a terracotta mould of the writer's tiny hand (which Voltaire himself once kissed in Ferney) like a shrine. For advice, she often turns to Genlis's little light-blue books (her collected works). The princess is convinced that the 'spirit of Félicité' (or her 'delicate essence') lives in these volumes and can readily answer all questions.

3.

Inclined, as he himself once confessed, to mysticism, 'Leskov' brings up in his conversation with the princess the pneumatological theory of Allan Kardec concerning 'mischievous spirits.' He confesses that he burns with the desire to find out 'how to have the good fortune to be shown the spirit of the witty Marquise de Silleri, the countess of Brûlart.'[4] The 'spirit' of the long-forgotten writer Genlis becomes the story's main character, and its 'testing' the engine of the plot. As the narrator points out, the task falls to the reader to decide to what extent such 'spirits' 'perform successfully and remain true to their literary heritage.' The problem of the spirit of Genlis, then, is closely connected in the story with the problem of the spirit of literature itself.

4.

The spiritualist princess asks 'Leskov' to acquaint her innocent, angelic daughter with modern Russian literature – 'naturally, only with the good, that is, real, literature, not infected with the evil of the day.'[5] Above all, the princess fears the 'suggestive phrases' and 'provocative subjects' by which, in her opinion, almost all recent literature is spoiled. Even Ivan Goncharov doesn't satisfy her ultra-Victorian taste, for in his novel *Oblomov* seductive female elbows are mentioned several times.[6] 'Leskov' tries to challenge the princess, but in the end only the opinion of her oracle can convince her. Opened at random, the book 'expounds': 'Reading is too serious and consequential an activity to leave to the unguided taste of young people. There is reading that young people like, but it makes them irresponsible and predisposes them to frivolity, after which it is hard to correct their character. All this I have learned from experience.' The princess is triumphant. The first trial of the spirit, and of literature, is over.

5.

However, in the words of the narrator, the 'spirit' continues to live and act and in the end 'pulls off such a puerile joke that it results in a deep tragicomedy.' On New Year's Eve, in the princess's little salon, the conversation turns to literature and its practitioners. One of the guests, a diplomat, declares that all literature is 'a serpent' [*zmeia*], not even excepting the works of the pious Genlis. To refute this opinion, the princess asks her angelic daughter to read aloud from *The Spirit of Mme Genlis* so that Félicité herself can have her say on the subject. The innocent girl, opening the book at random, reads aloud the story of how the blind Mme Du Deffand, who had a habit of feeling her salon guests' faces on making their acquaintance, mistook the plump physiognomy of the young historian Gibbon for another soft part of his body: 'Mme Du Deffand brought her hands up to him and ran her fingers over the round face. She diligently searched for somewhere to stop, but this was impossible. Then the face of the blind lady expressed first astonishment, then fury, and in the end, quickly pulling back her hands with revulsion, she cried out, "What a vile joke!"' (89–90).[7]

6.

The result of the 'vile joke' (which serves as an excellent example of the technique of defamiliarization, as well as a biting parody on spiritualists' palpating of the spirits' parts, discussed earlier) are the tears of the innocent girl, the horror of the mother, the muffled laughter of the guests, and the malicious pleasure of the diplomat, the enemy of literature. 'Leskov' subsequently finds out that afterwards the princess, before leaving Russia entirely, has destroyed the works of Genlis and broken the terracotta hand to pieces 'from which, however, it seems, there remained, as a memento, one little finger, or, more precisely, the finger' (a 'fig'). It turns out that the 'spirit' drove out the person who called it forth.

7.

In 1866 Leskov included 'The Spirit of Mme Genlis' in his collection of Christmas stories. This genre, according to the writer, ought to meet several demands; it should (1) formally coincide with the events of Christmas Eve, (2) contain some element of fantasy, (3) possess 'some kind of moral, even a sort of refutation of harmful prejudice,' (4) place an emphasis on the truth of the incident described, and (5) contain a comic finale, in accordance with the holiday mood. It is easy to convince oneself that 'The Spirit of Mme Genlis' fulfils the letter and the spirit of the Christmas genre.[8] But what is the moral of this story? What prejudice is being derided?

8.

In the finale of the story, the narrator comes to three conclusions (in a style extremely reminiscent of truisms): it is necessary first to read the books about which we resolve to talk; maidens shouldn't be held in childish ignorance for so long; and it is as impossible to rely blindly on spirits as on people. The diplomat interprets the spiritual event otherwise: the 'spirit' only bears out his opinion about literature – that 'the best of snakes is still a snake,' and the better the snake, the more dangerous it is, for it 'holds its poison in its tail.' The story's aphoristic epigraph, chosen from the already mentioned book of the learned Benedictine Augustine Calmet *Dissertation sur les apparitions* (1746), states that it is hard to get rid of a spirit once it is called up.[9] Hugh

McLean concludes that 'literature,' in the guise of the spirit Genlis, teaches the princess a cruel lesson. The story is a comic jibe at 'Victorian prudery' and 'spiritualist credulity.'[10] Inès Muller de Morogues sees in the story a pedagogical satire, one that warns of the dangers of a Puritanical education,[11] while W. Pozdiejew views it as a satire on mysticism.[12] From the story of the spirit of Mme Genlis one can also derive a religious lesson, characteristic of the Christmas genre: 'the necessity of a strong faith in God,'[13] rather than in spirits, behind whom hide cunning demons. However, the multiplicity of the 'truths' derived from this story only underlines its parodic character: 'The Spirit of Mme Genlis' eludes straightforward explication.

9.

We recall that the subtitle of the story is 'A Spiritualistic Event.' The author constantly situates the story in the contemporary discussion of spiritualism[14] and, in the opinion of Hugh McLean, represents an 'unadulterated satire of the spiritualist fad.'[15] The object of Leskov's satire turns out to be so-called philosophical spiritualism – that is, as we recall, the Kardecian doctrine founded on the existence, apparition, and admonition of spirits. In Russia of the 1860s, entire circles of Kardecists occupied themselves with (in the words of a contemporary) 'systematic study of the secrets of the dead, conversations with long-deceased people, and other such nonsense.'[16] The messages from the famous deceased contained various pieces of advice and guidelines, remarks on life after death, and a critique of earthly life.

10.

As we know, Leskov actively engaged in heated discussions of Kardecian spiritualism in the 1860s. Without a doubt, the dogmatic and practical sides of this 'chatty fairy-tale doctrine' turned the writer off: 'Is it worth it, in the end, to die [...] so that the first idle medium can once again wrest you "from the mansions of the Father," as a mischievous little boy takes an old bark sandal off the sleeping board, and starts to spin you in front of everyone?'[17] But we also remember that in Kardec's spiritualism Leskov found elements in harmony with his own mystical interests and intuitions: close attention to the 'journey' of the human spirit languishing in the prison of the flesh; the idea of death as a desirable transition to a new state; the possibility of spiritual apparitions in our world; and the idea of the provisional character of punishment and the temporary nature of hell (here a source for Leskov is, of course, Origen[18]). One may assume that the 'psychological potential' of Kardec's doctrine was also attractive to the writer, particularly the representation of the soul's inner work on the path to perfection and the attitude towards earthly life as a temporary trial, as one of the stations on the path to another world. Finally, the spiritualistic stories about the miracles of nature and communication with other worlds could have attracted Leskov the storyteller as a model of modern 'scientific mysticism.'[19] Interest in spiritualism was reflected in a whole series of the author's works: the novel *At Daggers Drawn*, the stories 'Laughter and Woe,' 'The Apparition of the Spirit,' 'On the Edge of the World,' and 'White Eagle,' the essay 'Monastic Islands on Lake Ladozhsky,' and others.[20]

11.

In the story of the spirit of Genlis, spiritualist convictions are not only the object of parody but also a distinctive element in the construction of the text. The irony of the narrative lies in the fact that the event narrated could easily have been interpreted by contemporaries as a 'confirmation' of the spiritualist theory of 'mischievous spirits,' which the narrator mentions at the beginning of his story. In accordance with the teachings of Allan Kardec (an author whose work Leskov knew well), spirits fall into different classes depending on the moral perfection they have achieved. Among the spirits of low rank Kardec conceived of a category of frivolous or mischievous spirits who are 'inconsistent and sarcastic.' These spirits 'love to conjure up minor difficulties,' 'to create gossip, to cunningly lead astray with mystifications and pranks.' They 'seize on the slightest strangeness' and 'express' the humorous 'in vile and satirical qualities.' They are born buffoons and mystifiers who, 'if they take on other names, do so more out of mischief than malice.'[21] It is impossible to trust these *esprits mystificateurs*, but there is no point being afraid of them either, for they are under the direction of higher spirits, 'who often use them, as we use servants and workers.'[22] A true spiritualist, according to Kardec, should learn to distinguish between the voices of buffoons and serious spirits.[23] On the other hand, religious opponents of spiritualism (from theologians to mystically minded commentators) saw a diabolic hallucination[24] in the games of mischievous spirits, while sceptical materialists saw the crooked tricks of mediums.

12.

Stories of the tricks of prankster spirits who were constantly clogging up the 'pneumatic ether' occupied an important place in spiritualist folklore. More often than not these spirits called themselves by the names of famous writers. Thus, for example, A.N. Aksakov told of an irksome rhyming prankster – the spirit Spiridon, posing as Alexander Pushkin.[25] In the case of another famous Russian spiritualist, N.P. Vagner, we recall the story of the pranks of the 'spirit of Ivan Barkov,'[26] dictating 'by means of a saucer' to an innocent seventeen-year-old girl and her pious mother such 'indecent vulgarities' that the mother's brother laughed until he cried when these messages were communicated to him.[27] Much later, in his novella *The Eye* (1930), Nabokov depicted a mischievous spirit preaching under the name Ivan Turgenev.

13.

It is worth noting that the 'mischievous spirits' of Allan Kardec are mentioned in, and act in, a few of Leskov's works of the 1870s. In the 'Sternian' story 'Smekh i gore' (Laughter and Woe, 1871) they 'disturb' the public prosecutor with their liberal attitude towards punishment. In the antinihilistic novel *At Daggers Drawn*, which is riddled with spiritualistic ideas, these spirits mock the 'unnatural' imposter Joseph Vislenev, who is playing the role of a medium–prophet.[28] They also poke fun at the novel's main villain, Glafira Bodrostina. Their role in Leskov's literary mythology is to unmask vice through parody.

14.

The mention of the pranks of mischievous spirits at the beginning of the story 'The Spirit of Mme Genlis' thus imparts a new dimension to the narrative: a natural explanation of the 'spiritualistic event' (a funny coincidence) cannot fully rule out the supernatural (the action of a mischievous spirit or a prank of the devil). This duality of perception of an unusual phenomenon, according to Tzvetan Todorov, distinguishes the genre of the fantastic – presented, in the case of the Leskovian story, in a comic mode.[29] But what is the 'point' of this spiritual joke?

15.

Whether or not we believe in the mystical interpretation of this 'strange adventure,' the 'spirit' in the story acts as a rational and independent force, coming out 'on the side' of the men of letters and arousing aesthetic delight in the narrator himself. One might say that Leskov transforms a spiritualistic ontology into a literary plan. In a broad sense, the object of his parody is neither spiritualism as public superstition, nor heresy, nor the Victorian approach to literature as the object of strict pedagogical censure.[30] Instead, it is the tendentious attitude towards the author (or his works) by which the latter is understood as a dead spirit called up by the reader in support of his own outlook. As described in our chapter on Pushkin's shade, such a relationship, carried to absurdity by the practice of communication with famous souls, was in the highest degree characteristic of ordinary readers, as well as the 'tendentious' critics of the Age of Realism. According to Leskov, literature – even the most archaic, such as the works of Genlis – is alive, personal (the inimitable 'voice' of the author),[31] and self-willed. This mischief-making unpredictability of literature, incidentally, is wonderfully felt by the storyteller's main opponent, the diplomat. Only he, the foe of literature, sees in the merry spirit a traitor–devil with 'poison in its tail.'

16.

I contend that the anecdote about the spirit of Genlis can be understood as a distinctive manifesto of Leskov's *literary spiritualism*, which is fundamentally different from the naive spiritualist realism of Vagner (it could be said that Mme Genlis's broken terracotta hand thumbed its nose at the hapless hunter for materialized hands),[32] and the realistic phantasmagory of Shchedrin, as well as Dostoevsky's ontological realism and Tolstoy's artistic hypnotism. It is instead a parable (or a mystery play) about how the spirit of literature itself – immortal, free, mischievous, and overwhelming[33] – 'lives and acts.' Whatever might be expected of this spirit and whatever demands might be placed on it, it breathes where it wants, and no one knows where it comes from, where it is directed, and what joke it is capable of pulling off. Literary

works, in other words, are not the passive objects of reading and reverence, not the frozen fountain of wisdom, not the 'slave of the lamp,'
executing the command of its master, and not the 'equal conversational
partner of the reader.'[34] Rather, they are – by almost mystical means – a
subject, capable of directing a self-assured reader in whatever way
occurs to it. Such an 'animistic' or 'elemental' understanding of the literary text brings the heretical art of Leskov close to Renaissance spiritualism (from Paracelsus to Shakespeare)[35] and romantic spiritualism
(from Novalis and August W. Schlegel to Pushkin) and stands in opposition to the demonic conception of literature characteristic of Gogol
and (to a considerable degree) Dostoevsky.[36] It is in this respect that
Leskov the storyteller joins the ranks of the playful mediums rather
than 'the ranks of the [great realist] teachers and sages,'[37] evoking by
means of his art the spirit of literature and letting him go forth and act.
Thus, reading, according to 'Leskov' (and the reading of Leskov's own
story) is an activity that is cheerful, humane, healthy, and absolutely
unpredictable in its consequences.[38]

On the whole, I suppose, it makes sense to speak of two polar types
of artistic spiritualism in literature (that is, two attempts at the ontology of the 'spirit of literature'): the idea of literature as a cunning and
pernicious force ('the party of the devil,' in William Blake's words)[39]
and a relationship to it as to a live and free manifestation of spiritual
life that transcends and scoffs at material reality. One may call the pro-
ponents of this idea the 'PARTY OF THE SPIRIT.'[40]

Notes

Preface

1 The epigraphs are taken from Sechenov, 'Refleksy golovnogo mozga'; and L.N. Tolstoi, *Polnoe sobranie*, XI:138.
2 Among the most notable events in the history of these polemics, one may recall the fierce debate between the materialist Nikolai Chernyshevskii and the idealist philosopher Pamfil Iurkevich regarding the anthropological principle in philosophy (1860–2); the theological argument between Bishop Feofan (Govorov) and Bishop Ignatii (Brianchaninov) regarding the 'material substance of the soul' (1869); the passionate critique of Heinrich Struve's psycho-physiological approach to the soul by the philosophers Iurkevich, Aleksandr Aksakov, and Nikolai Strakhov (1870); and the intense debates between the philosopher Konstantin Kavelin and the scientist Ivan Sechenov on the nature and goals of psychology as a science (1872–3). See Zen'kovskii, *Istoriia russkoi filosofii*, I: pt2; Florovskii, *Puti russkogo bogosloviia*, VII: pt.2 ('Istoricheskaia shkola'); Fr Seraphim Rose, *The Soul After Death*; Iaroshevskii, *Istoriia psikhologii ot antichnosti do serediny xx veka*; and Joravsky, *Russian Psychology*.
3 By realism I mean a broad literary movement of the 1850 to 1880s that pursued an 'almost scientific description of the underside of the existing social reality,' that included various literary strategies (realisms) to achieve this goal, and that underwent profound transformations in the course of its history. For a similar approach, see Freeborn, 'The Nineteenth Century: The Age of Realism,' 248–332. In my discussion of realism, I depart from George Levine's thesis that 'realism exists as a process, responsive to the changing nature of reality as the culture understood it, and evoking with each question another question to be questioned, each threatening to

destroy that quest beyond words, against literature, that is its most distinguishing mark.' Levine, *The Realistic Imagination*, 22.

4 Freud, 'The Uncanny'; Derrida, *Specters of Marx*; Greenblatt, *Hamlet in Purgatory*; Garber, *Shakespeare's Ghost Writers*; Bergland, *The National Uncanny*; Rabaté, *Ghosts of Modernity*; and Warner, *Phantasmagoria*. For a good discussion of the trope of spectrality in the history of Western thought, see Buse and Stott, 'Introduction: A Future for Haunting,' 1–20.

5 Oppenheim, *The Other World*; Owen, *The Darkened Room*; Kerr, *Mediums, and Spirit-Rappers, and Roaring Radicals*; Kselman, *Death and the Afterlife in Modern France*; Monroe, *Laboratories of Faith*.

6 Castle, *The Female Thermometer*; Sword, *Ghostwriting Modernism*; Trail, *Possible Worlds of the Fantastic*.

7 Derrida, *Specters*, 14. In the 1990s the cultural significance of spectres and phantoms was recognized by scholars of different opinions. The 'dialogue with the ghost' that Derrida had begun became a fashionable genre that responded to postmodernist concerns.

8 Sword, *Ghostwriting Modernism*, 165. Ghosts, Sword stresses, 'are hermeneutic entities, both etymologically – like Hermes, the Greek messenger god, they possess a privileged ability to pass between the worlds of the living and the dead – and practically: all ghosts demand interpretation.'

9 Levine, *The Realistic Imagination*, 7. On the history of scholarly polemics regarding realism in the nineteenth and twentieth centuries, see Herman, *Concepts of Realism*.

10 Lilian R. Furst, *All Is True*, 26.

11 See, for example: Sakulin, *Iz istorii russkogo idealizma*; Gershenzon, *P.Ia. Chaadaev*; Chizhevskii, 'Neizvestnyi Gogol'; Berry, *Spiritualism in Tsarist Society and Literature*; Vaiskopf, *Siuzhet Gogolia*; Carlson, 'No Religion Other Than Truth'; Leighton, *The Esoteric Tradition in Russian Romantic Literature*; Bogomolov, *Russkaia literatura nachala XX veka i okkul'tizm*; Obatnin, *Ivanov-mistik*; Rosenthal, *The Occult in Russian and Soviet Culture*; and Masing-Delic, *Abolishing Death*. This list is by no means complete.

12 Levine, *The Realistic Imagination*, 22.

13 For a detailed survey of Russian literature in the Age of Realism, see Freeborn, 'The Nineteenth Century.' Wellek provides a brief discussion of the peculiarities of Russian realism in 'Realism in Literature.' IV:53–4. Brown discusses Belinsky's and Chernyshevsky's realist strategies in '"So Much Depends": ... Russian Critics in Search of "Reality."' For a painstaking analysis of Russian psychological realism, see Ginzburg, *O psikhologicheskoi proze*.

14 I will not embark here on a detailed discussion of the fantastic in realism, but will merely cite Trail's summary statement that the supernatural does

not disappear during this period; rather, it is transformed into the paranormal. Trail, *Possible Worlds of the Fantastic*, 34. In the end we are confronted with the literary analogue of scientific spiritualism: the realist modification of the fantastic tale, expressing the epistemological uncertainty of the rationalist consciousness.

15   Castle, *The Female Thermometer*, examines a similar process of the 'interiorization' of spiritualism during the rationalistic epoch in her studies on the late Enlightenment. In his excellent article on the fantastic in *Anna Karenina*, Holquist suggests that the realist imagination perceived 'invisible' social forces, which acted behind the scene, as an equivalent for the romantic supernatural. Holquist, 'The Supernatural as Social Force in Anna Karenina,' 176–90.

16   The coexistence of these two tendencies recalls the mechanism of the fantastic tale as described by Tzvetan Todorov.

17   The tipping of the balance towards 'spiritualism' at the end of the nineteenth century led to the birth of a new, symbolist movement. On spiritualist implications of the new art, see Florenskii, 'Spiritizm kak antikhristianstvo.'

18   'The moral urgency of seeing with disenchanted clarity,' as Levine aptly calls it. Levine, *The Realist Imagination*, 22.

Introduction

1   Boltin, *Spiritizm*, 14.

2   The fullest accounts of the English and American Spiritualist movements may be found in Oppenheim, *The Other World*; Owen, *The Darkened Room*; and Kerr, *Mediums, and Spirit-Rappers, and Roaring Radicals*. On French Spiritualism, see Vartier, *Allan Kardec*; Hess, *Spirits and Scientists*, 59–79; Kselman, *Death and the Afterlife in Modern France*, 143–62; and Monroe, *Laboratories of Faith*.

3   In a chapter on spiritualism [spiritisme] in France, Thomas Kselman, *Death and the Afterlife*, summarizes the traditional explanations for the popularity of spiritualist teaching in the second half of the nineteenth century. Researchers of social and ideological trends held the view that 'in an age marked by religious skepticism, the growing prestige of science, and greater affectivity between family members, spiritism provided scientific sanction for reassuring beliefs about the future of the self and the eternal solidarity of the family.' From a more radical sociological perspective, spiritism represented a form of escapism: 'Oppressed workers, and later a bored middle-class, sought relief and entertainment by imagining a world

better than this one.' For the historian of religion, meanwhile, 'spiritism illustrates the continuing spread of doubt about the afterworld preached by orthodox Christianity, whose God was willing to condemn people to eternal punishment for even momentary and trivial lapses' (159). Kselman, for his part, points to the literary and linguistic nature of spiritualism (160).

4   The mediums, however, lost the unique mystical aura that surrounded the clairvoyants of the 1830s and 1840s. According to the scientistic ideology of spiritualism, a medium is neither a prophet nor a 'prophetic soul,' but simply a person endowed with psychic talents who is able to receive and transmit the signals of forces not yet known to science.

5   A literary 'encyclopaedia' of Russian mystical folklore of the first half of the nineteenth century was supplied by the prominent Slavophile historian Pogodin, *Prostaia rech' o mudrenykh veshchakh*. The book is organized under the following headings: 'Presentiments,' 'Portents,' 'Predictions,' 'The Faculty of Foresight,' 'Instances of Seeing Oneself,' 'The Inner Voice,' 'Conversions,' 'Apparitions Seen by the Dying at the Moment of their Death,' 'Dreams,' and so on. A popular book in 1860s Russia was a translation from the German of Augustine Calmet's *O iavleniiakh dukhov*, in which Calmet, a French Benedictine, cited numerous episodes of supernatural phenomena and provided commentary. One attentive reader of this work was Nikolai Leskov, who referred to it in his works *At Daggers Drawn* (1870–1) and *The Spirit of Madame de Genlis* (1881), which will be discussed at length in the epilogue to this book.

6   A detailed history of Russian spiritualism is still to be written. A brief sketch of the spiritualist movement in Russia is given in Pribytkov, *Spiritizm v Rossii*. See also M. Petrovo-Solovovo, 'Ocherki iz istorii spiriticheckago dvizheniia v Rossii' in his *Prilozheniia k perevodu sochinenii F. Podmora*; Britten, 'Spiritualism in Russia'; and Bykov's monumental anti-spiritualist monograph, *Spiritizm pered litsom nauki*. For a survey of spiritualist concerns in Russian literature, see Berry, *Spiritualism in Tsarist Society and Literature*.

7   During that same month – April 1853 – table turning became the subject of heated debates in France and Germany, eliciting numerous articles, feuilletons and caricatures, as well as speeches by leading scholars, politicians and religious figures.

8   *SPch*, 82 (1853): 326.

9   *SPch*, 88 (1853): 351.

10   *MV*, 62 (1853): 638.

11   On de Mirville's crtitique of spiritualism, see Monroe, 'Making the Seance "Serious."'

12 Mel'nikov-Pecherskii, 'Vospominaniia o Vladimire Ivanoviche Dale.'
13 'Neskol'ko slov o stolakh dvigaiushchikhsia prosto i o stolakh, kotorye
    predskazyvaiut budushchee, ugadyvaiut proshedshee i otvechaiut pis-
    menno [sic] na vsiakie voprosy,' *Moskvitianin*, I, 21, otd. VIII (1853): 124.
14 Filaret, *O stologadanii*, 5.
15 See the review in the July 1855 issue of *The Contemporary* of Alexandre
    Brierre de Boismont's, *Des hallucinations*.
16 Littré, 'Govoriashchie stoly i stuchashchie dukhi,' 47. A model of the Rus-
    sian positivist critique is Prince V.F. Odoevsky's letter on table turning,
    addressed to O.S. Pavlishcheva [Pushkina] (1854). The learned prince
    ascribed psychological causes to the mysterious phenomena that so
    impressed his correspondent. See Tur'ian, 'Predislovie.'
17 See Kerr, *Mediums and Spirit-Rappers*, 10–11.
18 The historical subtext of Hugo's communications with spirits is analysed in
    Matlock's superb article, 'Ghostly Politics.'
19 Pierre Leroux exerted a considerable influence on George Sand – an idol of
    the young in the 1860s. For the influence of Leroux on Sand, see Lacassa-
    gne, *Histoire d'une amitié*.
20 'Realisty,' in Pisarev, *Polnoe sobranie sochinenii i pisem*, VI:303–4. Pisarev bor-
    rows from Leroux the thought that he would, by his own account, make
    the basis of his realist-minded reflections on science and art.
21 Hence Chernyshevsky's interest in the mystical revelations of Newton (the
    idol of the 'age of science'). Chernyshevskii, '"Chto delat"?' XI:196–7.
22 In the late 1850s, Home performed several seances for the Tsar. The table,
    recalled lady-in-waiting A.F. Tiutcheva, did in fact turn. Mysterious taps
    beat out the anthem 'God, Save the Tsar.' During one seance the spirit of
    the late Tsar, Nicholas I, was summoned. Tiutcheva, *Pri dvore dvukh impera-
    torov*, II:125–6. On the fashion for spiritualism under Alexander II, see
    Berry, 'Mediums and Spiritualism in Russian Literature,' 129–44.
23 On Kardec and French Spiritualism, see David J. Hess, *Spirits and Scientists*,
    59–79; and Monroe, *Laboratories of Faith*, 95–149.
24 Kardec, *Dukhovnaia filosofiia*, OR RGB, fonds 344 Shibanov, no. 351:i–xxxvi.
25 Hess, *Spirits and Scientists*, 61.
26 'The Book of Spirits, containing the principles of the spiritist doctrine of the
    immortality of the soul, the properties of Spirits, and their relations with
    people; moral laws, the present, future life and the future of humanity.
    Based on the teachings of higher spirits, transmitted through mediums.
    Collected and ordered by Allan Kardec. Translated from the French by
    Apollon Boltin, 1862'; 'Experimental Spiritism: Book on Mediums or a
    Guide for Mediums and Summonings [*vyzyvanii*]. Containing: a special

exhortation of the spirits about the theory of manifestations of all kinds; means of communicating with the invisible world; development of mediumship; difficulties and stumbling blocks that may be encountered in the practice of spiritism. Continuation of the Book of Spirits. A work by Allan Kardec. Translated from the French by Apollon Boltin, 1863'; 'What is Spiritism? Guide for inexperienced observers of the phenomenon of the manifestation of Spirits, containing an exposition of the principles of the Spiritist doctrine. By Allan Kardec, author of The Book of Spirits and The Book of Mediums, publisher of the monthly periodical *Revue Spirite*. Translated from the French by Apollon Boltin, 1863.' OR RGB, fond 344, Shibanov, nos. 351–7.

27 On St Petersburg circles of Kardecists, see Shepard, 'Experiences in High Life in Russia.' Shepard draws a vivid image of 'the chief of Russian Spiritists,' the head of the construction division of the Russian Technical Department, General D.I. Zhuravskii (Jouravski): in his office 'he is in every sense of the work, a business man, a man of the world, yet strictly honest and rigid in all his principles of practice with the world; a man who is positive in all his dealings, as the head of the great Russian railway. And a great friend of his majesy the Emperor, yet with all these attainments in the outside world, he is a changed man when once out of his office and at home, or at his city seance [...] and prayers and supplication, and devotion commences. Then all is changed, and you see the holy priest, the saint, I was almost going to say the martyr to the philosophy of Allan Kardec.'

28 Bykov, *Spiritizm pered sudom nauki*, 120.

29 According to one contemporary account, Ivan the Terrible would make polite appearances in various drawing rooms simultaneously, 'announcing his presence with a tap of the table or through the medium's idle chatter.' *Vsemirnaia illiustratsiia*, 19 (1869): 304.

30 The first Russian spiritualist journal, *Rebus*, began publication only in 1881.

31 Britten, *Nineteenth-Century Miracles*, 351.

32 'Our fellow countrymen,' Leskov observed ironically in an article on spiritualism, 'are probably more down-to-earth than the French even *there*'; Leskov, *Polnoe sobranie sochinenii*, VII:266.

33 In America and England, great success was enjoyed by the so-called literary mediums, who performed mediumistic improvisations before various audiences. They affirmed that through them deceased writers (including Shakespeare, Rousseau, Keats, Byron, Coleridge, Shelley, and Saadi) transmitted their works from the other world. The favourite among American mediums of the 1860s was Edgar Allan Poe; among the English, it was Shakespeare. See Hess, *Spirits and Scientists*, 15–21. The anti-Semitic writer

V.I. Kryzhanovskaia (pseudonym: Rochester) was an exception, achieving considerable fame in Russia as a literary medium. She putatively wrote 'one novel with one hand, and another novel with the other.' See Gren, *Sborniik statei po spiritizmu i eskhatologii*, II:26. For more on the work of this 'essentially unique representative of the occult novel in Russia,' see Reitblat, 'Kryzhanovskaia,' II:173–4. I am not touching here on the phenomenon of Helene Blavatsky (who received messages from *mahatmas*), since it belongs more to the Western tradition than to the Russian. See Carlson, *'No Religion Other Than Truth'*; and Washington, *Madame Blavatsky's Baboon*.

34 On the occult interests and practices of Russian writers at the turn of the century (Vladimir Solov'ev, Valerii Briusov, Viacheslav Ivanov, Mikhail Kuz'min, and others), see, for example, Bogomolov, *Russkaia literatura nachala XX veka i okkul'tizm*; Obatnin, *Ivanov-mistik*; and Rosenthal, *The Occult in Russian and Soviet Culture*.

35 Karatygin, 'Vecher u generala Katenina.'

36 In contrast, for example, to the reports and mystical collections of the Masonic lodges of the first decades of the nineteenth century.

37 Fel'kner nevertheless preserved two poems received by his brother at the seances: one from Ivan Krylov, and another from Pushkin himself. Fel'kner, 'Golosa iz-za groba.' On spiritualist poems, see the chapter below on the Russian dead poets' society.

38 On asking which poet wrote these lines, Vagner received the reply: 'Surikov.' 'A famous poet?' 'Yes!' Vagner, however, remained doubtful that the poem had been written 'by our famous national poet,' given their dissimilarity with Surikov's poetic manner: 'The spirit ... clearly represented a personality who had been mightily entangled by other individuals.' Vagner, *Nabliudeniia nad mediumizmom*, 31–2.

39 Ibid., 93.

40 Ibid., 122.

41 'The moral teaching of spiritism does not represent the outcome of his theories, as one might have expected, but some mixture of unhealthy naturalism and un-Christian morality.' Boltin, '"Spiritizm," stat'ia Apollona Boltina,' *Raduga* 4 (1864): 1.

42 Boltin, *Zamechaniia na stat'iu 'Refleksy golovnogo mozga,'* 5.

43 Precise information about the number of spiritualists and sympathizers in 1860s and 1870s St Petersburg is lacking. It should be noted, though, that 130 individuals signed a letter against the conclusions of D.I. Mendeleev's antispiritualist commission (not all, of course, were spiritualists). *SPbV*, no. 122 (4 May 1876). Madame Blavatsky, who published her translation of this letter in *The Banner of Light* (24 June 1876), stressed that 'the names

attached to this protest represent the best blood of Russia. It is the most influentially signed document, probably, that ever appeared in an official journal of my country.' Blavatsky, *Collected Writings*, I:215–16. It was only at the beginning of the twentieth century, with the movement's institutionalization in Russia, that more or less reliable statistical data on Russian spiritualism began to appear (see Bykov, *Spiritizm pered sudom nauki*).

44   *Vsemirnaia illiustratsiia* 19 (1869): 303.

45   Ibid.

46   Lesevich, 'Modnoe sueverie,' *OZ* 199, no. 12 (1871): 198–200.

47   Ignatii, *Slovo o chuvstvennom i o dukhovnom videnii dukhov*. [http://www.wco.rv/biblio/books/ignlr7/main.htm]

48   Lebedev, 'Spirity i spiritizm,' *Khristianskoe chtenie* 9 (1866): 707.

49   Ibid., 723.

50   Leskov devoted several essays to Kardecism in Russia: a sketch of St Petersburg society life (24 May 1869); and the articles 'Allan Kardec, Recently Deceased Leader of the European Spiritualists' (12 June 1869), 'A Fashionable Enemy of the Church' (28–9 June 1869); and 'The Greats of the World in Their Future Existence: A Fantastic Regiment on Mars' 8 August 1869). Leskov, *Polnoe sobranie sochinenii*, VII:261–7, 270–300; VIII:117–27.

51   Leskov, 'Modnyi vrag tserkvi,' *Polnoe sobranie sochinenii*, VII:298.

52   Potulov, 'Otvet na vopros,' *DB*, 43 (1869): 1106. It is worth noting that in 1876, Potulov sent his collection of antispiritualist essays *Prodolzhenie bor'by s lgushchei uchenost'iu* to Dostoevsky, to whom he ascribed similar views. He was inspired to do so by Dostoevsky's article on spiritualism in the January issue of *A Writer's Diary*.

53   Potulov, 'Spiritizm i ego znachenie,' *DB*, 30 (1869): 802.

54   Zhukovsky, the exemplary Romantic poet, was renowned as the 'poetic usher [*diad'ka*] of the English and German devils and witches' and was revered by Russian spiritualists as one of the harbingers of the era of spiritualism. See his article 'Something about Ghosts,' written during the year of spiritualism's birth in America and published posthumously in *Russkaia Beseda* (1853), with the comment that 'in his spiritual purity and religious sincerity the author appears as the morning star of the new literary epoch in Russia.' See a chapter on Zhukovsky's spiritualism in my book *Dom tolkovatelia*, 203–34. In 1853, at the dawn of Russian Spiritualism, *The Muscovite* published the letter 'Concerning V.A. Zhukovsky's Article on Ghosts,' in which the correspondent spoke of the importance of the issue raised by Zhukovsky and of the need to collect and publish 'with complete historical fidelity' every episode that bore a relation to the world of the spirits. The

correspondent himself adduced two such episodes; see *Moskvitianin*, 1 (1856): 305. An instance of the literary refraction of this tradition is represented by the 'mystical anecdotes' of Leskov and Turgenev from the 1860s to the 1880s.

55 Berg, 'V.I. Dal' i Nashchokin,' 614. In fact, Dal' met Zhukovsky much earlier, while studying in Dorpat (1826–9). See Il'in-Tomich, 'Dal' Vladimir Ivanovich,' II:77. During this period, Dal'´s first poems were published in Voeikov's *Slavianin* (The Slav). In 1837 he was far from young, having been born in 1801. Encounters and conversations with Zhukovsky did, however, take place that year.

56 They studied at the Mikhailovskii Engineering Academy (Engineer Castle).

57 *Tserkovnyi vestnik* 34 (1875).

58 On spiritualist photography and the Bouget scandal, see Chéroux, 'Ghost Dialectics,' 45–71; and Monroe, *Laboratories of Faith*, 150–98.

59 See also Strakhov's letter to Tolstoy from 25 December 1876, in *L.N. Tolstoi – N.N. Strakhov*, I:239.

60 Ibid., I:243–4.

61 *RV* 115, no. 1 (1875): 301–2. On Tolstoy's attitude towards Modern Spiritualism see Berry, *Spiritualism in Tsarist Society and Literature*, 86–94. I will discuss Tolstoy's critique of spiritualism in chapter 7.

1. Seance as Test, or, Russian Writers at a Spiritualist Rendezvous

1 Vagner, 'Po povodu spiritizma. Pis'mo k redaktoru,' 855–75.

2 Mendeleev, *Sochineniia*, XXIV:186.

3 On the historico-cultural significance of the spiritual controversy of 1875–6, see the excellent work of Gordin, *A Well-Ordered Thing*, 85–110.

4 The role of the press in the 'spiritual renaissance' of the 1870s into the early 1880s was enormous. In addition to critical articles on Modern Spiritualism, descriptions of seances, spiritualist tracts, stories, and even works that had supposedly been written by the spirits of dead writers were published and discussed in print during this period. About the public character of the controversy, see Gordin, *A Well-Ordered Thing*, 103–4.

5 Mendeleev, *Sochineniia* XXIV:178–80.

6 On this 'Victorian doubt,' see, for example, Houghton, *The Victorian Frame of Mind*, 8.

7 Thomas Kselman argues that 'spiritist texts can be understood if we associate them with the *conte fantastique*, a literary form roughly equivalent to the Victorian ghost story popular throughout the nineteenth century.'

Kselman, *Death and the Afterlife in Modern France*, 160. Pumpianskii dedicated a special work to the spiritualist background of Turgenev's 'strange tales.' See Pumpianskii, 'Gruppa tainstvennykh povestei,' v–xx. See also Ledkovsky, *The Other Turgenev*.

8 Gordin offered a profound contextual reading of the polemics about spiritualism between Dostoevsky and Mendeleev. Gordin, 'Loose and Baggy Spirits.' Whereas Gordin concentrates on the ways Dostoevsky uses polemical rhetoric to persuade readers to reject spiritualism (p. 758), I will focus on this writer's immediate response to what happened in the particular seance and then elaborate on the psychological and literary implications of Dostoevsky's approach to spiritualism.

9 In his lecture of 25 April 1876 about Modern Spiritualism, Mendeleev emphasized that the spiritualists 'have understood the impact of literature on the fate of their question, and have taken pains that literary men should establish a personal opinion about spiritualism.' Mendeleev, *Sochineniia* XXIV:218.

10 Dostoevskii, *Polnoe sobranie sochinenii*, XXIV:207.

11 Sir William Crookes, one of the most illustrious scientists to investigate the phenomenon of spiritualism, pays tribute to St Claire in his *Researches into the Phenomena of Modern Spiritualism*, 38–9. Mikhail Petrovo-Solovovo, a historian of the Russian spiritualist movement, reveals her identity as Mrs Marshall. Petrovo-Solovovo, *Prilozhenie k perevodu sochineiia F. Podmora 'Spiritizm,'* 120; idem, 'Obituary.'

12 An author of the article in Dickens's periodical wrote angrily: 'It was something inexpressibly sad to see how these two wretched women were able to play on the holiest and deepest feelings of their audience; how, for the paltry sum which they gained from each as the price of their deceptions, they mocked the most sacred truths, and cheated the most earnest faith.' Linton, 'Modern Magic,' 373–4. In turn, Robert Bell sympathetically described one of the Marshalls' seances in his sensational article 'Stranger than Fiction': 'It is the province of men of science to investigate alleged phenomena irrespective of extrinsic incidents, and to clear away all impediments on their progress to pure truth, as nature casts aside the rubbish on the descent of the glacier' (215).

13 On Mary Marshall, the medium, the manageress, and the actress, see *Psychological Review* 4 (1882): 420; Podmore, *Modern Spiritualism*, 2: 27–8; and Sherson, *London's Lost Theatres of the Nineteenth Century*, 129, 293.

14 'In any case, she had nothing in common with that radiant, private [*lichnyi*], light-hearted English type that the foreigner meets in London at every step.' Boborykin, 'Ni vzad – ni vpered,' 1.

15   Ibid.
16   For more detail, see Gordin, *A Well-Ordered Thing*, 98.
17   Gamma, 'V mire chertovshchiny,' 1.
18   Swedenborg, *O nebesakh, mire dukhov i ob ade*; Aksakov, *Evangelie po Sveden-borgu*; idem, *Ratsionalizm po Svedenborgu; kriticheskoe issledovanie ego ucheniia o Sv. Pisanii*.
19   In 1867 Aksakov began to print, in German, *The Spiritualist Library for Germany*.
20   See Hare, *Opytnye issledovaniia o spiritualizme*, 7.
21   Ibid.
22   *Psychische Studien. Monatliche Zeitschift vorzüglich der Untersuchung den weine gekannte Phänomene des Seelenlebens gewidmet*. In 1876 Aksakov requested permission to print the first Russian spiritualist journal, *Vestnik mediumizma*. He did not receive it. About another attempt by Aksakov to legitimize Modern Spiritualism, see Luk'ianov, *O Vl. Solov'eve v ego molodye gody*, 1990), II:107.
23   See Petrovo-Solovovo, 'Obituary,' 45–9.
24   Aksakov, 'Mediumizm i filosofiia.' Solov'ev also wrote about Iurkevich's interest in Modern Spiritualism in 1874. The philosopher attended seances of the medium Home in Butlerov's apartment in 1871. See *Zhurnal minister-stva narodnogo prosveshcheniia* (1874) 30: 273.
25   *RV* 11 (1875): 300–48.
26   See Butlerov, *Koe chto o mediumizme*, 55.
27   About Butlerov's scientific approach to mediumistic phenomena, see Petrovo-Solovovo, *Prilozheniie k perevodu sochineniia F. Podmora*, 174–82; and Gordin, *A Well-Ordered Thing*, 86–7, 89.
28   In 1891, Vagner became the first president of the Russian Society of Experi-mental Psychology. This part of his scholarly activity deserves a separate discussion.
29   As early as 1 January 1876, Vagner informed Dostoevsky of the upcoming visitation of the medium, to whose seances he had promised to bring the writer. In a letter of reply from 2 January, Dostoevsky thanked Vagner and asked him to notify him of the arrival of the 'interesting guest from Eng-land.' On 8 January, Vagner sent word that the English medium 'mistress C[laire] arrived the other day' and that seances would be held at the apart-ment of Aksakov, who would be glad to see Dostoevsky in attendance. On 12 February he wrote that a seance with the medium would take place on Saturday, 14 February, at eight p.m. at Aksakov's. It was apparently rescheduled for Friday. See Budanova and Fridlender, *Letopis' zhizni i tvorchestva F. M. Dostoevskogo*, III:47–8, 54–6.
30   Tkachev, 'Belletristy-empiriki i belletristy-metafiziki.'

31 Boborykin praised Zola's innovative techniques as early as 1872 ('New Methods in French Fiction,' *Nedelia* [10 September 1872]). See, for example, Gauthier, 'Zola's Literary Reputation in Russia prior to "L'Assommoir,"' 38.
32 Boborykin, *Zhertva vecherniaia*, 62.
33 *SPbV* 75, 82, 89 (1876).
34 Faresov, *Protiv techenii*, 82. On Leskov's mysticism, see Abramovich, 'Mistitsizm v tvorchestve N. Leskova.'
35 For more on Leskov's criticism of philosophical spiritualism, see Morogues, 'Leskov et le spiritisme.'
36 Leskov, 'Pis'mo v redaktsiiu.' On Leskov's literary use of the spiritualist doctrine, see my article 'Russkie dukhi.'
37 The writer had in his library several books dedicated to the theme of afterlife existence and spiritual communication: *Slovo o smerti* by Bishop Ignatii (Brianchaninov) (editions from 1862 and 1863); A. Bem's *Dusha i telo* (1880); and *Kak zhivut nashi umershie i kak budem zhit' i my po smerti. Po ucheniiu pravoslavnoi tserkvi, po predchuvstviiu obshchechelovecheskogo dukha i vyvodam nauki* (1880) by Father Mitrofan (V.I. Alekseev). See Desiatkina and Fridlender, 'Biblioteka Dostoevskogo (Novye materialy),' in *Dostoevskii*, IV:256–62.
38 In Dostoevsky's notebooks, comments on articles about Modern Spiritualism (of Shkliarevskii, Rachinskii, Surovin, and others) appear repeatedly. In the writer's library were separate imprints of the above-mentioned articles by Vagner ('On the Subject of Modern Spiritualism') and Aksakov ('Mediumism and Philosophy: Recollections about Moscow University Professor Iurkevich'), as well as a booklet by the propagandist of French *spiritisme* Apollon Boltin, 'Doctrines of the Church of Christ, Set Forth According to Spiritualist Teaching.' See Desiatkina, and Fridlender; 'Biblioteka Dostoevskogo,' 256. Dostoevsky also mentions Modern spiritualism in *A Raw Youth* (XIII:424–5; see also Gordin, 'Loose and Baggy Spirits,' 759).
39 See, for example, Solov'ev's letter to Dostoevsky from 17 January 1875. *OR RGB*, f. 93/II Dostoevsky, no. 8, ed. khr. 122, l. 12–13.
40 In this essay, Dostoevsky refers to the recent sensational trial of a French 'spirit photographer,' Édouard Isidore Buguet. In June 1875 the latter admitted that he had never taken a genuine spirit photograph, but this confession did not shake all believers. For Dostoevsky, this case was a perfect example of the power of belief over any 'mathematical,' rational arguments. The writer planned to write a piece about this case called 'The Long Hand in Paris.' On Buguet's trial, see Chéroux, 'Ghost Dialectics.'
41 Leskov, 'Pis'mo v redaktsiiu,' 255.
42 Boborykin, 'Ni vzad – ni vpered.'

43 Leskov, 'Pis'mo v redaktsiu,' 255.
44 Ibid.
45 Ibid.
46 Ibid.
47 Ibid.
48 Boborykin, 'Ni: vzad – ni vpered,' 2.
49 Interestingly, in spite of the evident differences in beliefs, the spiritualist hosts and their artist guests shared certain important methodological assumptions. The spiritualist studying mediumistic phenomena and the realist (in a broad sense of the word) writer creating a character agree: the devil is in the details, in close observation, meticulous representation, and patient interpretation of psychic causes and effects. Thus, the naturalist writer Boborykin shared Butlerov's reliance on empirical facts and his interest in psychophysiology. Vagner's fantastic mediumism resonated with Leskov's mystical realism, and Aksakov's metaphysical inclinations and Swedenborgianism corresponded to Dostoevsky's literary quests, which we will discuss in the second part of this book.
50 Possibly this was the prominent Slavophile historian Mikhail Pogodin, who died on 8 December 1875.
51 Leskov, 'Pis'mo v redaktsiiu,' 255. In his April lecture on Modern Spiritualism, Mendeleev remarked that Leskov 'describes this seance by ascertaining the facts just as the spiritualists want.' Mendeleev, *Sochineniia*, XXIV:218.
52 On the mystical overtones of Leskov's narrative craft, see Poddubnaia, 'Stanovlenie kontseptsii lichnosti u N.S. Leskova.' I discuss Leskov's literary spiritualism in the epilogue.
53 Boborykin, 'Ni vzad – ni vpered,' 1.
54 Morson, 'Introductory Study,' I:183.
55 Sergei Suchkov argues that Dostoevsky considered that 'the spiritualists are calling into being slumbering satanic forces,' which are assuming, 'as if in mockery of humanity, the forms that it so much desires.' Suchkov, 'Puteshestvennik v tsarstvo dukhov,' in Aleksandr Aksakov, *Animizm i spiritizm*, 15.
56 The danger of falling under the power of demons was a focus for Orthodox criticism of Modern Spiritualism. The direct source of the demonic perspective for Dostoevsky might have been the treatise of Bishop Ignatii (Brianchaninov) about the 'perceived and spiritual visions of spirits,' which the writer had in his library. See Ignatii's *Slovo o smerti*: http://www.wco.ru/biblio/books/ignbr7/Main.htm.
57 Pointing out the connection between Modern Spiritualism and the reign of the Antichrist was a focus for Orthodox criticism of the doctrine. As Bishop

Feofan wrote as early as 1869: 'Now only preparation is taking place, and there will appear the Antichrist, and he will undertake the building of his kingdom from the spiritualists.' See *Domashniaia beseda* 43 (1869): 1106.

58 Later Dostoevsky wrote that 'the Modern Spiritualist doctrine is a terrifying doctrine. No Satan but the real one could come up with anything like it' (XXIV:126). On Dostoevsky's position concerning the reality of 'spiritualist phenomena' see Orwin, 'Did Dostoevsky or Tolstoy Believe in Miracles?' 130–4, 137–8.

59 Mendeleev considered Dostoevsky's article a step towards the side of mysticism. The mystic N.I. Potulov, in a letter to Dostoevsky, lightly reproached him for his insufficient criticism of the satanic character of Modern Spiritualism and suggested that he read his own antispiritualist articles, which came out in a separate book in 1874. See *OR RGB*, Dostoevskii II. 7.117, l. 1 ob. 2. In turn, the writer E.S. Nekrasova complained that the essay on Modern Spiritualism 'betrays the fact that the author has gone out of date quite a bit: he wants to inform and convince the reader that he does not believe in devils?!!!' In Dostoevskii, *Polnoe sobranie sochinenii* XXII:295.

60 Dostoevsky, *A Writer's Diary.* I:457–9.

61 Characteristically, both spiritualists and Dostoevsky tried to express their hypotheses in scientific language: observation, facts, laws. However, whereas Butlerov and other spiritualists spoke about mediumistic phenomena as subject to (as yet undiscovered) natural laws, Dostoevsky was concerned with eternal moral laws that should not be shaken by mediumistic temptations.

62 According to Dostoevsky, 'Modern Spiritualism is the transformation of stones into bread and the killing of ideas and the soul' (XXIV:161).

63 The appeal to the experience of Apostle Thomas can also be found in Aksakov's article on Iurkevich.

64 The italicized words are echoed twice in the writer's final novel: in Alesha's description of Christian realism and in Ivan's discussion with the devil, who is preparing to join a spiritualist society in order to create opposition among them: 'I'll say I'm a realist, but not a materialist, he-he!' (*The Brothers Karamazov*, Pt IV, Bk XI, ch. 9).

65 *Rb*, 26 (1885): 240.

66 Ibid.

67 To use Leatherbarrow's terminology, which is in turn based on the Bakhtinian notion of the chronotope, the space of the seance represents a socially marked 'liminal place' that is associated with the world of unclean forces. Leatherbarrow, *A Devil's Vaudeville*, 7. In Morson's terminology, the spiritual-

ist seance can act as a 'boundary genre,' 'compared to puns or homonyms on the scale of an entire discourse' (Morson, 'Introductory Study,' 48–9).

68 The last part of this argument is often omitted by critics (see E.I. Kiiko, 'Realizm fantasticheskogo,' IV:260.)

69 Todorov, *The Fantastic*, 24–40.

70 See Emerson, '"The Queen of Spades" and the Open End,' 31–7.

71 A cultural-semiotic analysis of the theme of the card game in the 'Napoleonic era' is given in the well-known work of Iu.M. Lotman, 'Tema kart i kartochnoi igry v russkoi literature nachala XIX veka,' VII:120–42.

72 Kiiko, 'Realism fantasticheskogo,' 260.

73 As Orwin justly observes, for Dostoevsky spiritualist phenomena 'have no physical, natural existence that can be validated by a scientific commission' such as that of Mendeleev, 'but they are nonetheless real,' since 'it is through these phenomena, good and evil, that moral progress (or regress) takes place, and the human world actually changes to reflect their presence.' Orwin, 'Did Dostoevsky or Tolstoy Believe in Miracles?' 138.

74 On the 'demonic nature' of Dostoevsky's literary ontology see recent works of Leatherbarrow (*A Devil's Vaudeville*) and Weiner *By Authors Possessed: The Demonic Novel in Russia*. The literary representations of Dostoevsky's demonic anthropology and its theosophical sources will be discussed in the second part of this book.

75 According to the chronicler of London's 'lost theatres,' Marshall acquired the theatre 'chiefly to show herself off in the part of Romeo' (her daughter Blanche played Juliet in the same performance). Sherson, *London's Lost Theatres*, 293. An English spiritualist newspaper *Life* reported in 1881 (p. 287) that Mary Marshall was working on her memoirs (unfortunately, we have not found any evidence about such work).

76 See, for example, Vagner, *Otvet na prigovor spiriticheskoi komissii*. Vagner's position is described briefly in Gordin, *A Well-Ordered Thing*, 102. Later on, in the first issue of the first spiritualist journal *Rebus*, Vagner published (anonymously) a feuilleton, 'Does it Exist or Not? A Mysterious Event,' in which Mendeleev was depicted comically through the character Brendeleev. The latter is a grumbler and scandalist who makes every possible effort to destroy a spiritualist seance. He presses on a table with all his weight to keep a medium from lifting it. After the medium expells him from the room, he watches the proceedings through a key-hole and makes outrageous comments. In the finale, Brendeleev himself becomes a victim of the 'unseen presences.' A certain spirit (*dukh*) reveals to a cheering public that 'Brendeleev ate beans today.' This 'supernatural' discovery of the spirit (the Russian word 'dukh' means both *spirit* and *foul odor*) raised

several questions in the narrator's monologue that parody the issues
recently debated by Mendeleev's commission and its opponents: Did he
actually eat beans or not? If he did, then how did the spirit learn about this
fact? Is there a physical explanation for this revelation? *Rb*, 1–3 (1881).
77 Aksakov, *Pamiatnik nauchnogo predubezhdeniia*, 40.
78 Boborykin, 'Ni vzad – ni vpered,' 1.
79 An English translation of this document can be found in Blavatsky, 'The
Russian Scientists,' 8.
80 Dostoevsky's polemic with Vagner's spiritualism and Mendeleev's scientific method is examined in Volgin and Rabinovich, 'Dostoevskii i Mendeleev,' as well as in Gordin, 'Loose and Baggy Spirits.'
81 *OR RGB*, f. 93/II. 2.4. This letter was concluded with a plea to Anna
Grigor'evna asking permission for an evening seance in a circle of 'Orthodox spiritualists,' gathering 'two steps away' from Dostoevsky's apartment. This group included the seer Elizaveta Ivanovna Tyminskaia as well
as Elena Ivanovna Molokhovets, the author of a famous cookbook and several mystical brochures. See Khartman, 'Elena Ivanovna Molokhovets,'
Zvezda 3 (2000): 107–11.
82 By the beginning of the 1880s, Vagner was combining experimental spiritualism with the religious kind ('in the sense of Orthodoxy' – but obviously
infused with Kardecian doctrine).
83 Later on, Vagner received an ultimate testimony of the existence of life after
death from his dear friend Butlerov, who passed away in 1886. Vagner,
'Vospominan'e ob Aleksandre Mikhailoviche Butlerove,' II.

2. Russian Glubbdubdrib

1 *Gr*, 3 (18 January 1876): 84.
2 'Spiritizm i ego znachenie,' *DB* 31 (1869): 829.
3 See, for example, Arthur Conan Doyle, *The History of Spiritualism*, I:277–8.
4 Blavatsky, 'Trance Mediums and "Historical" Visions,' in *Collected Writings*,
III: 359–65.
5 See Kostomarov, *Kto byl pervyi Lzhedimitrii?* (Who Was the First False
Dimitry). In 1873, Kostomarov published an article in *Vestnik Evropy* titled
'O sledstvennom dele po povodu ubieniia tsarevicha Dimitriia' (On the
Criminal Investigation of the Murder of the Tsarevich Dimitry), a polemic
against E. Belov, author of 'O smerti tsarevicha Dimitriia' (On the Death of
Tsarevich Dimitry), 1873.
6 Kostomarov perceived the history of medieval Russia as a struggle

between democracy and autocracy, which corresponded, in his view, to the individualism of the south (Little Russia) and the collectivism of greater Russia.

7   Dobroliubov, *Sobranie sochinenii*, VI:41.

8   'There exist in history sacred dates, sacred names, and sacred convictions,' Pogodin wrote, 'which one should touch upon only with the very greatest caution.' His multiyear polemics with Kostomarov goes back to 1860, when he challenged his opponent to debate on the subject of the origins of Rus'. It is interesting that in his formal challenge to an academic duel (which was held on 19 March 1860 in the Great Hall of St Petersburg University), he wrote to Kostomarov that the spectres of authoritative historians of the past would replace his own seconds, while his opponent could stay with his populist supporters from *The Contemporary*: 'I throw down the glove and challenge you to a duel ... I have no need of seconds, for the shades of Bayer, Schlotzer, and Krug stand before me ... While you, for your amusement, can invite as seconds your beloved kings of *The Whistle*!' (i.e., a polemical section of *The Contemporary*). Barsukov, *Zhizn' i trudy M.P. Pogodina*, XXVII:295–8, cited in Primak, *Mykola Kostomarov*, 95. In 1874 Pogodin published a book containing his objections to Kostomarov's judgments, titled *Bor'ba ne na zhivot, a na smert'*. On their polemics in the 1860s and 1870s, see Primak, *Mykola Kostomarov*, 95–7, 139, 154. Kostomarov's 'general thesis, the paucity of primary sources in support of the official historical icons, he maintained to the last' (154).

9   *Gr* 1 (1874): 1. The italics are mine.

10   *Russkaia istoriia v zhizneopisaniiakh ee glavneishikh deiatelei* (Vols. 1–3, 1873–88).

11   Markevich, 'Kostomatov, Nikolai Ivanovich,' in *Russkii biograficheskii slovar'* 9 (1885): 318–19.

12   Cf. the debate about Kostomarov's 'Lives' in *VE* 9–10 (1873), 1 (1874).

13   Kostomarov, *Russkaia istoriia v zhizneopisaniiakh ee glavneishikh deiatelei*, (1874): 629.

14   Ibid., 629–31.

15   Markevich, 'Kostomatov, Nikolai Ivanovich,' 319.

16   In his 'autobiography' (1875–90) Kostomarov describes how 'he came to the conviction that one should study history not only through dead chronicles and manuscripts, but in the living [common] people.' Kostomarov, 'Avtorbiografiia,' in *Izbrannye proizvedeniia. Avtobiografiia*, 446. Cf. Meshchersky's parody: 'It's the live testimony of a contemporary ... *Genuine history*!'

17   Cf. the works of Kavelin (1818–85), Solov'ev (1820–79), Shchapov (1831–76), Bestuzhev-Ryumin (1829–97), Zabelin (1820–1908), and other histori-

182 Notes to page 49

ans who laid the foundations of Russian historiography. See also historical sources in the multivolume *Documents* [akty] *Collected in the Libraries and Archives of the Russian Empire by the Archaeographical Expedition*; issues of *Russkii Arkhiv*; the high activity beginning in 1866 of the historical journal *Vestnik Evropy*; and Mazour, *Modern Russian Historiography*.

18 Gossman, *Between History and Literature*, 230–1.

19 Wachtel, *An Obsession with History*, 15–18.

20 Cf. Leo Tolstoy's famous reply to those who accused him of deviating from historical truth: 'Wherever historical figures speak and act in my novel, this is not my invention. Rather, I have availed myself of various materials, amounting in the course of my work to an entire library of books, the titles of which I do not deem it necessary to copy out here, but to which I am always prepared to refer.' Tolstoi, 'Neskol'ko slov po povodu knigi "Voina i mir,"' 523.

21 For a survey of Kostomarov's writings, see Sokolov, 'Kostomarov, Nikolai Ivanovich.'

22 In 'Le discours de l'histoire,' Barthes offers a semiotic interpretation of the 'realistic effect' created by this kind of 'objective' historical discourse: 'Historical discourse does not follow the real, it can do no more than signify the real, constantly repeating that *it happened*, without this assertion amounting to anything but the signified "other side" of the whole process of historical narration.' Barthes, 'The Discourse of History,' 20.

23 Romantic divination of this sort was celebrated by Karamzin in his preface to the first volume of his *History of the Russian State* (1818): 'History, opening coffins and raising the dead, breathing life into their hearts and placing words on their lips, creating kingdoms afresh from decay and presenting to the imagination the long line of ages, with their distinct passions, customs and acts, broadens the limits of our own existence [...] Through its creative force we live with the people of every age, we see and hear them, love and hate.' Karamzin, *Istoriia gosudarstva Rossiiskogo*, 14. Pushkin, elaborating on Karamzin, wrote that 'history belongs to the poet!' (XIII:145). On Jules Michelet's romantic vision of historiography as 'the lyric resurrection of past bodies' and the dialogue with the dead, see, respectively, Barthes, 'Lecture in Inauguration of the Chair of Literary Semiology,' in *October* 8 (1979): 15; and Certeau, *The Writing of History*, 2.

24 Castle describes Carlyle's historical imagination as a 'nightmarish magic-lantern show'; Castle, *The Female Thermometer*, 140. On French Romantic representations of history (phantasmagoria shows, historical book illustrations, historical novels and popular plays about the Revolution and Napoleon), see Samuels, *The Spectacular Past*.

25 Tolstoy, writing to Strakhov about his work on a new historical novel, resorted precisely to a spiritualist analogy: 'I have spent nearly all my working hours this winter [1872] on Peter, that is, I've been summoning spirits from that time' (LXII:16).

26 Consider in this regard the title given by a famous novelist of the time, Vsevolod Krestovsky, to a work in two volumes dedicated to contemporary Russia's encounter with destructive nihilism: *A Bloody Humbug: A Chronicle of the New Time of Troubles of the Russian State* (1875).

27 Emerson, 'Pretenders to History,' 15.

28 Clayton argues that 'perhaps, taking our cue from Kireevsky, we might call the tragedy "The Shade of Dimitry," borrowing from a common form of title for poems at the time.' Clayton, *Dimitry's Shade*, 16.

29 On the image of the Pretender in the Russian public consciousness and political rhetoric of the 1860s and 1870s, see Maiorova, 'Tsarevich-samozvanets v sotsial'noi mifologii poreformennoi epokhi.'

30 Leskov, *Polnoe sobranie sochinenii v 30 tomakh*, IX:280.

31 See Kostomarov, 'Kto byl pervyi Lzhedimitrii?'; Bitsyn (N.M. Pavlov), 'Pravda o Lzhedimitrii' (1864); Dobrotvorskii, 'Kto byl pervyi Lzhedimitrii?' (1866); and Kazanskii, 'Issledovanie o lichnosti pervogo Lzhedimitriia' (1877). On the history of the polemics see Dunning, 'Who Was Tsar Dmitrii?' On imposture as a Russian phenomen, see Mordovtsev, *Samozvantsy i ponizovaia vol'nitsa.*

32 According to Kostomarov, 'the theatre has the means to disseminate throughout society information about life in the past, just as it can acquaint [society] with the trends and notions of the present; just as, in general, it can serve as an important weapon in broadening the intellectual horizons of society' (in 'Po povodu noveishei russkoi istoricheskoi stseny,' 94). Cited in Taruskin, *Musorgsky*, 124.

33 *VE*, 2, no. 2 (1867): 98.

34 Kholodov, 'Repertuar,' 129.

35 On Tolstoy's overwhelming interest in history in the 1860s, see Eikhenbaum, *Tolstoy in the Sixties*, parts 3 and 4.

36 Platt examines the relationship between Russian historical painting of the 1860s to 1880s and modern historiography in *Terror & Greatness* (in manuscript).

37 On the links between Russian realist opera and the historiography of the time, see Taruskin, 'The Present in the Past,' in *Musorgsky*, 123–200.

38 On Russian historical drama of the 1860s and the historical plays of Ostrovsky and Tolstoy, see Anikst, *Teoriia dramy v Rossii ot Pushkina do Chekhova*, 330–97; Kholodov, 'Repertuar,' 129–47; and Stepanova,

'Stikhotvornaia dramaturgiia Ostrovskogo (1866–1873),' in Ostrovskii, *Polnoe sobranie sochinenii*, VI:534–69.

39 Anikst, *Teoriia dramy v Rossii ot Pushkina do Chekhova*, 383.

40 Ostrovskii, *Polnoe sobranie sochinenii*, VII:526.

41 Ibid., 35.

42 *Golos* 1870, 19 September.

43 Kholodov, 'Repertuar,' V:147.

44 Ibid., 129–38. Stasov recalled Kostomarov's ecstatic response to Musorgsky's *Boris Godunov*: 'Now that is a page of history!' Stasov, *M.P. Musorgskii v vospominaniiakh sovremennikov*, 46–7. As Taruskin has shown so convincingly, Kostomarov found in Musorgsky's opera an inspired reflection of his own scholarly investigations: 'When Kostomarov said of *Boris* that it was a "page of history," one understands what he meant – it was a page of *his* history' (198).

45 'Dimitry the Pretender and the time of the pretenders in general,' wrote an anonymous reviewer of *Sovremennik* in response to the staging of Chaev's play *Dimitrii Samozvanets* (1866), 'represent our playwrights' favoured and most well-worked subject-matter.' *Sovremmenik* (1866): 241. On the heightened interest in Russian literature and drama towards the Time of Troubles and the mysterious personality of Dimitry, see Maiorova, 'Tsarevich— samozvanets,' 223–4. Maiorova also mentions A.N. Serov's unrealized plan for an opera, *Dmitrii Samozvanets* (224).

46 Historical painting, it seems, remained more or less indifferent to the image of the self-proclaimed Dimitry. The realist N.V. Nevrev, while following the official interpretation of events to the letter, presented the Young Pretender as a kind of enigma: he stands in the shadows, with his back half-turned (*Prisiaga Lzhedimitriia I pol'skomu koroliu Sigizmundu*, 1877).

47 L. Lotman, 'Istoricheskaia dramaturgiia A.N. Ostrovskogo,' in Ostrovskii, *Polnoe sobranie sochinenii*, VII:528.

48 'If it is permissible for the historian to engage in examination of the issue of such an enigmatic historical figure and to leave this issue unresolved, allowing the readers to make their own minds up on the basis of the facts presented by the historian, then a dramatist should certainly not set himself such a task. Rather, he should take a *famous* situation, and place his character on solid ground: either he is a conscious Pretender, or he is the real Dimitry, or else an involuntary Pretender.' In Anikst, *Teoriia dramy v Rossii ot Pushkina do Chekhova*, 349–50.

49 See Emerson's article, 'Pretenders to History.'

50 A.K. Tolstoy, *Dramaticheskaia trilogiia*, 394.

51 In her most recent article, Emerson argues that Tolstoy's Dimitry is presented

in *Tsar Boris* as 'a Pretender-function,' a disembodied rumour, rather than an actual character in flesh and blood: 'Everyone, from the tsar on down, needs him; but no one can control his image. The tsar's right to create a new rumor resolves nothing. Who was Tsar Dimitrii? Who was he not?' Emerson, 'Identity Crisis as Revisionist Historical Dramaturgy.' See also Epstein-Matveyev, 'The Construction of Identity in A.K. Tolstoy's Dramatic Trilogy.'

52 'The future, in short, would be the past. This is national tragedy as a Westernizer might cast it.' Emerson, 'Pretenders to History,' 273. I thank Caryl Emerson for pointing out this episode in Tolstoy's tragedy.

53 'The battle in which my hero dies is a battle with the specter of his crime, embodied in a mysterious being which threatens him from afar and destroys the entire edifice of his life' (Tolstoy to Sain-Wittgenstein, 17 October 1869). In A.K. Tolstoy, *Dramaticheskaia trilogiia*, 407.

54 In order of composition: *Koz'ma Zakhar'ich Minin, Sukhoruk* (1861, 1866), *Voevoda (Son na Volge)* (1865), *Dimitrii Samozvanets i Shuiskii, Tushino* (1866), *Vasilisa Melent'eva* (1867; with Gedeonov).

55 See L. Lotman's commentary on the play in Ostrovskii, *Polnoe sobranie sochinenii*, VII:580–7.

56 The comedy ends with the German, Gregory, organizer of the first Russian theatre, addressing the sceptic Volynsky: 'O, much has been written by those / Who live far away from us. / We too will write, and find for ourselves / Various subjects. And every man will see there / His life, and his quiet doings, / And his thoughts alone with the pillow. / And he who has forgotten his conscience, and knows not / Its judgement – there he will find it.' To Volynsky's question, 'And who will be my judge?' Gregory answers curtly, 'The comedian.' Ostrovskii, *Polnoe sobranie sochinenii*, VII:362. (It is interesting to note the polemical thrust of this play in relation to the words of Pushkin's chronicler, Pimen: it is not the scribe of history, working away in monastic seclusion, who fulfils the role of moral arbiter of the epoch, but the playwright and comedian, who writes for the stage.)

57 Likhachev, *A History of Russian Literature, 11th–17th Centuries*, 540.

58 On the spiritualist ontology of Elizabethan drama, see Greenblatt, *Hamlet in Purgatory*, 258–61.

3. Dead Poets' Society

1 I have in mind Barthes's definition of myth as a special 'type of speech chosen by history, [which] can consist of modes of writing or of representation.'

Barthes, 'Myth Today,' 110. I will therefore be referring to both written and pictorial sources, which exploit the image or theme of the materialized shade of Pushkin: poems, critical articles, reminiscences, legends, drawings, monuments, and so on.

2 The history of the myth of Pushkin's 'immortality' is the subject of Stephanie Sandler's recent book, *Commemorating Pushkin: Russia's Myth of a National Poet* (2004). Sandler 'attempts to show how foundational texts and cultural institutions have created myths of Pushkin around paradoxes of life and death, of the individual and the national group; how thinking about Pushkin has been a vehicle for self-expression and self-discovery; how Russia's national culture has emerged through myths of Pushkin as friend, prophet, and national genius' (13). I am not interested here in how the myth of Pushkin was created, nor in how it was refracted in the individual consciousness and work of various authors (Akhmatova, Tsvetaeva, Siniavsky, Bitov, etc.), but in how and why 'Pushkin' served and serves society's purposes. This is the distinction between my approach and that taken by the authors of the classic works on 'Pushkin's shade,' which examine the spiritualist views of the poet himself. See Gershenzon, 'Ten' Pushkina,' in *Stat'i o Pushkine*, 69–95; Senderovich, 'On Pushkin's Mythology,' 3; and Gasparov, *Poeticheskii iazyk Pushkina kak fakt istorii russkogo literaturnogo iazyka*, 214–27.

3 The spiritualist movement, of course, was not monolithic and evolved in time. In this chapter I will address only the general ideas of spiritualism in relation to literary works from 'beyond' the grave (*zagrobnoe tvorchestvo*). On the phenomenon of 'posthumous literature,' see Helen Sword's superb article 'Necrobibliography: Books in the Spirit World' (republished in *Ghostwriting Modernism*).

4 In the mid-nineteenth century, for example, the famous German spiritualist Ludwig von Güldenstubbe placed clean sheets of paper and pencils 'beneath tombstones, on tombs, in mausoleums' and simply in dark places, 'and thereby received, on his own assurance, handwritten missives from otherworldly figures.' See Bykov, *Spiritizm pered sudom nauki*, 107.

5 On the manner in which the methods of attribution 'parodied' the textual scholarship of the time, see in particular Aksakov, *Animizm i spiritizm*, 351–4. The theoreticians of spiritualism recognized the possibility of false communications, literary imposture, or mere monkey tricks on the part of the spirits. 'An experienced spiritualist,' we read in one of the first Russian spiritualist novels, 'who is capable of analysing the facts he has obtained, will never seek in the spirits' communications infallible truths for his religious or other convictions, but will treat them as critically as he

treats everything which lacks an absolute derivation.' Pribytkov, *Legenda starinnogo baronskogo zamka*, 44. Nevertheless, the practice of spiritualism shows that the received texts were usually interpreted as bearers of absolute truths.

6 In Lesevich, 'Modnoe sueverie,' 194.

7 See Strakhov's critique of contemporary myths or idols in his letters about spiritualism. 'Tri pis'ma o spiritizme,' *Gr* 41–4 (1876).

8 In the manifesto of the American spiritualists, endorsed at the Philadelphia Congress of 1865, it was stated that spirits after death do not move away 'from the field of their activity.' Lesevich, 'Modnoe sueverie,' 194.

9 Naturally, deists, convinced atheists, and straightforward sceptics all repented of their previous views when they were summoned by spiritualists, and affirmed the truth of the latter's beliefs. The replies of these repentant authors (such as Voltaire, who was said to have signed his renunciation of his former anticlericalism with his own hand) were greatly cherished in spiritualist circles.

10 Doten, *Poems From the Inner Life*, 104–5.

11 S.A., *Zhivye rechi otzhivshikh liudei*, 131.

12 Oduar, *Spiritizm*, 131–4. This is a translation of Audouard's *Les mondes des Esprits ou la Vie après la mort*.

13 Tynianov, *Poetika*, 357–8. Tynianov's interest in the 'parodic personality' of Koz'ma Prutkov is relevant here.

14 Ibid.

15 Opponents of spiritualism constantly pointed towards this: 'The spirits are Catholics in Rome, Anglicans in London and New York, freethinkers in Paris, schismatics in Petersburg […] The same contradiction [is apparent] when they are asked their opinion on social questions.' Aksakov, *Pozitivizm v oblasti spiritizma*, 59.

16 Sword, *Ghostwriting Modernism*, 12–13.

17 Mendeleev, *Materialy dlia suzhdeniia o spiritizme*, 326.

18 Counter-arguments were found in instances where the capabilities and cultural horizon of the mediums did not correspond to the level and particularities of the works they received. The most popular example of this in spiritualist circles was the story of how, in the early 1870s, the 'spirit' of Dickens dictated the conclusion of the unfinished novel *The Mystery of Edwin Drood* to a barely educated American mechanic and medium. This instance of mediumistic communication, whose content was 'higher than the intellectual level' of the medium, drew the attention of the leading theoretician of spiritualism, Aksakov. See Aksakov, *Materialy*, 351 and passim. In his major work on spiritualism, *Animizm i spiritizm*, Aksakov mentions

Essays from the Unseen delivered through the mouth of W.L., a sensitive, and recorded by A.T. P.P. (London, 1885), which included communications received from various historical figures, philosophers, poets, and theologians.

19 This illusion is especially prominent when a writer seeks in his poetics to recreate a personal authorial voice and to indulge in 'poetic chatter' addressed to the imagined reader (cf. the repeated appeals to the reader in the works of Byron and Pushkin).

20 Greenblatt, *Hamlet in Purgatory,* 251.

21 Preminger and Brogan, eds., *New Princeton Encyclopedia of Poetry and Poetics,* 994.

22 'Posthumous Work of Koz'ma Prutkov.' See Prutkov, *Sochineniia,* 321.

23 Dostoevsky referred to a report in *Golos* from 6 January 1876. Western spiritualists also received posthumous works from Russian classics. In 1936 the English medium Ida M. Everett Keeble published a story dictated to her by Turgenev, titled 'Beyond Earth's Fears.' One of the most recent examples is a publication of communications channelled by the famous Russian bard Vladimir Vysotsky (1938–80) through a Russian medium Tatyana Tanika, *Channeling Vysotsky.* According to the spirit of Vysotsky, he met Elvis Presley in the other world and dedicated a poem to him.

24 Iu.M. Lotman, 'K probleme raboty s nedostovernymi istochnikami,' 325.

25 On the kindred phenomenon of the 'spectre of Shakespeare' in English culture, see in particular Sword, *Ghostwriting Modernism*: 'As both Everything and Nothing, both many and no one, Shakespeare raises the dual hermeneutic specters of overdetermination and indeterminacy. His murky features mirror the interpretative paradoxes of every age and culture that has tried to lay claim to his image' (50).

26 *Rb* 22 (1899): 909.

27 *Rb* 40 (1883): 1.

28 Annenkov, 'Materialy dlia biografii A.S. Pushkina.' This perceived duality remains relevant to this day: on the bicentenary of his birth, the former Samara governor Aiatskov proposed canonizing the poet, while the littérateur Anatolii Mandorskii drew attention to Pushkin's 'Satanic zigzags.'

29 Further evidence of the merging of the literary and spiritualist traditions in the Pushkinian myth is provided by the curious 'Infernal Poem' that was communicated to the credulous Vagner by the shade of the pornographer poet of the eighteenth century, Ivan Barkov (1732–68). (I quoted a fragment as the epigraph to the first part of this book.) The poem, which struck Vagner as eminently Pushkinian, is written in the *Onegin* stanza, bears the title of one of Pushkin's unfinished poems, and plays out the theme of the noto-

rious *Shade of Barkov*, which since the mid-1860s had been attributed to Pushkin himself (debate about the attribution of this poem has raged for a century and a half). Barkov's shade testified in this communication that Pushkin now merrily abided in hell, and was immediately rebuked by the shade of the pious Ioann Damaskin, who called Barkov a slanderer of the glorious poet. Vagner, *Nabliudeniia nad mediimizmom*, 101–4. On the polemics about *The Shade of Barkov*, see Pil'shchikov's and Shapir's commentaries in Pushkin, *'Ten' Barkova.'*

30 *Strekoza* 23 (1880): 6.

31 *Sochineniia A.S. Pushkina v 6 tomakh. Izdanie Ia. A. Isakova. S prilozheniem portreta i snimka s poslednego pis'ma Pushkina* (SPb., 1859–60). The 'publishers' of Pushkin's posthumous letter in *Dragonfly* informed readers that they had received it via spirit mail: 'The letter has a somewhat crumpled appearance. The envelope is sealed with the letters "A.S" and a crest, and contains a postmark depicting Charon in the boat [...] and a note in the hand of the manager of spirit mail, Mr. Aksakov: "letter delayed on account of the flooding of the Acheron River and the damage caused thereby to railway embankments in the country of spirits."' The content of the letter is as follows. Having received a delivery of books from a friend on planet earth, Pushkin – together with Derzhavin, Griboedov, Gogol' and Krylov – studies the six published volumes of the Isakov edition of Pushkin's collected works, cursing the edition and its editor, Efremov. In his conclusion, Pushkin tells his publisher meekly: 'Rather than inserting Efremov's doggerel among my verse, you would do better to insert my poems in the *Complete Collected Works* of Mr. Efremov.' There follows a facsimile of the signature of the deceased poet. *Strekoza* 23 (1880): 6.

32 *Strekoza* 23 (1880): 1. The opening of the monument was itself perceived by the public of the time as material proof of the poetic immortality of the bard of Aleko and Tatyana: 'He stands tall and silent on the granite, / With head bowed and hat in hand, / *Like a wondrous, mysterious specter from beyond*, / With immortal lyre and laurel wreath' (A. Ivanitskii). Kallash, *Russkie poety o Pushkine*, 199.

33 'Writing' [*pishushchii*] spiritualism found many adepts among the Russian military.

34 *RI*, 11 January (1859): 31.

35 *BZ* 2 (1859): 64. In that same year, 1859, the poem was recorded by the littérateur I.F. Pavlov in his notebook: 'A posthumous poem by Pushkin, written by the table *chez* Pavlishcheva (during a spiritualist seance).' See Berkov and Lavrov, *Bibliografiia proizvedenii Pushkina i literatury o nem*, 204.

36 Berg, 'V.I. Dal' i P.V. Nashchokin,' 615–16.

37 Pavlishchev. *Vospominaniia ob A.S. Pushkine*, 75.
38 Karatygin, 'Vecher u generala A.A. Katenina,' 753–7.
39 Nabokov, 'Dar,' in *Sobranie sochinenii*, III:93.
40 Lann, *Literaturnaia mistifikatsiia*, 56.
41 In Berkov and Lavrov's *Bibliografiia*, references to this text are given in the section 'Sham Pushkin,' which includes numerous forgeries of Pushkin's verse and incorrectly attributed poems.
42 From Pletnev's letters about Pushkin to Grot in the 1840s: 'His mood at that time was highly religious. He spoke to me about the workings of Providence; he valued in men the quality of benevolence above all others and perceived this quality in me.' 'The conversations he most enjoyed holding with me, in the weeks before his death, revolved around the words: "Glory to God on high, and peace on earth, and benevolence among men." Pletnev, 'Iz perepiski s Ia. K. Grotom,' 291–2.
43 Zhukovskii, 'Pis'mo k S.L. Pushkinu,' 423–36.
44 *Russkii vestnik* 11 (1869): 95. On the evolution of Pushkin's image in Russian poetry, see Iezuitova, 'Evoliutsiia obraza Pushkina v russkoi poezii XIX veka,' 113–39.
45 The image of the 'cell beyond the clouds' in which the lyrical hero of the poem 'Monastery on Kazbek' (1829) dreams of taking refuge 'in proximity to God' symbolizes an absolute removal from secular life, yet, so to speak, within the confines of earthly existence.
46 Pushkin, *Collected Narrative and Lyrical Poetry*, 225.
47 See Gershenzon, 'Ten' Pushkina,' 69–95.
48 Cf. the reaction of Mariia Volkonskaia's father, N.N. Raevskii, who sent the poem to his daughter in Siberia: 'I am sending you an epitaph for your son written by Pushkin; *he wrote nothing else like this in all his life.*' Pushkin's poem was engraved on the child's gravestone. See Udimova, 'Stikhotvorenie Pushkina pamiati syna S.G. Volkonskogo,' 405.
49 This epitaph was first published in 1855, in the seventh volume of Annenkov's collected works of Pushkin – that is, it was published after the appearance of 'Entering the Heavenly Realms' in 1859. But this does not alter the essence of the matter, since by 1859 the coincidence of the motifs in the two poems might have struck Pushkin's spiritualist-minded admirers as an argument in favour of the authenticity of the shade's communication. In terms of the myth with which I am concerned here, it does not matter so much who actually wrote this poem; it is much more important to identify the reasons why this poem could have been accepted as belonging to Pushkin.
50 Udimova, noting the poem's political subtext (a supplication on behalf of the Decembrist Sergei Volkonskii, who had been sentenced by the Tsar),

emphasizes the fact that the poet clothes his feelings in 'the traditional idiom of Christian epitaphs' (406).

51 My italics.

52 See Tomashevskii, *Pushkin*, II:496–7. See also Gershenzon's discussion of the fundamental ambivalence of Pushkin's attitude towards the afterlife in *Stat'i o Pushkine*, 71–6.

53 This fragment, it should be noted, was very much on the public's lips. Ia.K. Grot cited it in his speech during the 1880 celebrations, making the following comment, symptomatic of our theme: 'This mood was accompanied in Pushkin's soul by an inclination towards superstition.' Grot, 'Rech',' 240–1.

54 The theme of the shade of the genius-poet is highly prevalent in Pushkin's work (the shades of Ovid, Homer, Dante, Chenier, and Byron; and, as parodic figures, those of Barkov and Fonvizin).

55 A parodic elaboration of this theme was also widely known: the shade of a great comic writer would appear 'in order to affirm the spirit of true poetry' – thus, for example, the shade of Molière in the eponymous French satire. See Vatsuro, *Lirika pushkinskoi pory*, 120.

56 Ibid., 133.

57 I refer to Anton Del'vig's famous 'Elizium poetov' (1814–17). Posthumous 'Delvigiana' included not only appeals in prose and poetry to the poet's shade, but also a story about the shade's 'actual' appearance to his friends. See Selivanov, *Vospominaniia proshedshego*, 19–22. Pushkin's interpretation of the myth of Del'vig's shade has been discussed by Gasparov: 'Del'vig's death – his transformation into a 'shade' – contributed the final ingredient to his persona, permitting the relationship between the two friends to be embodied in the image of a mystical "meeting."' Gasparov, *Poeticheskii iazyk Pushkina*, 225.

58 Curiously, the comparison of Pushkin to a shade was made at the very beginning of his poetic career by Zhukovsky: 'He torments me with his gift, like a ghost.' *Russkii arkhiv* 10 (1896): 208.

59 Sandler discusses this issue in 'The Making of Museum Culture,' in *Commemorating Pushkin*.

60 Annenkov, *Materialy*, 112.

61 Cf. the indicative titles under which some of these efforts were published: 'A photographic portrait of Pushkin'; 'A Shadow Portrait of Pushkin (to be cut out and reflected on a wall)'; 'Opening of a Monument to Pushkin: The Moment of Unveiling.'

62 *Moskovskaia izobrazitel'naia pushkiniana*, 32.

63 On the semiotic juxtaposition of 'shade' and 'monument' in the poetic myth of Pushkin, see Senderovich, 'On Pushkin's Mythology,' 107–12.

64 Güldenstubbe, *La realite des esprits et le phenomene merveilleux de leur ecriture directe*, 83. My colleague David Powelstock commented wittily that the note, with three Christian names in its title (*Vera* [Faith], *Nadezhda* [Hope], and *Liubov'* [Love]) could be interpreted as a hitherto unknown fragment of Pushkin's famous 'Don Juan list.'

65 Kallash, *Russkie poety o Pushkine*, 126.

66 See Levitt, *Russian Literary Politics and the Pushkin Celebration of 1880*, 83–5; *Otechestvo*, 87–8.

67 Kallash, *Russkie poety o Pushkine*, 329–30. These motifs were rendered canonical by Mayakovsky in *The Jubilee Poem* (1930). On the theme of the statue in Pushkin's oeuvre, see Jakobson, *Puškin and His Sculptural Myth*.

68 At this time the idea was mooted of making cinematic use of phonograms with recordings of the poet's verse. If the idea had been carried through, 'Pushkin' would have recovered his voice, to the surprise and delight of many. On Pushkin's early filmography, see Barykin, *Pushkinskii kinoslovar.'*

69 Of the numerous works devoted to the Pushkin myth, see especially Levitt, *Russian Literary Politics and the Pushkin Celebration of 1880*; Paperno, 'Nietzscheanism and the Return of Pushkin in Twentieth-Century Russian Culture'; Horowitz, *The Myth of A.S. Pushkin in Russia's Silver Age*; Debreczeny, *Social Functions of Literature*, and Sandler, *Commemorating Pushkin*.

70 Lazarev and Tuganova, 'Transformatsiia obraza Pushkina v tainikakh sovremennogo soznaniia,' 202.

71 In the twentieth century, the spiritualist character of the myth of Pushkin's shade was noted by writers of all camps. Of particular interest is the famous discussion of Pushkin's immortality in Russian culture in Nabokov's *Gift*. The hero comments: 'They say that a man whose leg is cut off at the hip can feel it for a long time, moving non-existent toes and flexing non-existent muscles. Thus will Russia long continue to feel the living presence of Pushkin.' Nabokov, *Sobranie sochinenii*, III:88–9. This process permits the possibility of the poet's ceaseless appearances (one of which is described in *The Gift*).

72 Sasha Chernyi, 'Pushkin v Parizhe.' This story recently attracted the attention of Iurii Leving, who saw in it a 'definite source' for the episode in which Pushkin returns as a phantom in Nabokov's *Gift*. Leving, 'Vladimir Nabokov i Sasha Chernyi,' 53.

73 Aldanov, *Ocherki*, 30–7.

74 See Denisenko, 'Posmertnaia maska Pushkina.' Opponents of the Bolsheviks also appealed to Pushkin, of course, as is testified by these ironical lines from a popular song about a 'fried chicken': 'The *barins* stroll along the boulevard and look at Pushkin through their glasses. "Tell us, Sasha,

our pride and joy, when will the Bolsheviks get out?" "Don't you coo and don't you crow!" Pushkin sang to them in verse. "When the camel and the lobster dance the Cracovienne, that's when the Bolsheviks will be gone."' See Nekliudov, 'Tsyplionok zharenyi,' http://www.ruthenia.ru/folklore/neckludov19.htm. The scholar of contemporary folklore S.B. Adon'eva points to Pushkin's specific function in mass culture: the poet assumes the role of oracle, to whom questions about the future are constantly addressed (divinations using his works, the calling up of his spirit at spiritualist seances). Adon'eva, *Kategoriia nenastoiashchego vremeni*, 66–9. On the summoning of Pushkin at peasant spiritualist seances in the early 1930s, see. Panchenko, 'Spiritizm i russkaia literatura,' 540.

75 Antokol'skii, *Sobranie sochinenii*, I:434.
76 I am grateful to Naum Korzhavin for referring me to this poem by G. Slavnikov.
77 *Literaturnaia Gazeta* (2 June 1999), 22.
78 Gasparov, *Poeticheskii iazyk Pushkina*, 17.
79 Garber, *Shakespeare's Ghost Writers*.
80 'Vprochem, / chto zh boltan'e! /Spiritizma vrode.' Maiakovskii, 'Iubileinoe,' in *Polnoe sobranie sochinenii*, V:55.

4. Flickering Hands

1 Vagner visited the Dostoevskys with a letter of recommendation from the poet Ia.P. Polonskii.
2 *Literaturnoe nasledstvo*, 207–8.
3 On Vagner, see *Kritiko-biograficheskii slovar' russkikh pisatelei i uchenykh*, 4, otd. 2:19–24; *Slovar' russkikh pisatelei*, I:85–6.
4 It was precisely positivism that spawned the idea of the resurrection of the dead by scientific means – a brilliant ideological finale to the nineteenth-century ghost hunting. See Solov'ev, 'Ideia chelovechestva u Avgusta Konta,' in *Sochineniia*, II:579. Suffice it to recall Nikolai Fedorov's utopia of resurrection of the dead by means of science in his *Philosophy of the Common Task*. For the impact of Fedorov's ideas on Russian writers of the twentieth century, see Masing-Delic, *Abolishing Death*.
5 According to Jakobson, realism, with its focus on detail, is inherently metonymic: 'The Realist author metonymically digresses from the plot to the atmosphere and from the characters to the setting in space and time.' Jakobson, *Language in Literature*, 111.
6 Vagner, 'Pis'mo k redaktoru,' *VE* 4 (1875): 855–77.

7 On the polemics between Kavelin and Sechenov, see Joravsky, *Russian Psychology*, 96–9.

8 Frank Podmore, *Modern Spiritualism*, II:95.

9 Kerr, *Mediums, and Spirit-Rappers, and Roaring Radicals*, 11.

10 Crookes, 'Notes on an Inquiry into the Phenomena Called Spiritual' (1874); Wolfe, *Startling Facts on Modern Spiritualism*; Olcott, *People from the Other World*. See Podmore, *Modern Spiritualism*, 95–116; and Oppenheim, *The Other World*, 16–21.

11 Aksakov, *Animizm i spiritizm*.

12 The period witnessed a lengthy series of shocking exposés of mediumistic frauds, including the trial of the photographer Bouget in 1875, which was covered by the Russian press; the 'Volckman affair' of 1873; and attempts to unmask Brédif by Doctor Likhonin.

13 On this subject, Aksakov refers to the experience of Crookes, 'who cut off a lock of hair from the figure of Katie King after feeling it to its very roots, to the skin of her head, and assured himself that it was from there that it really grew.' Aksakov, *Psychische Studien* 1 (1875): 22. This lock remained at his disposal even after the spirit had dematerialized. The motif of a ghost's preserved lock of hair entered literature; see Turgenev's 'strange story,' 'Klara Milich' (1883).

14 Vagner, 'Po povudu spiritizma,' 868–71.

15 The first attempted 'scientification' of Modern Spiritualism in Russia occurred in 1871 (the arrival of Home; seances attended by professors from the capital; Aksakov's translation of Crookes; and polemical discussion of spiritualism in the periodicals). But these efforts met with failure.

16 Vagner, *Vospominan'e ob Aleksandre Mikhailoviche Butlerove*, xl.

17 *Golos* 152 (1875): 1–2.

18 Rachinskii, 'Po povodu spiriticheskikh soobshchenii g. Vagnera,' 398.

19 In his campaign against pseudo-scientific fantasies, Mendeleev also appealed to the public's imagination: his antispiritualist speeches were framed by descriptions of astonishing atmospheric phenomena that awaited serious investigation. Mendeleev, *Sochineniia*, 173–7, 236–7.

20 The ideologues of spiritualism (such as Henry Olcott) compared the attacks on mediums to the witch hunts of the seventeenth century (the Salem trials).

21 See Gordin, *A Well-Ordered Thing*, 82–3.

22 Blavatsky, *Collected Writings*, I:508–9; Solovyoff, *A Modern Priestess of Isis*, 226–7.

23 Vagner, *Vospominan'e*, xli.

24 Vagner, 'Mediumizm,' *RV* 10 (1875): 806–951.

25 Vagner, *Vospominan'e*, xlii.

26 *RV* 10 (1875): 868.

27 Here Vagner refers to the recent dispute between Kavelin and Sechenov on the correspondence of body and soul. See Kavelin, *Zadachi psikhologii*; and Sechenov, 'Zamechaniia na knigu Kavelina Zadachi psikhologii.' See also Zen'kovskii, *Istoriia russkoi filosofii*, 152–6.

28 Vagner, 'Mediumizm,' 869–70.

29 Dostoevsky swiftly responded to this 'naive faith' in 'the mathematical precision' of psychic research in *A Writer's Diary* ('The mathematical argument is the less persuasive') and later in *The Brothers Karamazov*.

30 Vagner, 'Mediumizm,' 870.

31 Crookes also took four photographs of Katie.

32 Vagner, 'Mediumizm,' 878–86.

33 See Olcott, *People from the Other World*, chs. 10, 16, and 19. See also Blavatsky's first American article, 'Marvellous Spirit Manifestations.' Later, Blavatsky explained the phenomenon of materialization as the actions of elementary spirits, who create living 'portrait pictures' out of the thoughts and memories of the mediums.

34 Vagner, 'Mediumizm,' 894–5.

35 Ibid., 896. Olcott, Vagner reports, wrote up the story of the Georgian ghost for a newspaper and soon received a letter from a certain Mr Betanelli of Philadelphia. Betanelli declared that 'there are in the United States no other Georgians but three, of whom I am the one [while the other two] are not in Vermont now and never [*sic*] been there before' (in Olcott's *People from the Other World*, 305–6). Consequently, Vagner went on, there could be no talk of mystification: only the dead Georgian could have appeared at the Eddy homestead. Moreover, in the following letter cited by Vagner, Betanelli added that he had known Mikhalko in Kutais and that he was 'perfectly willing to give you all information and certificates concerning materialized Georgian spirits at Eddy's.' Betanelli provided Olcott with a translation of the mysterious Georgian words: '"Tiris" in English means "crys," "to cry." "Bar- bare is Georgian feminine name." Whole verse means: Crys, crys Barbare, &c.' (ibid.). Soon after, Blavatsky married Betanelli.

36 On the scandalous history of this medal, see Solovyoff, *A Modern Priestess of Isis*, 233–5, 266–9.

37 The New World was perceived in Russia not just as the home of experimental spiritualism, but also as the 'opposite' world, one that gathered those who had left 'our' world. Hence Dostoevsky's juxtaposition of Svidrigailov's suicide with the latter's joke about leaving for America.

38 Vagner, 'Mediumizm,' 896–901.

39 Ibid., 925, 931, 936.

40 In 1875, soon after their return from Chittenden, Blavatsky and Olcott
    announced the creation of the Theosophist Society, which was destined to
    play an important role in the modernist era. See Carlson, *'No Religion Other
    Than Truth.'*

41 According to Strakhov, 'spiritualism, with its manifold efforts to imagine
    the spiritual and to catch it in actuality, is a magnificent and startling exam-
    ple of how *not* to go about understanding the spiritual.' Strakhov, *O vech-
    nykh istinakh*, 127.

42 Vagner's literary practice is outside my purview here. I would simply note
    that spiritualist themes are prominent in his 'science fiction' works of the
    1870s: *Vpot'makh* (1877) and *Ol'd-Diks* (1877). The relationship between
    Modern Spiritualism and science fiction is an intriguing topic. The most
    representative Western examples of this fruitful cooperation include works
    of the French Kardecist Camille Flammarion and the British historian of
    experimental spiritualism Sir Arthur Conan Doyle. See, for example,
    Brantlinger, 'Imperial Gothic,' 251–6.

43 Blavatsky supplied a vivid image of the effect produced by Vagner's arti-
    cle: 'Fancy a herd of mad bulls rushing at the red flag of a picador, and you
    will have some idea of the effect of Wagner's Olcott pamphlet upon his col-
    leagues!' Blavatsky assumed the role of intermediary between American
    and Russian spiritualists. She kept readers of *Banner of Light* closely
    informed about the course of spiritualist polemics in Russia, and she
    warned the Philadelphia mediums about the potential machinations of the
    movement's sworn enemy, Mendeleev, who had arrived for the World
    Exhibition. Through her offices, Vagner entered into correspondence with
    Olcott, who, in turn, cited the professor's letters with evident sympathy.
    See *Banner of Light*, 22 June 1876, 1–2.

44 *Golos* (23 November 1875): 1.

45 His first collection was published in 1872.

46 In a letter of 1 January 1876 to Strakhov, written in Iasnaia Poliana, Tolstoy
    contrasted the simple beliefs of a 'fresh peasant' with the mediumistic
    'facts' of the professors, 'growing stupid as they crouch over their micro-
    scopes and retorts.' Tolstoy subsequently parodied Vagner and Butlerov in
    the figure of Professor Krugosvetlov in *Fruits of the Enlightenment* (1896). I
    discuss Tolstoy's attitude towards modern spiritualism in the last chapter
    of this book.

47 The name 'Wurst' ('sausage' in German) was given to Vagner by Leo
    Tolstoy. In *Anna Karenina*, Koznyshev refers to [Professor] Wurst's learned
    opinion in a comic (from Levin's perspective) conversation regarding the

boundaries between psychological and physiological phenomena in human life (pt I, ch. 7). I thank Irene Masing-Delic for referring me to this episode.
48 *Strekoza* 5 (1876): 3.
49 *Strekoza* 20 (1876): 3.
50 *Strekoza* 8 (1876): 6. It is curious that Dostoevskaia's description of Vagner should also highlight his comic ghostliness: Vagner appears to dissolve in the park alley.
51 *Golos* 152 (1875): 1.
52 *Golos* 23 (1875): 1.
53 Vagner, *Vospominan'e*, xl.
54 According to Shkliarevsky's calculations, to 'solidify free air into the form of a human hand' weighing about 1 kilogram, 'requires about two cubic English miles of it.' Shkliarevskii, 'Chto dumat' o spiritizme,' 478. This calculation attracted Dostoevsky's interest and may perhaps be related to the author's plan to write a 'fairy tale' about 'a hand in Paris.' Dostoevsky, *Polnoe sobranie*, XXIV:24: 165, 171.
55 *Nedelia* 52 (1875).
56 Polonskii, 'Starye i novye dukhi,' 389.
57 *Strekoza* 37 (1876): 3.
58 Hands were prominent in various aspects of the procedure and practice of seances: the spiritualist chain; the bound hands of the medium; the placing of hands on the planchette; automatic writing; and so on.
59 See Vries, *Dictionary of Symbols and Imagery*, 385; and 'Hands of Spirits,' in Shepard, ed., *Encyclopedia of Occultism and Parapsychology*, 4th ed., 566.
60 Freud, 'The Uncanny,' 244.
61 Vagner was not alone in holding this conviction. Even before, the flying hands at Home's seance had convinced both the poet A.K. Tolstoy and the writer V. Botkin of the truth of the spiritualist hypothesis. See A. Tolstoy, *Polnoe sobranie sochinenii*, IV:98. The famous medium D.D. Hume wrote that one of his Russian friends 'was converted from his previous unbelief, by seeing a hand visible to all of us in the room, slowly forming in the air, a few inches above the table, until it assumed the apparent materiality of a real hand.' This hand (apparently that of a woman) took a pencil from the table and wrote a message 'which deeply affected Mr. Home's visitor, who recognized it as being from his mother.' Britten, 'Spiritualism in Russia,' 352.
62 Like Pushkin's Don Juan, Vagner uses a single part to complete the beautiful whole in his imagination.

63 Aristotle, *The Complete Works*, I:432a1. The phenomenological link between the human hand (as the embodiment of the 'teleology of touch') and the doctrine of divine reincarnation was shown by Derrida in *On Touching*, 256–8.

64 Vagner continued to pursue his study of otherworldly hands. He 'succeeded' in photographing one such hand (see his 'Fotografiia nevidimoi ruki,' published in *Rebus* in 1883), and also in making a plaster cast of a materialized hand. On his spiritualist interests and activities in the 1880s and 1890s, see Petrovo-Solovovo, *Prilozheni k perevodu*, 182–94.

65 The resurrected Christ told his disciples, who supposed him to be a spirit (a ghost): 'Behold my hands and my feet, that it is I myself: handle me, and see; for a spirit hath not flesh and bones, as ye see me have' (Luke 24:39).

66 Butlerov, *Koe chto o mediumizme*, 55.

67 Polonskii, 'Starye i novye dukhi,' 390.

5. The Middle World

1 Saltykov-Shchedrin, *The Golovlyov Family*, 277.

2 Saltykov-Shchedrin, *The History of a Town*, 175.

3 See, for example, Boltin's article 'Spiritizm.' See also his polemical response to Sechenov's *Reflexes of the Brain*: *Zamechaniia na stat'iu Refleksy golovnogo mozga*.

4 In his last years, Saltykov experienced a persistent, almost maniacal, aversion to his wife.

5 See also Boltin's *Dogmaty Khristovoi tserkvi* (1864).

6 *OR RGB* 344, no. 351, I, xxvii.

7 Ibid., l. xxx.

8 Lesevich, 'Modnoe sueverie,' 198.

9 Ibid., 200–1.

10 For Marx's treatment of the phantomatic, see *The German Ideology* (1845–6). Engels devoted to this issue a short essay 'Natural Science in the Spirit World' (1872). For a discussion of the trope of spectrality in Marxist discourse, see Derrida, *Specters of Marx*; and Maley, 'Specters of Engels,' 23–49.

11 Pisarev, 'Skholastika XIX veka,' II:282–3. We are faced here with a materialist inversion of Romantic mysticism. Compare with Zhukovsky: 'These were ghosts through which the believing heart had to force its way

towards the true God. Death dispersed them; they vanished in the coffin; God appeared and took what was his.' Or: before faith 'that which is not ours disappears' Zhukovskii, *Polnoe sobranie sochinenii*, X:74.

12 Turgenev's attitude towards Romantic ghost seeing was of course much more complicated. During one of his reveries, Nikolai Kirsanov sees and almost embraces the ghost of his late wife (*Fathers and Sons*). This spiritualist motif would develop into one of Turgenev's favoured themes (see 'Klara Milich,' 1883).

13 On the theme of phantoms (*prizraki*) in Saltykov-Shchedrin, see Nikolaev, *Smekh Shchedrina*, 25–82.

14 'It is a form of life that strives to contain in itself something essential, vital, thrilling, but in fact contains only emptiness' ('Sovremennye prizraki,' VI:382–3).

15 For Shchedrin, of course, the residents of Golovlyovo themselves bear the blame for this (and in particular Iudushka). In their life, as Milton Ehre writes, 'reality has become reduced to what the Latin root of the word says – things … The reality of Golovlyovo is empty of emotional content and devoid of spiritual value. Lacking adequate contexts of meaning and value, the Golovlyovs stand before an incoherence of things, a reality turned into nightmare.' Ehre, 'A Classic of Russian Realism,' 111.

16 According to Nikolaev, the central tension in Shchedrin's satirical works derives from the fact that 'those who serve phantoms (non-people) trample the living man (living people).' Nikolaev, *Smekh Shchedrina*, 191. See also Poluektova, 'M.E. Saltykov-Shchedrin.'

17 On Shchedrin's novel as a polemical treatment of aspects of the Western and Russian literary tradition, see Todd, 'The Anti-Hero with a Thousand Faces,' 87–106. Makoveeva recently suggested viewing the work as a kind of anti-idyll. Makoveeva, 'Gospoda Golovlyovy as Devastated Idyll.'

18 As Richard Freeborn justly notes, 'Russian reality as he depicts it has only this-worldly dimension and is meaningless, sordid and utterly depressing.' Freeborn, 'The Nineteenth Century,' 248–9.

19 It is interesting to compare this device with the punishment of Khoma Brut in Gogol's 'Vii': Gogol's phantoms, it seems, materialize the hero's sins.

20 Gloomy graveyard poetry, centred on the themes of death and solitude, flourished in Russia in the late eighteenth and early nineteenth centuries. On the history of this tradition see Vatsuro's *Lirika pushkinskoi pory*. On the influence of the theosophical epic poem on Gogol, see Vaiskopf, *Siuzhet Gogolia*.

21 For an excellent discussion of these themes, see Ehre, 'A Classic of Russian Realism.'
22 As Marvin W. Meyer puts it, 'Gnostic texts employ various figures of speech to depict the sorry fate of the entrapped spirit: it is asleep, drunk, sick, ignorant, and in darkness. In order to be liberated, then, the spirit needs to be awakened and brought to sobriety, wholeness, knowledge, and enlightenment. This transformation in one's life, Gnostics maintained, is accomplished through a call from God – the God within and without – to discover true knowledge and rest. For Gnostic Christians, the source of the divine call is Christ.' Meyer, *The Secret Teachings of Jesus*, xvi.
23 This motif permeates the entire novel. See, for example, the materialization of Iudushka's ghost from a dressing gown in the hallucination of the dying Pavel Vladimirovich.
24 Saltykov-Shchedrin, *The Golovlyov Family*, 112.
25 The book is read by the public prosecutor in Gogol's *Dead Souls*.
26 Jung-Stilling's major writings, including his influential *Theorie der Geisterkunde* (1808–9), were translated into Russian by the Russian Freemasons A.F. Labzin and F.P. Lubianovskii in the 1800s to 1820s and were popularized by the spiritual journals *Sionskii vestnik* (The Messenger of Zion) and *Drug iunoshestva i vs iakikh let* (The Friend of Youth and All Ages). Among Jung's readers we can find the Emperor Alexander I and the philosopher Piotr Chaadaev, some Russian Orthodox bishops, and a considerable number of Russian sectarians. From 1810 to the early 1820s, the propagation of his books was stimulated and financed by the government. For a discussion of the Russian reception of Jung-Stilling, see, for example, Högy, *Jung-Stilling und Russland*.
27 Castle, *Female Thermometer*, 131, 161.
28 Saltykov-Shchedrin, *The History of a Town*, 175.

6. The Underworld

1 I refer to Dostoevsky's famous declaration of his aesthetic credo of 'fantastic realism,' formulated in his 11/23 December 1868 letter to Apollon Maikov: 'Oh, my friend, I have a totally different conception of reality and realism than our novelists and critics. My idealism – is more real than their realism. God! Just to narrate sensibly what we Russians have lived through in the last ten years of our spiritual development – yes, would not the realists shout that this is fantasy! And yet this is genuine, existing realism.

This is realism, only deeper; while they swim in the shallow waters ...
Their realism – cannot illuminate a hundredth part of the facts, that are real
and actually occurring. And with our realism, we have predicted facts. It's
happened.' Frank, *Dostoevsky: The Miraculous Years*, 351.
2 Fanger, *Dostoevsky and Romantic Realism*; Jones, *Dostoevsky after Bakhtin*;
Stepanian, 'K ponimaniiu "realizma v vysshem smysle,"' 54–64.
3 Mikhail Bakhtin, in his influential aesthetic reading of this story, presented
it as a sort of authorial manifesto: the 'menippea almost in the strict ancient
sense of the term.' Bakhtin, *Problems of Dostoevsky's Poetics*, 144. According
to Bakhtin, this classical genre reveals here (in its traditional form of 'conversations in the realm of the dead') 'its greatest potential, realizes its max-
imum': 'carnivalesque underworld,' a 'rather motley crew of corpses,' their
vulgarity and their scandals, the 'awareness of a complete absence of
responsibility, open graveyard eroticism, laughter in the coffins,' and so on
(138–41). In Bakthin's interpretation, the underworld of 'Bobok' represents
a grotesque or carnivalized masquerade of Dostoevsky's major ideas,
themes, and images: the idea that 'everything is permitted' if there is no
God and no immortality of the soul; 'the theme of a consciousness on the
brink of insanity'; 'the theme of the final moments of consciousness (connected in other works with the themes of capital punishment and suicide)';
'the theme of sensuality, penetrating the highest spheres of consciousness
and thought; the theme of total "inappropriateness" and "unseemliness" of
life cast off from its folk roots and from the people's faith' (144).
4 Dostoevsky, *A Writer's Diary*, I:185.
5 Jackson, *The Art of Dostoevsky*, 301.
6 Sources for 'Bobok's' otherworldly chatter were sought in contemporary
publications. Tunimanov names the satire of Nil Admirari (L.K. Paniutin's
pseudonym), witch deals with ritual walks in a Smolensk cemetery. Suvorin's
paradoxical 'Progulka v adu' (Promenade in Hell, 1872) must also be mentioned. There have been attempts to connect the provocatively naturalistic
picture of life in the otherworld with the *danses macabres* of baroque painting;
see, for example, Mochul'skii, *Gogol'. Solov'ev. Dostoevskii*. 'Bobok' has also
been examined in the context of the spiritualistic issues in fashion at the time
of its publication. Thomas Berry argues that the conversations of the deceased
can 'be interpreted as a parody of a seance where the absurd is placed on a
par with empirical reality.' Berry, 'Dostoevsky and Spiritualism,' 48. Finally,
attempts have been made to view the story as an Orthodox parable. Metropolitan Antonius sees in it a portrayal of the 'remorselessness of sinners and
their indifference towards evil' and suggests that the story was written 'under

the effect of some church legends' (unfortunately, he does not specify precisely which). Tunimanov, 'Portret s "borodavkami,"' XIV:175.

7   Among the literary predecessors of this fantastic story, scholars have named Lucian's *Menippus, or a Journey to the Kingdom of the Dead*; Dante's *Divine Comedy* (1308–21); Boileau-Despréaux's *Dialogue sur les héros de romans* (1664); Bouvier de Fontenelle's *Dialogues des morts* (1983); Prince Odoevskii's 'The Live Corpse' (1844); Gogol''s *Mertvye dushi* (Dead Souls, 1842); the works of Poe; and Pushkin's 'Kogda za gorodom, zadumchiv, ia brozhu' (1836). Traces of Pushkin are apparent in the story: one is reminded of the lewd banquet in *Feast during the Plague* (1830). On 'Bobok,' see also Portnova, 'K probleme paradoksal'nosti stilia Dostoevskogo,' 91–101; and McNair, 'Dostoevsky, "Bobok," Pierre Bobo, and Boborykin,' 84–96.

8   'Mr. Dostoevsky recounts how he overheard conversations at the cemetery between already buried dead people, how these decaying corpses gossiped, declared their love, and so on. Granted, these are all fantastic stories, but the very choice of such subject matter makes a morbid impression on the reader and makes him think the author is off his head [lit.: something is wrong with his *"top floor"*].' Anonymous, 'Zhurnal'noe obozrenie,' 102.

9   'What kind of horror is this? What kind of cynicism? … Why publish all of this swinishness, in which there is not an ounce of artistic merit. It does nothing but frighten, offend, profane. For Dostoevsky "Bobok" is a kind of fusilade of the Eucharist, and the play with the words "spirit" [*dukh*] and "spiritual" [*dukhovnyi*] is a sacrilege of the holy ghost [*Dukh Sviatoi*]. If it is possible to punish an author for what he publishes, then for "Bobok," for "Bobok" alone, he deserves penal servitude. Yes, Dostoevsky was exiled to hard labor because he wrote "Bobok."' Belyi, *Kritika*, I:407–8.

10   '"Bobok" is the most frightening of Dostoevsky's metaphysical insights. The godless world is decomposing alive. The rotting of souls is more horrible than the decay of bodies.' Mochul'skii, *Gogol'. Solov'ev. Dostoevskii*, 460.

11   Ibid., 459.

12   Bakhtin suggests that in 'Bobok' 'menippea converges with the mystery play' and 'the central figurative idea of the story' is that 'today's corpses [are] unfruitful seed, cast on the ground, but capable neither of dying [...], nor being born anew.' Bakhtin, *Problems of Dostoevsky's Poetics*, 145.

13   Characteristically, the corrupted dead of this story are portrayed through their voices (jokes, remarks, stories), which the deranged narrator has overheard. In this respect, 'Bobok' presents a kind of a radio reportage *de profundis*.

14   In his commentary, Tunimanov acknowledges that Platon Nikolaevich's ideas resemble Swedenborgian views of the afterlife more than Strakhov's rationalistic ideas (XXI:406). He does not develop his observation in the

commentary, however, and immediately disregards it by naming other sources for Platon Nikolaevich's explanation, including, for example, Tiutchev's poem 'Nash vek' (*Our Age*, 1851).

15 Dostoevsky, *A Writer's Diary*, 182. Could this character in fact be based on Swedenborg's translator and spiritualist Aleksandr *Nikolaevich* Aksakov? Up until their acquaintance while taking the waters at Bad Ems in 1875, Dostoevsky thought of Aksakov as a 'nihilist'; see *Polnoe sochinenii*, XXIX:210.

16 Swedenborg, *O nebesakh*, 424–5. English citations are from Swedenborg, *Heaven and Its Wonders and Hell*, 321.

17 Swedenborg, *Heaven and Its Wonders and Hell*, 340.

18 On the themes of shame, lying, and exposure in Dostoevsky's works, see Martinsen, *Surprised by Shame*.

19 Dostoevsky, *A Writer's Diary*, 183.

20 Idid.

21 Swedenborg, *Heaven and Its Wonders and Hell*, 182.

22 Dostoevsky, *A Writer's Diary*, 182–4.

23 Andrei Belyi, who calls 'Bobok' a cynical parody of Revelation, incorrectly identifies the heroes' conception of consciousness with that of the author himself (or more precisely, believes that Dostoevsky considers Klinevich's ideas to be the truth). It is surprising that such an admirer of Swedenborg as Belyi fails to note the presence of the former's theosophical dialectics in 'Bobok.' Struve suggests that 'the literal meaning of this derived word is "single bean in a pod." This can be not only a symbol of death, representing the corpses in their coffins, but also a burgeoning life, a bean growing in its pod as a seed which will insure the next cycle of life.' Struve, *Russkie rasskazy*, 354.

24 Swedenborg, *Heaven and Its Wonders and Hell*, 273.

25 *Sorokoviny* refers to a commemorative service in the Orthodox Church forty days after death. In the first half of the 1870s, Dostoevsky contemplated writing a work named 'Sorokoviny,' which would have dealt with the theme of twenty tribulations for the Orthodox soul. Though the plan was not realized, this theme surfaced in *The Brothers Karamazov*, in Dmitrii's lifetime 'sufferings and ordeals of the soul' (*khozhdenie dushi po mytarstvam*) (bk 9, chs. 3 to 5) and in Ivan Karamazov's dialogue with the devil (bk 11, ch. 9). Dostoevsky likely drew on Bishop Ignatii's *Slovo o smerti* (Sermon on Death). He had two editions of this influential theological tract in his library (1862, 1863).

26 As Bakhtin correctly notes, however, 'under conditions of the menippea, the "seemly" simple man is presented with a slight overtone of comicality, as if he were somewhat inappropriate.' Bakhtin, *Problems of Dostoevsky's Poetics*, 145.

27 Benz, *Emanuel Swedenborg*, 402.
28 In his book, Swedenborg repeats his major ideas many times. In 'Bobok,' Dostoevsky refers to concrete lines of *Heaven and Its Wonders*, but he adopts and artistically transforms (creates a literary 'image of the idea') the general sense of Swedenborg's doctrines concerning the otherworld.
29 'The uncertainty and the feeling of disgust with that new thing which was bound to come any minute were dreadful; but he said that the thing that was the most unbearable to him at the time was the constant thought, "What if I had not had to die! What if I could return to life – oh, what an eternity! And all that would be mine! I should turn every minute into an age, I should lose nothing, I should count every minute separately and waste none!"' Dostoevsky, *The Idiot*, 87–8. I thank Kevin Platt for this observation.
30 Stockenström, '"The Great Chaos and the Infinite Order,"' 43.
31 A literary portrayal of the same idea of spiritual self-exposure appears in Dal''s short 'cemetery story' 'Bred' (The Raving, 1861). Dal' was an ardent Swedenborgian, a propagator and translator of the theosophist's writings.
32 Dostoevsky attacks experimental (Anglo-American) spiritualism as a quasi-religion based on positivism in his notes for 1876–77 (XXIV:96–7, 160, 161, 172).
33 Grossman, *Biblioteka Dostoevskogo*, 175–7. See also Sholomova, 'Dostoevskii i Svedenborg,' 248–51.
34 'It is possible that it was precisely the well-known spiritualist's book that inspired Dostoevsky to write a "fantastic tale" whose hero is a dreamer and prophet who travels to a small star' (XXV:403).
35 Miłosz, 'Dostoevsky and Swedenborg,' 128.
36 Robin Feuer Miller makes an interesting observation regarding the role of the image of the seed in both Swedenborg and Dostoevsky (*The Brothers Karamazov*). Miller, 'Dostoevsky's "The Dream of a Ridiculous Man,"' 281–2. A relationship between the Swedenborgian image of the seed and the 'little bean,' *bobok*, is possible. See, for example, in *On Heaven, the World of Spirits, and on Hell* (§475): 'To think and to will without doing, when there is opportunity, is like a flame enclosed in a vessel that goes out; also like seed cast upon the sand, which fails to grow, and so perishes with its power of germination. But to think and will and from that to do is like … A seed in the ground that grows up into a tree or flower and continues to live.' Swedenborg, *Heaven and Its Wonders and Hell*, 296. On the Eleusinian symbolism of the seed in 'Bobok,' see Bakhtin: '"contemporary dead men" are as sterile seed, cast on the ground, but capable neither of dying (that is, of being cleansed of themselves, of rising above themselves), nor of being renewed (that is, of bearing fruit).'

Bakhtin, *Problems of Dostoevsky's Poetics*, 147. One may also note that in ancient mythologies the bean was considered a symbol for the dead person's soul (hence Pythagoras's notorious ban on eating beans) and was associated with resurrection and salvation. See Freidenberg, *Poetika siuzheta i zhanra*. Phillips suggests that the word *bobok* 'sounds like the word Bog [God], with redupli- cation.' 'The implication here might be that God is what will remain meta- physically after all else has perished, or morally as a final judge of these debauched souls.' Phillips, 'Dostoevskij's "Bobok,"' 142.

37 Swedenborg, *Heaven and Its Wonders and Hell*, 352.

38 Dostoevsky, *The Notebooks for* The Possessed, 243. The image of a butterfly plays an important role in Swedenborg's theosophy. See Swedenborg, *The True Christian Religion*, 15–16: 'Any one can find evidences in favor of a Divine in the visible things of nature when he observes those worms which are moved by the joy of a peculiar love to aspire after a change of their earthly state into one somewhat analogous to a heavenly state. For this purpose they crawl into suitable places, enclose themselves in a covering, and thus place themselves in a womb from which to be born again; and there they become chrysalids, aureliae, nymphs, and finally butterflies [...] Who that sees evidences in favor of a Divine in the visible things of nature can help seeing in these as worms an image of man's earthly state, and in these as butterflies an image of his heavenly state? Those who have con- firmed themselves in favor of nature behold the same things, but having rejected man's heavenly state from their thought they call them mere oper- ations of nature.'

39 In the passage just quoted, Dostoevsky's demonic hero rejects the idea of salvation. I believe that on this point Dostoevsky's Orthodox beliefs in for- giveness and resurrection latently confront Stavrogin's 'Swedenborgian' determinism (see 'At Tikhon's'). Analysing a possible Swedenborgian 'dimension' of *The Devils* is beyond the scope of the present study, however.

40 Swedenborg, *Heaven and Its Wonders and Hell*, 283–4.

41 Religious, folk, and literary sources of the demonic in Dostoevsky are traced by Leatherbarrow in *A Devil's Vaudeville*.

42 Polkanov, 'O zhizni dushi po vossoedinenii eia s telom.' A censor's approval is dated 10 January 1873.

43 Concrete Swedenborgian implications of 'The Dream' are beyond the scope of the present discussion.

44 Khrisanf, 'Emmanuil Svedenborg i ego verouchenie.'

45 On the early period of Russian Swedenborgianism, see Chizhevskii, 'Swe- denborg bei den Slaven.' Hallengren, 'Russia, Swedenborg and the Eastern Mind,' includes among those studying Swedenborg from the 1850s to the

1870s author and philologist Vladimir Dal', philosopher Pamfil Iurkevich, Princess K.M. Shakhovskaia, and philosopher and poet Vladimir Solov'ev. See Roshchin, 'Svedenborg v Rossii.' From 1863 to 1870, Aksakov published his translations and interpretations of Swedenborg's works in London and Leipzig. In his 1863 translation of *De coelo* he included an introductory article about Swedenborg as a forerunner of modern spiritualism as well as the theosophist's biography. See also Aksakov's critical analysis of Swedenborg's system in his *Ratsionalizm Svedenborga*.

46 Shleiden, *Etiudy,*'

47 Shleiden, in Chernyshevskii, *Polnoe sobranie sochinenii*, IX:482.

48 Ibid., 483.

49 'From the medical point of view,' Kovalevskii argues, Swedenborg's case is characterized by the following symptoms of *epilepsia nocturna:* convulsions, fits of ecstasies and hallucinations, and 'the gift of clairvoyance and communication with the world of spirits,' as well as religious messianism. Kovalevskii, *Generalissimus Suvorov*, 434, 452.

50 In his introduction to Swedenborg's *De coelo*, Aksakov wrote: 'In the present time the issue of the world of spirits has been raised again and is rapidly advancing. This issue is progressing, not by philosophical speculation, nor by mystical sermons, nor by the logic of a single day, but rather by the simple path of empirical facts, by the discovery of laws of nature, by the logic of historical evidence. Striking phenomena are occurring around us! The veil that has concealed from human beings the mysteries of the spiritual world and the further destinies of our souls in the afterlife is vanishing; the communication between the spiritual world and the earth, between man in flesh and man the spirit, has been regained; the new world reveals itself to man's soul, which hears, sees, and perceives its own immortality in this world.' Aksakov, 'Ot perevodchika.'

51 Russian Swedenborgians observed that Swedenborg's cosmology and ethical system perfectly corresponded with Russian Orthodox beliefs. Thus, Vladimir Dal' found the idea of *mytarstva dushi* (ordeals of the soul) very close to Swedenborg's afterlife experiences. See Mel'nikov-Pecherskii, 'Vospominaniia o Vladimire Ivanoviche Dale,' 66. On the other hand, in the late 1850s and 1860s critical discussions of Swedenborg's teachings appeared in Russian religious journals. See Khrisanf, 'Emmanuil Svedenborg i ego verouchenie,' 72–105, 251–72; Osinin, 'Shvedenborg i ego uchenie.'

52 Florovskii, *Puti russkogo bogosloviia*, 2, ch. 6.

53 Jung-Stilling, *Die Theorie der Geisterkunde*. In the 1830s and 1840s this idea was popularized by the influential doctor and writer Justinus Kerner.

54 Kardec, *The Book of Spirits*; Owen, *The Debatable Land Between This World and the Next*, Davis, *Stellar Key to the Summerland*.

55 Both Swedenborg and Dostoevsky are characterized by a strong apocalyptic feeling: the Swedish seer explained his revelations by the fact that the Last Judgment had already begun. In his *Writer's Diary* Dostoevsky hints at the approaching denouement of world history. Swedenborg's famous apocalyptic tract *The White Horse* (1758) 'echoes' the eccentric Lebedev's interpretation of the apocalyptic horse in *The Idiot*.

56 In this respect it is suggestive to compare Leskov's 'progressivist' and Dostoevsky's 'apocalyptical' views. As we have seen it, at the end of the 1860s, Leskov was highly interested in Allan Kardec's idea of punishment in the next world according to one's moral behaviour and improvement of the soul by degrees through a series of physical reincarnations. Dostoevsky also may have been familiar with Kardec's spiritualist doctrine: in his library he had Apollon Boltin's *Dogmaty Khristovoi tserkvi, izlozhennye soglasno spiriticheskomu ucheniiu* (1864). There are no traces of Kardec's doctrine of compulsory reincarnation in Dostoevsky's works, however.

57 As Vladimir Solov'ev wrote in his article on the Swedish seer, 'it is quite original in Swedenborg's theosophy that he does not accept the prehuman and superhuman origins of angels and devils. Instead, he sees in them only the evolution of a man in two opposite directions. This means that any man during his lifetime is already, in his essence, either angel or devil, and the one who, like Swedenborg, becomes a spiritual seer, can distinguish this essence clearly. Therefore, it is earthly or natural mankind that is the source and hotbed [*Seminarium*] of heaven and hell.' Solov'ev, 'Svedenborg,' 498.

58 Benz, *Emanuel Swedenborg*, 404.

59 Iurii Lotman and Boris Uspenskii, in their famous essay on dual models in Russian cultural consciousness, propose that Russian 'binary' cultural consciousness is rooted in the Orthodox cosmology, in which there is no room for an evolutionary 'neutral sphere' of Purgatory. One may contend that from a Dostoevskian perspective, a Swedenborgian 'world of spirits,' in which souls expose their inner content completely, does not contradict this binary scheme but instead provides it with 'an inner logic' for the final bifurcation – either heaven or hell. See Lotman and Uspenskii, 'Rol' dual'nykh modelei v dinamike russkoi kul'tury,' 220. I thank Caryl Emerson for this observation.

60 Dostoevsky, *A Writer's Diary*, 156–7.

61 Ibid., 165.

62 Though the theme of Protestantism is important for his *Diary*, it is likely that Dostoevsky is simply referring to Swedenborg's 'political' visions: the Protestant seer always portrayed Catholics as suffering in hell. It is difficult to perceive Swedenborg as an orthodox Protestant, for his doctrine was strongly opposed by Swedish Lutheran priests. See Benz, *Emanuel Swedenborg*, 498–518.

63 Ibid., 237. On Dostoevsky's ontological spiritualism, as opposed to Tolstoy's mysticism, see Bitsilli, 'Problema zhizni i smerti v tvorchestve Tolstogo,' 478.

64 Minaev, 'Komy na Rusi zhit' khorosho,' 7.

65 Anonymous, '"Besy" Fedora Dostoevskogo,' *Iskra*, no. 6 (1873): 5.

66 See, for example, Kant's refutation of the seer in *Träume eines Geistersehers*.

67 Morson, 'Introductory Study,' 11.

68 The portrait referred to is by Vasilii Perov. *Golos* 14, quoted in XXI:402.

69 As certain commentators have noted, the conversation overheard by Dostoevsky's narrator resembles the dogs' correspondence in Gogol''s 'Diary of a Madman.'

70 'The Dream of a Ridiculous Man' (1877) may be considered in the context of this unrealized plan.

71 Bakhtin, *Problems of Dostoevsky's Poetics*, 147. Bakhtin notes that the narrator in 'Bobok' is shown on the threshold of insanity. This borderline state of mind is ambiguous, however, for it may be interpreted either as a disease or as a penetration into the mystery of this world, which is concealed from the sane mind of the living.

72 The ontological nature of Dostoevsky's humour and irony in their relationship to prophetic discourse and metaphysical fears (see Dostoevsky's article on the devils and Modern Spiritualism or 'The Dream of a Ridiculous Man') is outside the scope of the present discussion. The 'holy fools" connection of Dostoevsky's provocative humour is discussed in Murav, *Holy Foolishness*. One may also add that this double-edged aggressive (self-)irony was deeply rooted in the medieval mystical discourses of communication with the Devil (from Egyptian hermits to Jakob Boehme and Russian 'fools in Christ').

73 In this context, the then fledging career of the secular mystic Vladimir Solov'ev is representative. Incidentally, in the early 1870s, Solov'ev was interested in Swedenborg's theosophy. Swedenborg was one of the favourite philosophers of his teacher Pamfil Iurkevich. Later on, Solov'ev wrote an article on the theosophist for Brokgauz and Efron, *Entsiklopedicheskii slovar'*.

7. The (Dis)infection

1 The epigraphs are taken from Stark, 'Psychical Infection,' 555; and Emerson, 'Tolstoy's Aesthetics,' 250.
2 Davydov, 'Iz proshlogo,' 205.
3 *Tolstoy's Diaries*. 211.
4 Dole, *The Life of Count Tolstoi*, 326.
5 A promise to visit friends after one's death is a traditional motif of spiritualist folklore (e.g., Anton Delvig's promise, which we mentioned in the chapter about Pushkin's ghost). Note that in the 1880s and 1890s materials about Russian writers' interest in the afterlife were regularly published in the spiritualist journal *Rebus*. Tolstoy, with his well-known obsession with the problem of death and his disbelief in miracles from beyond the grave, both attracted and enraged Russian spiritualists. The culmination of the anti-Tolstoyan critique was the tract by Aksakov, father of Russian spiritualism, 'K chemu bylo voskresat'?' In the present chapter we do not consider an intriguing issue of Tolstoy's spiritualism, first posed by Leskov in his 1869 review of *War and Peace*. (Leskov considered Tolstoy's description of Prince Andrew's death to be the apotheosis of Tolstoy's mystical intuition. He considered Tolstoy to be a spiritualist writer rather than a realist-psychologist, as Strakhov argued.) On Tolstoy's attitude towards miracles, see Orwin, 'Did Dostoevsky or Tolstoy Believe in Miracles?' 125–41.
6 Not Mal'chich, as is indicated in the *Iubileinoe* edition of Tolstoy's complete works (XXVII:648).
7 The eyewitness was E.I Boratynskaia. See S.M. Luk'ianov, *O Vl. Solov'eve v ego molodye gody*, IV:27.
8 Davydov, 'Iz proshlogo,' 205.
9 An anonymous Russian correspondent for *Severnaia pchela* (Northern Bee) mentioned the same seance at the Trubetskoys' in his account of a new French mania: 'There is much gossip about a certain Hume, an American who does all kinds of tricks [...] He allegedly has a gift (but who can believe it?) to summon the dead from the beyond, give life to inanimate objects; as he sings, "You, the spirits of the underground, come here," his request is immediately fulfilled. Some time ago, in response to a persuasive request of a gentleman who had recently lost his daughter, he called her back from the grave. She immediately appeared in the very same image as she used to be during her lifetime. The poor father, they say, lost his mind. On another occasion, he made a little bell jump off the table, walk around the room, climb onto the knees of Mr. N*** and finally ring out a familiar

aria. He asked one lady to raise a carpet slightly in the room in which they were sitting. She did it and – oh, what a horror! – she saw right in front of her *un bras livide*, a bluish and pale and cold hand of the dead! She surely fainted. Several days earlier, he had spent an evening at one of our fellow citizens', Princess Tr***, place. Regretfully, he refused to satisfy the princess's and guests' curiosity under a pretext of nervousness. O charlatanism of charlatanisms! if I may say so, and everything in Paris is charlatanism!' 'Pis'ma russkogo turista,' *Severnaia pchela*, 511. Turgenev sarcastically described the March seance in his letter to Annenkov from 9/21 March 1857. Turgenev. *Polnoe sobranie sochineni*, III:210.

10 *L.N. Tolstoi – N.N. Strakhov*, I:243. See Tolstoy's 1875 notes on mediumism as superstition, 'i.e., the absence of rational worldview' (XVII:72).

11 Davydov, 'Iz proshlogo,' 244.

12 Behrs, 'Vospominaniia o grafe L.N. Tolstom,' 187.

13 See, for example, Tolstoy's thoughts on afterlife and immortality in XVII:338–58, and, especially, L:191–3: 'G[od]'s force comes through the beings, as through transparent [...] bodies, and directs them. I am one of the beings. The matter and the material are just the limitations of my and other similar beings' form.'

14 On Tolstoy's spiritualism, see, for example, Bitsilli, 'Problema zhizni i smerti u Tolstogo'; and Zen'kovskii, 'Problema bessmertiia u L.N. Tolstogo.' See also McLaughlin, 'Tolstoy and Schopenhauer.'

15 On the 'heyday of hypnotism' see Gauld, *A History of Hypnotism*, 273–515.

16 On the history of hypnotism in Russia, see Zielinski, 'Russia.'

17 Rozenbach, 'Gipnotizm,' 741. On the dangers of hypnotism, see a monograph by the noted psychiatrist A.A. Tokarskii, *K voprosu o vrednom vliianii gipnotizirovaniia*.

18 Blavatsky, *Isis Unveiled*, 217.

19 Rozenbach, 'Gipnotizm,' 741.

20 See Butlerov, *Stat'i po mediumizmu*, 273–394.

21 Quoted in Zielinski, 'Russia,' 25–6.

22 Britten, *Nineteenth-Century Miracles*, 349.

23 Tolstoy, *The Complete Works*, 261, 275. The major source of Krugosvetlov's speech, however, is Butlerov's articles on mediumism, in which he repeatedly referred to modern theories of ether, matter and energy, and the fourth dimension. See Butlerov, *Stat'i po mediumizmu*, 330–1, 340–75. The explications of Vagner/Krugosvetlov, which can be traced to theories of magnetism, are reminiscent of the views of the then prominent neurologist J. Luys, in particular his theory of the 'subtle fluid' that surrounded people, which

was called ether: 'It would seem possible that this ambient medium – the nature of its substance being unknown – may transmit the perturbations of nerve power.' See Bramwell, *Hypnotism and Treatment of Suggestion*, 48.

24 Butlerov, *Stat'i po mediumizmu*, 331.

25 See, on Feldman, Kaufman, 'Sovremennyi Kaliostro,' 73–80.

26 *Rb* 31, 42, 43. In 1891, Vagner, the leader of the Russian Society of Experimental Psychology (which he himself had founded), performed a series of experiments with Feldman, the summary of which he presented to the society in the following year. Vagner did not agree with Feldman's materialist interpretation of phenomena observed during hypnosis. See 'Protokoly zasedanii russkogo obshchestva eksperimental'noi psikhologii.' This book contains a valuable bibliography of hypnosis literature in Russian. Feldman is presented in satirical fashion in the third act of 'Fruits of Enlightenment' (XXVII:208–9).

27 *Rb* 506 (1885): 454.

28 *Russkoe bogatstvo*, October (1897): 98.

29 Utevskii, *Vospominaniia iurista*, 105–6. This story went around in several versions. The writer A.V. Amfiteatrov attested that the saved Pobedonostsev, instead of thanking the Jewish Feldman, told him to get baptized. As Amfiteatrov crudely joked on the occasion, 'One shouldn't drag out everything that swims in the water.' Amfiteatrov and Anichkov, *Pobedonostsev*, 50.

30 Ibid.

31 For Feldman's tour, see the medical newspaper *Vrach* (Physician) from 1889 (pp. 697, 806, 978, 983, 1074).

32 O. Fel'dman, 'Otnoshenie Tolstogo k gipnotizmu,' 355.

33 Tolstoy, 'The Kreutzer Sonata.'

34 Both Grosman and Feldman belong to the Charcot school (he had attended a course in Salpêtriére), which was then at odds with the Liébault school (both Charcot and Liébault are mentioned in the comedy). In the play, Grosman recalls his performances in Odessa (where Feldman had gone on tour). An actor at the Maly Theater, Garin-Vinding, dressed up as Feldman when he played the role of Grosman in *Fruits of Enlightenment*. Feldman took offence, and sued Garin-Vinding in court (XXVII:658).

35 In Tolstoy's view, the healing Hypnotist was nothing but a new version of the Physician, whom the writer had banished from his utopia of righteous life. However, unlike the 'body doctor,' the hypnotist dealt with man's psyche and was therefore much more dangerous.

36 See in particular V. Zubov, 'Tolstoi i russkaia estetika 90-kh godov,' 177–8 (Zubov mentions Souriau's *La Suggestion dans l'art* as a possible source of

Tolstoy's aesthetics, p. 178); Rainov, 'Estetika Tolstogo i ego iskusstvo'; Gary R. Jahn, 'The Aesthetic Theory of Leo Tolstoy's What Is Art?'; Gustafson, *Leo Tolstoy: Resident and Stranger*; Šilbajoris, *Tolstoy's Aesthetics and His Art*, 97–133; Emerson, 'Tolstoy's Aesthetics'; Denner, 'Accidental Art'; Robinson, 'Tolstoy's Infection Theory.'

37 Daniel Beer points out in his survey of the heyday of social psychology in Russia that 'the sciences of bacteriology and epidemiology served as a model for mass psychology as the former enjoyed great influence following their discovery of a coherent and testable description for the contagion of illnesses. According to the epidemiological approach, the suggestion of ideas, attitudes, or behavioral patterns, whether normal or pathological, is just another instance of contagion. The literature thus mentions not only a *contagium vivum* but also a *contagium psychicum*, analogous to organic agents of contagion such as microbes, that causes a person's mind to be contaminated with the ideas, habits, and attitudes of another person.' Beer, '"Microbes of the Mind,"' 541.

38 Kandinskii, *Obshcheponiatnye psikhologicheskie etiudi*, 153–4. Quoted in Beer, '"Microbes of the Mind,"' 545.

39 Ibid.

40 We should note that in 1864 Tolstoy had written the anti-nihilist comedy *An Infected Family.*

41 Stephen Baehr observes 'that Tolstoy uses a form of the word "infection" to describe the functions of both artist and doctor': 'The opposition between these two professions is thus captured through *double entendre*: while the genuine artist unifies people by "infecting" them with emotion, the doctor moves people apart by curing "infection." The doctor thus prevents life from becoming "art"'. Baehr, 'Art and *The Kreutzer Sonata*,' 41. This is certainly true, but, I believe, there is one more metaphorical actor in Tolstoy's infection play – the hypnotist who subjects the man's mind to his will.

42 'The sight of a person yawning produces an irresistible desire to yawn ... Consciousness and the will are irrelevant here, because the person infected with yawning performs the act not only bypassing his will, but often in spite of it, or absolutely unconsciously.' Kandinskii, *Obshcheponiatnye psikhologicheskie etiudi*, 177. Quoted in Beer, '"Microbes of the Mind,"' 545.

43 One of the first examples of psychological infection in Tolstoy is servant Iegor's reaction to Levin's enthusiasm in *Anna Karenina* (pt IV, ch. XIV). Tolstoy was interested in psychological theories of imitation (XLIX:79).

44 Tolstoy, *The Kreutzer Sonata and Other Stories*, 144.

45 Richard Gustafson, *Leo Tolstoy: Resident and Stranger*, 373.

46 Tolstoy, *What Is Art?* 50–1.

47 Ibid., 130.

48 Gustafson, *Leo Tolstoy*, 374.
49 Tolstoy, *What Is Art?*, 129. It is curious how the activities of two Wagners – the spiritualist and the composer – merge in Tolstoy's perception of the false art.
50 *Voprosy filosofii i psikhooigii* (1894): 189. Professor A.N. Giliarov was an author of a survey *Gipnotizm po ucheniiu shkoly Sharko i psikhologicheskoi shkoly. 1881–1893.*
51 *Voprosy filosofii*, 189.
52 Journal entry of 18 December, 1899.
53 In April 1884, Tolstoy read E.P. Letkova's article 'Psychiatrico–Zoological Theory of Mass Movements,' published in *Otechestvennye zapiski*, 1884, 3: 1–27. He commented on this article (a discussion of Lombroso's ideas) in his diary: 'Inertia is a psychological law. Any innovation is painful. The conclusion is clear. There are two laws: inertia and movement. Madness, i.e. abnormality, is one only of the two – the resultant of the two is normality' (XLIX:76); *Tolstoy's Diaries*, I:207.
54 G. Lebon, *Psikhologiia narodov i mass*, 165. Tolstoy was in correspondence with Le Bon regarding his book about psychology of socialism (LIII:185).
55 Danaher in his painstaking analysis of Tolstoy's metaphorical representations of truth and falsehood, observes, 'hypnosis is linked to both a superficial light image (hypnotists typically dangle a shiny bauble in front of their subjects to lull them into a trance) and force (note Tolstoy's use of the word *armies* to describe the officially sanctioned hypnotists, that is, church and government functionaries). The Tolstoyan extension DECEPTION IS HYPNOSIS is a node which exists *potentially* between two everyday metaphorical conceptualizations of Truth and Falsehood.' Danaher, 'A Cognitive Approach to Metaphor in Prose,' 254.
56 Thrailkill. *Affecting Fictions*, 225.
57 Quoted in Sirotkina, *Diagnosing Literary Genius*, 76.
58 Fel'dman, 'Otnoshenie Tolstogo k gipnotizmu,' 357–8. On Tolstoy's negative attitude towards psychiatry, see Sirotkina, *Diagnosing Literary Genius*, 85–6, 95.
59 Fel'dman, 'Otnoshenie Tolstogo k gipnotizmu,' 358.
60 The moralist Shchedrin was similar to Tolstoy in his rejection of idealistic art. However, Shchedrin's materialism and socialism were undoubtedly alien to Tolstoy, the propagator of moral Christianity. Tolstoy's belief in the infectious (and transformative) power of Christian art protected him from the former's gloom and despair.
61 Furst, *All Is True*, 26. Rainov wrote in a 1928 article, 'the goal of his [Tolstoy's] life was, as we believe, an overcoming of the transparency of art by the means of art itself.' Rainov, 'Estetika Tolstogo i ego iskusstvo,' 91.

Epilogue

1 The story was first published in 1881 in the journal *Oskolki* (Fragments), 49–50, with the subtitle 'A Characteristic Event (from Literary Memoirs).' In 1886 Leskov included it, with insignificant revisions, in the collection *Christmas Stories*.

2 Eikhenbaum, 'Chrezmernyi pisatel,' 252. On Leskov's narrative craft see Walter Benjamin's classic essay 'The Storyteller.'

3 *Genlis, Esprit du Madame de Genlis*, 1–2.

4 Leskov. *Sobranie sochinenii*, VII:79–92.

5 'Leskov' emphasizes that his Paris acquaintance Prince Ivan Gagarin recommended him to the princess. 'For some reason,' the princess also liked Leskov's recently published story 'The Sealed Angel.' The illusion of reality that the narrator creates with these references is dispelled on closer examination: the action of the story takes place in the 1860s. 'The Sealed Angel' came out in 1873, and Leskov met the Jesuit Gagarin in 1875.

6 It is possible that Goncharov offended the spirit of Genlis in that in his novel he commented disrespectfully on her antiquated novels (in the chapter 'The Dream of Oblomov').

7 This anecdote is well known. Compare: 'When Madame du Deffand was introduced to someone for the first time, it was her custom to form a mental picture of the new acquaintance by touching his or her face. When she put her hand to Gibbon's face, she is said to have exclaimed, "Fi donc!" believing that someone was tricking her by presenting the behind of a naked baby.' Craddock, *Edward Gibbon*, 93. See also Craddock, *Edward Gibbon: A Reference Guide*, 49, 121. In Russia this anecdote 'from Genlis' first appeared in *Vestnik Evropy* (The Herald of Europe) in 1804: 'Mr. Lozen, being briefly acquainted with Mr. Gibbon, brought him one day to Mme. du Deffand, who was already blind then and would feel with her hands the faces of renowned people who were presented to her in order to form an understanding of their qualities. She did not fail to show Mr. Gibbon this brand of flattering courtesy. Mr. Gibbon extended his face to her with all the good will in the world. Mme. du Deffand, lightly running her hands over this broad face, searched in vain for some quality and found nothing but two misshapen cheekbones. As she continued this examination, her face expressed extreme amazement, and finally, hastily removing her hands with strong indignation, Mme du Deffand screamed "What a rotten joke!!!"' Genlis, 'Nechto o grafe Benevskom,' 56–60. Bukhshtab points out that Leskov cites this anecdote, with a few revisions, from the 'Memoirs of Felicity ***' (pt 2).

8 On the genre of the Christmas story in the works of Leskov see Dushechkina, *Russkii sviatochnyi rasskaz*, 181–94.
9 Leskov knew Calmet's book well (see references to it in the novel *At Daggers Drawn*, for example, in ch. 12, pt 6). Nevertheless, in the Russian translation of the book (pts 1–2, M., 1867), I have been unable to find the words
   offered as the epigraph to 'The Spirit of Mme. Genlis.' They are possibly
   Leskov's invention.
10 McLean, *Nikolai Leskov*, 378.
11 Morogues, '*Le Probléme feminine*,' 91–2. Pension tutors right up to the end
   of the century insistently recommended that their pupils read the pious
   works of Genlis, placing these last in opposition to the 'immoral' novels of
   Turgenev. As a result, the pupils were filled with a deep loathing for the
   repugnant moralist; see Kuprin, 'Vpot'makh' (In the Dark).
12 Pozdiejew, 'Mistika i satira v sviatochnom rasskaze,' 136–43. Alexander
   Zholkovsky has kindly familiarized us with the manuscript of his insight-
   ful article about this story, 'Malen'kii metatekstual'nyi shedevr Leskova.'
   In this article, Zholkovsky discusses intertextual richness and biographic
   subtexts of Leskov's story.
13 Dushechkina, *Russkii sviatochnyi rasskaz*, 185.
14 Russian journals printed many reports of spiritualist appearances in the
   1870s. In 1881 the first Russian spiritualist journal *Rebus*, filled with such
   stories, began to appear.
15 McLean, *Nikolai Leskov*, 379.
16 Anonymous, 'Portret gospodina Kardeka,' 304.
17 Ibid., 265.
18 On Leskov's interest in the teachings of Origen, see Andrei Leskov, *Zhizn'
   Nikolaia Leskova*, II:544.
19 In his witty 1869 article on spiritualism, Leskov retells a story about a fantastic regiment on Mars from Allan Kardec's *Revue spirite*. 'Le caporal Fran-
   cois Pamphile' is suddenly transported from his bed to the planet Mars. It
   turns out that the latter is populated by the souls of great conquerors and
   generals under the leadership of Alexander the Great. From conversations
   with the dead commanders, Pamphile learns that they march and rehearse
   battles all the time. Their retainers are great women, including Queen Elizabeth I and the Russian Empress Catherine II. An orchestra composed of
   Mozart, Beethoven, Gluck, and Puccini plays inspiring military music for
   them. However, their life is a disaster, since, in accordance with (spiritualist) God's design, they are not allowed to fight and are tormented by their
   recollections. Mars appears a reformatory for warlords of both sexes.
   Leskov writes that he does not know how to define the genre of this story:

is it a fairy tale, an anecdote, a legend, or, more like, just a terrible non-sense? *Polnoe sochinenii*, VIII:117–25. Leskov found this story in the September 1868 issue of *Revue spirite*: 'Le Régiment fantastique,' *Revue spirit* 9 (1868): 271–9.

20 See Morogues 'Leskov et le Spiritisme,' 113–32; Vinitskii, 'Dukhovnyi kartser'; Vinitskii, 'Russkie dukhi.'

21 *OR PGB*, f. 344, Shibanov's collection, no. 351, 69–70.

22 Ibid., 69. In *The Book of Mediums* it is said that that these spirits are clever and often tell bitter truths in the guise of a joke (ch. X, pt 135).

23 Kardec asserted that these mischievous spirits had long been known to people under the names of minor devils, goblins, elemental spirits, and so on. But in the mischievous spirits he saw not demons or elemental creatures, but human souls located at the bottom of the spiritual stairway. Kardec's mysticism is pan-anthropological. There is no place here for impure forces and Christian demonology.

24 Recall N. Potulov, the ultraconservative contributor of *Domashniaia beseda* (and Dostoevsky's correspondent), who exposed spiritual games with the devil in his writings.

25 The spirit turned out to be so prolific that the participants 'interrupted the seance and went to drink tea; they thought they had gotten rid of the rhymer,' but they were mistaken. A.N. Aksakov, *Materialy dlia suzhdeniia ob avtomaticheskom pis'me*, 6.

26 Ivan Barkov's unprintable writings (as well as numerous works of the sort traditionally attributed to him) circulated in manuscript collections throughout the eighteenth and nineteenth centuries.

27 They asked the spirit why it played such tricks, to which it answered that it 'wrote these profanities all its life and now should dictate them for the convincing of non-believers in the authenticity of spiritual appearances.' N.P. Vagner, *Nabliudeniia nad spiritizmom*, 105. In his book Vagner seriously tells about a few instances of such spiritual hooliganism, in which connection he openly sweeps aside a version about mystifications from the side of the medium.

28 'Yes, there are mischievous, light, frivolous spirits, to whom not only does it mean nothing to lie and clown around, but who even find pleasure in it and intentionally, for fun, are ready to arouse God knows what in a person. There were cases of terrible mistakes, when some great spirit was long heeded, and suddenly it came out that it was some imposter, vagrant, trash.' Leskov, *Polnoe sobranie sochinenii*, IX:507.

29 On the whole Leskov's artistic strategy as the narrator of stories about the

supernatural lay in guiding the reader between two mistaken extremes –
rationality, absolutely rejecting the existence of the supernatural, and
superstition, rudely giving material form to spiritual content.

30 The 'pedagogical irony' of the story becomes evident if we remember that
its author was a member of the special division of the learned committee
[uchenyi komitet] of the Ministry of Popular Education for the inspection
of books published for the *narod*.

31 In this sense Leskov's story forces us to say 'the spirit' of the *real* Genlis, as
opposed to the image of the convinced moralist 'assigned' by the princess.
'The witty Marquise Silleri' loved frivolous jokes, and her life, full of
adventures, including amorous ones, was extremely far from the aureole of
strict morality, with which she tried to surround herself in old age. About
the 'after-death existence' of Genlis we, to be sure, know nothing, but we
note that the writer's choice by way of an object of spiritualist experience
could be connected with the fact that her reputation was founded not only
on moralistic works, but also on stories and novels with apparitions.

32 The development of the 'hand motif' in Leskov's story is discussed in
Zholkovsky's article in *Malen'kii metatekstual'nyi shedevr Leskovi*.

33 See the analysis of Leskov's 'philosophy of the word' in Sperrle, *The Organic
Worldview of Nikolai Leskov*, 199–200. On the profound kinship between
Leskov's storytelling and his mysticism, see Benjamin, 'The Storyteller.'

34 The idea of the artistic text as a 'thinking device,' in conversation with the
reader was stated by Iu.M. Lotman in his series of works of 1980–90:
'Displaying intellectual attributes,' the scholar wrote, 'the highly organized
text ceases to be only an intermediary in the act of communication. It
becomes an equal partner in conversation, possessing a high degree of
autonomy. Both for the author (the addresser) and for the reader (the
addressee) it can appear as an independent intellectual construct, playing
an active and independent role in the dialogue.' Lotman. *Izbrannye trudy*
I:131. In Leskov's case it turns out that the text is not so much an 'intellect'
and 'equal conversational partner,' as an unpredictable and mischievous
'spirit,' clearly taking advantage of the reader-addressee.

35 For the Neoplatonic roots of Sheakespeare's artistic spiritualism, see, for
example, an elegant essay by Johnson, 'The Genesis of Ariel,' 205–20.
According to Johnson, the spirit Ariel (*The Tempest*) 'is the embodiment of
what is, in a double sense, Shakespeare's magic' (210).

36 For a discussion of Gogol's latent demonism, see, for example, Epstein,
'The Irony of Style,' 55–71. On 'demonism' in the novelistic ideology of
Dostoevsky, see Weiner, *By Authors Possessed; and* Leatherbarrow, *A Devil's*

Vaudeville. It is amusing that in his antispiritualist article, Dostoevsky cites a public letter received from Nikolai Gogol at a spiritualist seance in which the latter called the spirits devils – that is, if one follows the logic of the article, acknowledged that he was a devil-mystifier and not the spirit of a deceased writer (XXII:32).

37 Benjamin, 'The Storyteller,' 107.

38 Not for nothing did such a connoisseur of the free spirit of literature as Iu.N. Tynianov admire this small, dynamic, and clever joke. According to the memoirs of N. Stepanov, Tynianov rapturously read aloud 'The Spirit of Mme. Genlis.' Stepanov, 'Idei i plany,' 238.

39 On 'the historical development of the view of literary activity as intristically demonic' in Russia see Davidson, 'Divine Service or Idol Worship?', 125–64.

40 To be sure, between these poles there are a few intermediate and 'mixed' variations, probably corresponding in their foundation to differing spiritualistic doctrines. But this is, of course, a theme for further research.

Works Cited

Abramovich, N.Ia. 'Mistitsizm v tvorchestve N. Leskova.' In *Literaturno-kriticheskie ocherki v dvukh knigakh*, vol. 1. Moscow: Zaria, 1909.

Adon'eva, S.B. *Kategoriia nenastoiashchego vremeni (antropologicheskie ocherki)*. St Petersburg: Peterburgskoe vostokovedenie, 2001.

Aksakov, A.N. *Animizm i spiritizm. Kriticheskoe issledovanie mediumicheskikh iavlenii i ikh ob'iasneniia gipotezami 'nervnoi sily,' 'galliutsinatsii' i 'bessoznatel'nogo.' V otvet E.F. Gartmanu*. St Petersburg: Tipografiia V. Demakova, 1901.

– *Materialy dlia suzhdeniia ob avtomaticheskom pis'me (iz lichnogo opyta) i dlia suzhdeniia o materializatsii*. St Petersburg: Tipografiia V. Demakova, 1899.

– 'Mediumizm i filosofiia. Vospominaniia o professore Moskovsogo universiteta Iurkeviche.' *Russkii vestnik* 121 (1876): 442–69.

– *Pamiatnik nauchnogo predubezhdeniia. Zakliuchenie mediumicheskoi kommisii fizicheskogo obshchestva pri S.-Peterburgskom universitete*. St Petersburg: Tipografiia V. Bezobrazova, 1883.

– *Pozitivizm v oblasti spiritizma. Po povodu knigi E. Dass'e 'O posmertnom chelovechestve.'* St Petersburg: Rebus, 1884.

– *Ratsionalizm Svedenborga. Kriticheskoe issledovanie ego ucheniia o Sviashchennom pisanii*. Leipzig: F. Wagner, 1870.

Aldanov, Mark. *Ocherki*. Moscow: Novosti, 1995.

Amfiteatrov, A., and E. Anichkov. *Pobedonostev*. St Petersburg: Shipovnik, 1907.

Anikst, A. *Teoriia dramy v Rossii ot Pushkina do Chekhova*. Moscow: Nauka, 1972.

Annenkov, P.V. *Aleksandr Sergeevich Pushkin v Aleksandrovskuiu epokhu: 1799–1826 gg*. St Petersburg: Tipografiia M. Stasiulevicha, 1874.

– *Materialy dlia biografii Aleksandra Sergeevicha Pushkina*. Moscow: Terra, 2007.

Anonymous. 'Portret gospodina Kardeka, znamenitogo sharlatana-spirita.' *Vsemirnaia illiustratsiia* 19 (1869).

– 'Zhurnal'noe obozrenie.' *Delo* 12 (1873).

Antokol'skii, Pavel. *Sobranie sochinenii v 4 tomakh*. Moscow: Khudozhestven-naia Literatura, 1971.

Aristotle. *The Complete Works*, Revised Oxford translation, edited by Jonathan Burry, vol. 1. Princeton: Princeton University Press, 1995.

Audouard, Olympe. *Les mondes des esprits ou la vie après la mort*. Paris: Dentu, 1874.

Baehr, Stephen. 'Art and "The Kreutzer Sonata": A Tolstoian Approach.' *Cana-dian–American Slavic Studies* 10, no. 1 (1976): 39–46.

Bakhtin, Mikhail. *Problems of Dostoevsky's Poetics*, edited and translated by Caryl Emerson. Minneapolis: University of Minnesota Press, 1984.

– *Voprosy literatury i estetiki*. Moscow: Khudozhestvennaia literatura, 1975.

Belyi, Andrei. *Kritika. Estetika. Teoriia simvolizma*, vol. 1. Moscow: Iskusstvo, 1994.

Barsukov, Nikolai. *Zhizn' i trudy M.P. Pogodina*, vol. 17. St Petersburg: A.D. i P.D. Pogodiny, 1903.

Barthes, Roland. 'The Discourse of History.' *Comparative Criticism* 3 (1981): 7–20.

– 'Lecture in Inauguration of the Chair of Literary Semiology, Collège de France, January 7, 1977.' *October* 8 (1979): 3–16.

– 'Myth Today.' In *Mythologies*, selected and translated by Annette Lavers, 142–3. New York: Hill and Wang, 1995.

– 'The Reality Effect.' In *French Literary Theory Today*, edited by Tsvetan Todo-rov. Cambridge: Cambridge University Press, 1982.

Barykin, E.M. *Pushkinskii kinoslovar'*. Moscow: Sovremennye tetradi, 1999.

Beer, Daniel. '"Microbes of the Mind": Moral Contagion in Late Imperial Russia.' *Journal of Modern History* 79, no. 9 (2007): 531–71.

Behrs, S.A. 'Vospominaniia o grafe L.N. Tolstom.' In *L.N. Tolstoi v vospominaniiakh sovremennikov*, I:174–93. Moscow: Khudozhestvennaia literatura, 1987.

Belov, Evgenii. 'O smerti tsarevicha Dimitriia.' *Zhurnal ministerstva narodnogo prosveshcheniia* 168 (1873): 1–44.

Benjamin, Walter. 'The Storyteller: Reflections of the Works of Nikolai Leskov.' In *Illuminations*, translated by Harry Zohn, 83–109. New York: Schocken, 1969.

Bell, Robert. 'Stranger than Fiction.' *Cornhill Magazine*, July (1860).

Benz, Ernst. *Emanuel Swedenborg: Visionary Savant in the Age of Reason*, trans-lated by Nicholas Goodwick-Clarke. West Chester: Swedenborg Foundation, 2002.

Berg, N.V. 'V.I. Dal' i P.V. Nashchokin.' *Russkaia starina* 28, no. 7 (1880): 613–16.

Bergland, Renée L. *The National Uncanny: Indian Ghosts and American Subjects*. Hanover: University Press of New England, 2000.

Berkov, P.N., and V.M. Lavrov. *Bibliografiia proizvedenii Pushkina i literatury o nem. 1886–1899*. Pod redaktsiei B.V. Tomashevskogo. Moscow and Lenin-grad: Izdatel'stvo AN SSSR, 1949.

Berry, Thomas. 'Dostoevsky and Spiritualism.' *Dostoevsky Studies* 2 (1981): 43–50.

– 'Mediums and Spiritualism in Russian Literature during the Reign of Alexander II.' In *The Supernatural in Slavic and Baltic Literature: Essays in Honor of Victor Terras*, edited by Amy Mandelker and Roberta Reeder, 129–44. Columbus: Slavica, 1988.

– *Spiritualism in Tsarist Society and Literature*. Baltimore: Edgar Allan Poe Society, 1985.

Bitsilli, P.M. 'Problema zhizni i smerti v tvorchestve Tolstogo.' In *L.N. Tolstoi: Pro et Contra. Lichnost' L'va Tolstogo v otsenke russkikh myslitelei i issledovatelei. Antologiia*, sostavlenie, vstupitel'naia stat'ia, kommentarii i bibliografiia K.G. Isupov, 473–99. St Petersburg: Izdatel'stvo gumanitarnogo universiteta: Slavica, 2000.

Bitsyn N. (N.M. Pavlov). 'Pravda o Lzhedimitrii.' *Den'* nos. 51–2 (1864).

Blavatsky, H.P. *Collected Writings*, I:1874–1878. Wheaton: Theosophical Press, 1966.

– *Isis Unveiled: A Master-Key to the Mysteries of Ancient and Modern Science and Theology*. London: Bernard Quaritch, 1892.

– 'Marvellous Spirit Manifestations: A Second Ida Pfeiffer with the Eddys – Apparitions of Georgians, Persians, Kurds, Circassians, Africans, and Russians – What a Russian Lady thinks of Dr. Beard.' *Daily Graphic* 5, 20 October (1874): 873.

– 'The Russian Scientists.' *Banner of Light* 39, 24 June (1876): 8.

Boborykin, P.D. 'Ni vzad – ni vpered.' *Sankt Peterburgskie vedomosti*, nos. 75, 82, 89 (1876).

– *Zhertva vecherniaia*. St Petersburg: N.A. Shigin, 1872.

Bogomolov, Nikolai. *Russkaia literatura nachala XX veka i okkul' tizm: Issledovaniia i materially*. Moscow: Novoe literaturnoe obozrenie, 1999.

Boltin, Apollon. *Dogmaty Khristovoi tserkvi, izlozhennye soglasno spiriticheskomu ucheniiu*, 1864.

– *'Spiritizm,' stat'ia Apollona Boltina. (Napechatana v zhurnale 'Raduga.')* St Petersburg: 1864.

– *Zamechaniia na stat'iu I. Sechenova 'Refleksy golovnogo mozga.'* St Petersburg: Tipografiia Doma prizreniia maloletnikh bednykh, 1867.

Bramwell, John Milne. *Hypnotism and Treatment of Suggestion*. London: Cassell, 1909.

Brantlinger, Patrick. '"Imperial Gothic: Atavism and the Occult in the British Adventure Novel, 1880–1914.' In *Gothic: Critical Concepts in Literature and Cultural Studies*, vol. 1, edited by Fred Botting and Dale Townshend. London: Routledge, 2004.

Brierre de Boismont, Alexandre. *Des hallucinations, ou histoire raisonée des appari-tions, des visions, des songes, de l'extase, des rêves, du magnétisme et du somnam-bulisme*. Paris: Germer Baillière, 1845.

Britten, Emma Hardinge. 'Spiritualism in Russia.' In *Nineteenth-Century Mira-cles, or Spirits and Their Work In Every Country of the Earth: A Complete Histori-cal Compendium*. Whitefish, MT: Kessinger, 2003.

Brokgauz, F.A., and I.A. Efron. *Entsiklopedicheskii slovar'*, 86 vols. St Petersburg: Brokgauz i Efron, 1890–1907.

Brown, Edward J. '"So Much Depends": Russian Critics in Search of "Reality."' *Russian Review* 48, no. 4 (1989): 353–81.

Budanova, N.F., and G.M. Fridlender, eds. *Letopis' zhizni i tvorchestva F.M. Dos-toevskogo*, vols. 1–3. St Petersburg: Akademicheskii proekt, 1999.

Buse, Peter, and Andrew Stott. 'Introduction: A Future for Haunting.' In *Ghosts: Deconstruction, Psychoanalysis, History*, edited by Peter Buse and Andrew Stott, 1–20. New York: St Martin's, 1999.

Butlerov, A.M. *Koe chto o mediumizme, i ob izuchenii mediumicheskikh iavlenii*. St Petersburg: Rebus, 1884.

– *Stat'i po mediumizmu. S fototipicheskim portretom avtora i Vospominaniem ob A.M. Butlerove N.P. Vagnera*. St Petersburg: A.N. Aksakov, 1889.

Bykov, V.P. *Spiritizm pered sudom nauki, obshchestva i religii*. S fotografiiami i risunkami. Moscow: Izdanie E.I. Bykovoi, 1914.

Calmet, Augustine. *O iavleniiakh dukhov, v trekh chastiakh*. Moscow: Tipografiia Bakhmeteva, 1866.

Carlson, Maria. *'No Religion Other Than Truth': A History of the Theosophical Movement in Russia, 1875–1922*. Princeton: Princeton University Press, 1993.

Castle, Terry. *The Female Thermometer: Eighteenth-Century Culture and the Inven-tion of the Uncanny*. New York: Oxford University Press, 1995.

Certeau, Michel de. *The Writing of History*, translated by Tom Conley. New York: Columbia University Press, 1988.

Chadwick, Owen. *The Secularization of the European Mind in the Nineteenth Century*. Cambridge: Cambridge University Press, 1975.

Chernyi, Sasha. 'Pushkin v Parizhe (Fantasticheskii rasskaz).' In *Taina Pushkina. Iz prozy i publikatsii pervoi emigratsii*. Moscow: Ellis Lak, 1998.

Chernyshevskii, N.G. "Chto delat'? Iz rasskazov o novykh liudiakh." In *Polnoe sobranie sochinenii v 15 tomakh*. Pod obshchei redaktsiei V.Ia. Kirpotina, vol. 11. Moscow: Khudozhestvennaia literatura, 1939–53.

Chéroux, Clément. 'Ghost Dialectics: Spirit Photography in Entertainment and Belief.' In *The Perfect Medium: Photography and the Occult*. New Haven: Yale University Press, 2005.

Chizhevskii, D. 'Neizvestnyi Gogol'.' *Novyi zhurnal* 27 (1951): 126–58.

- 'Swedenborg bei den Slaven.' In *Aus zwei Welten: Beiträge zur Geschichte der slavisch-westlichen literaturischen Beziehungen*, 269–90. The Hague: Mouton, 1956.

Christian, R.F., ed. *Tolstoy's Diaries*, vol. 1. London: Athlone, 1985.

Chulkov, G.I. 'Avtomaticheskie zapisi Vl. Solov'eva,' *Voprosy filosofii* 8 (1992): 121–32.

Clayton, J. Douglas. *Dimitry's Shade: A Reading of Alexander Pushkin's Boris Godunov*. Evanston: Northwestern University Press, 2004.

Conan Doyle, Arthur. *The History of Spiritualism*, 2 vols. New York: Doran, 1926.

Craddock, Patricia B. *Edward Gibbon: Luminous Historian: 1772–1794*. Baltimore: John Hopkins University Press, 1989.

- *Edward Gibbon: A Reference Guide*. Boston: G.K. Hall, 1987.

Crookes, William. *Researches into the Phenomena of Modern Spiritualism*. London: J. Burns, 1874.

- *Spiritualizm i nauka. Opytnye issledovaniia nad psikhicheskoi siloi Uil'iama Kruksa, chlena Korolevskogo obshchestva*. Sostavil, perevel i izdal A.N. Aksakov. St Petersburg: Tipografiia A.M. Kotomina, 1871.

Danaher, David. 'A Cognitive Approach to Metaphor in Prose: Truth and Falsehood in Leo Tolstoy's "The Death of Ivan Il'ich."' *Poetics Today* 24, no. 3 (2003): 439–69.

Davidson, Pamela. 'Divine Service or Idol Worship? Russian Views of Art as Demonic.' In *Russian Literature and Its Demons*, edited by Pamela Davidson, 125–64. New York: Oxford University Press, 2000.

Davis, A.J. *Stellar Key to the Summerland*. Boston: William White, 1868.

Davydov, N.V. 'Iz proshlogo.' In *L.N. Tolstoi v vospominaniiakh sovremennikov*, II:197–210. Moscow: Khudozhestvennaia literatura, 1978.

Dazur, Victor. 'Le Régiment fantastique,' *Revue spirite*. 9 (1868): 271–9.

Debreczeny, Paul. *Social Functions of Literature: Alexander Pushkin and Russian Culture*. Stanford: Stanford University Press, 1997.

Denisenko, S.V. 'Posmertnaia maska Pushkina (zametki po materialam russkoi emigratsionnoi pechati 1937).' In *Pushkin i drugie*, 148–52. Novgorod: Novgorodskii gosudarstvennyi universitet, 1997.

Denner, Michael A. 'Accidental Art: Tolstoy's Poetics of Unintentionality.' *Philosophy and Literature* 27, no. 2 (2003): 284–303.

Derrida, Jacques. *Specters of Marx: The State of the Debt, the Work of Mourning, and the New International*, translated by Peggy Kamuf. London: Routledge, 1994.

- *On Touching – Jean-Luc Nancy*. Stanford: Stanford University Press, 2005.

Desiatkina, A.P., and G.M. Fridlender. 'Biblioteka Dostoevskogo (Novye materialy).' In *Dostoevskii: Materialy i issledovaniia*, vol. 4, 256–62. Leningrad: Akademiia nauk SSSR, 1980.

Dobroliubov, N.A. *Sobranie sochinenii. V dev'ati tomakh*, vol. 6. Leningrad: Gosudarstvennoe izdatel'stvo khudozhestvennoi literatury, 1961–4.

Dobrotvorskii, Amvrosii. 'Kto byl pervyi Lzhedimitrii?' Nezhin, 1865.

Dole, Nathan Haskell. *The Life of Count Tolstoi*. New York: Scribner, 1929.

Dostoevskii, F.M. *Polnoe sobranie sochinenii v 30 tomakh*. Leningrad: Nauka, 1972–90.

– *The Idiot*, translated with an introduction by David Magarshack. New York: Penguin, 1955.

– *The Notebooks for* The Possessed, edited and with an introduction by Edward Wasiolek. Chicago: University of Chicago Press, 1968.

– *A Writer's Diary*, translated and annotated by Kenneth Lantz. Evanston: Northwestern University Press, 1993.

Doten, Lizzie. *Poems from the Inner Life*. Boston: William White, 1864.

Druzhinin, A.V. 'Rasskaz, pered kotorym vse vymyshlennyi prakh i nichtozhestvo.' In *Polnoe sobranie sochinenii*, VIII:623–33. St Petersburg, 1865–7.

Dunning, Chester. 'Who Was Tsar Dmitrii?' *Slavic Review* 60, no. 4 (2001): 705–29.

Dushechkina, E.V. *Russkii sviatochnyi rasskaz. Stanovlenie zhanra*. St Petersburg: Sankt Peterburgskii gosudarstvennyi universitet, 1995.

Edgerton, William B. 'A Ghostly Urban Legend in Peterburg: Was N.S. Leskov Involved?' *The Supernatural in Slavic and Baltic Literature: Essays in Honor of Victor Terras*, edited by Amy Mandelker and Roberta Reeder, 129–44. Columbus: Slavica, 1988.

Efremov, P.A. 'Mnimyi Pushkin v stikhakh, proze i izobrazheniiakh.' *Novoe vremia* 9851 (1903).

Ehre, Milton. 'A Classic of Russian Realism: Form and Meaning in the *Golovlyovs*.' In *Saltykov-Shchedrin's* The Golovlyovs: *A Critical Companion*, edited by I.P. Foote. Evanston: Northwestern University Press, 1997.

Eikhenbaum, B. 'Chrezmernyi pisatel'.' In *O proze. O poezii*, 237–53. Leningrad: Khudozhestvennaia literatura, 1986.

– *Tolstoi in the Sixties*, translated by Duffield White. Ann Arbor: Ardis, 1982.

Emerson, Caryl. 'Identity Crisis as Revisionist Historical Dramaturgy: The Pretenders of A.K. Tolstoi with a Sidewalk Glance at Pushkin.' *Slavic and East European Journal* 52, no. 1 (2008).

– 'Pretenders to History.' *Slavic Review* 44, no. 2 (1985): 257–79.

– '"The Queen of Spades" and the Open End.' In *Pushkin Today*, edited by David M. Bethea, 31–7. Bloomington: Indiana University Press, 1993.

– 'Tolstoy's Aesthetics.' In *The Cambridge Companion to Tolstoy*, edited by Donna Tussing Orwin, 237–51. Cambridge: Cambridge University Press, 2002.

Encyclopedia of Occultism and Parapsychology, 4th ed., 2 vols. Detroit: Gale Research, 1996.

Engels, Friedrich. 'Natural Science in the Spirit World.' In *Dialectics of Nature,* translated by Clemens Dutt. Moscow: Progress, 1954.

Epstein, Mikhail. 'The Irony of Style: The Demonic Element in Gogol's Concept of Russia.' In *Gogol: Exploring Absence – Negativity in 19th Century Russian Literature,* 55–71. Bloomington: Indiana University Press, 1999.

Epstein-Matveyev, Rebecca. 'The Construction of Identity in A.K. Tolstoi's Dramatic Trilogy.' *Slavic and East European Journal* 52, no. 1 (2008).

Fanger, Donald. *Dostoevsky and Romantic Realism: A Study of Dostoevsky in Relation to Balzac, Dickens, and Gogol.* Cambridge, MA: Harvard University Press, 1965.

Faresov, A.I. *Protiv techenii: N.S. Leskov, ego zhizn', sochineniia, polemika i vospominaniia o nem.* St Petersburg: Tipografiia M. Merkusheva, 1904.

Fedorov, Nikolai. *Filosofiia obshchego dela,* vols. 1–2. Vernyi: Tipografiia Semirechenskogo oblastnogo pravleniia, 1906–13.

Fel'dman, Osip. 'Otnoshenie Tolstogo k gipnotizmu.' In *Mezhdunarodnyi tolstovskii al'manakh, sostavlennyi P. Sergeenko,* 354–8. Moscow: Kniga, 1909.

Fel'kner, K. 'Golosa iz-za groba.' *Kolos'ia* 11 (1889): 297–9.

Feofan Zatvornik [G.V. Govorov]. 'Pis'ma o dukhovnoi zhizni.' *Domashniaia beseda* 43 (1869).

Feuer Miller, Robin. 'Dostoevsky's "The Dream of a Ridiculous Man": Unsealing the Generic Envelope.' In *Freedom and Responsibility in Russian Literature: Essays in Honor of Robert Louis Jackson,* edited by Elizabeth Cheresh Allen and Gary Saul Morson, 86–104. Evanston: Northwestern University Press, 1995.

Filaret [V.M. Drozdov]. *O stologadanii (vypiska iz pis'ma ot 29 oktiabria 1853 goda.* Moscow: Tipografiia V. Gotie, 1853.

Florenskii, Pavel. 'Spiritizm kak antikhristianstvo. Po povodu dvukh poem: "Lestvitsa" Al. Miropol'skogo, 1902; A. Belyi. "Severnaia simfoniia (1-aia geroicheskaia)."' In *Sochineniia v 4-kh tomakh,* vol. 1. Moscow: Mysl', 1994.

Florovskii, Georgii. *Puti russkogo bogosloviia.* Paris: YMCA Press, 1983.

Frank, Joseph. *Dostoevsky: The Miraculous Years, 1865–1871.* Princeton: Princeton University Press, 1995.

Freeborn, Richard. 'The Nineteenth Century: The Age of Realism: 1855–80.' In *The Cambridge History of Russian Literature,* 248–332. Cambridge: Cambridge University Press, 1996.

Freidenberg, Ol'ga. *Poetika siuzheta i zhanra.* Podgotovka teksta i obshchaia redaktsiia N.V. Braginskoi, 2-e izdanie. Moscow: Labirint, 1997.

Freud, Sigmund. 'The Uncanny.' In *The Stanford Edition of the Complete Psychological Works of Sigmund Freud,* translated under the general editorship of James Strachney, vol. 17. London: Hogarth, 1917–19.

Furst, Lilian R. *All Is True: The Claims and Strategies of Realist Fiction*. Durham: Duke University Press, 1995.

Gamma [G.K. Gradovskii]. 'V mire chertovshchiny.' *Golos*, 23 November (1875).

Garber, Marjorie. *Shakespeare's Ghost Writers: Literature as Uncanny Causality*. New York: Methuen, 1987.

Gasparov, B.M. *Poeticheskii iazyk Pushkina kak fakt istorii russkogo literaturnogo iazyka*. Vienna: Wiener Slawistischer Almanach, 1992.

Gauld, Alan. *A History of Hypnotism*. Cambridge: Cambridge University Press, 1992.

Genlis, Stéphanie Félicité de. *Esprit du madame de Genlis, ou, portraits, caracteres, maximes et pensees, extraits de tous ses ouvrages publies jusqu'a ce jour*. Par M. Demonceuax, avocat. Paris: Maradan, 1806.

Genlis, Mme. 'Nechto o grafe Benevskom i angliiskom istorike Dzhibbone.' *Vestnik Evropy* 15, no. 9 (1804): 56–60.

Gershenzon, Mikhail. *P.Ia. Chaadaev: Zhizn' i myshlenie*. St Petersburg: 1908.

– *Stat'i o Pushkine*. Leningrad: Gosudarstvennaia akademiia khudozhestven-nykh nauk, 1926.

Giliarov, A.N. *Gipnotizm po ucheniiu shkoly Sharko i psikhologicheskoi shkoly (1881–1893)*. Kiev: Tipografiia Imperatorskogo universiteta sv. Vladimira, 1894.

Ginzburg, Lidia. *On Psychological Prose*. Princeton: Princeton University Press, 1991.

– *O psikhologicheskoi proze*. Leningrad: Sovetskii pisatel', 1974.

Gogol', Nikolai. *Sobranie sochinenii*, vols. 1–7. Moscow: Khudozhestvennaia lit-eratura, 1976.

Gordin, Michael D. 'Loose and Baggy Spirits: Reading Dostoevskii and Mende-leev.' *Slavic Review* 60, no. 4 (2001): 756–80.

– *A Well-Ordered Thing: Dmitrii Mendeleev and the Shadow of the Periodic Table*. Princeton: Princeton University Press, 2003.

Gordon, Avery F. *Ghostly Matters: Haunting and the Sociological Imagination*. Minneapolis: University of Minnesota Press, 1978.

Gossman, Lionel. *Between History and Literature*. Cambridge: Harvard University Press, 1990.

Gauthier, E. Paul. 'Zola's Literary Reputation in Russia prior to "L'Assom-moir."' *French Review* 33, no. 1 (1959): 37–44.

Gren, A.N. *Spirit: sborniik statei po spiritizmu i eskhatologii*, vol. 1. Piatigorsk: Tipografiia A.P. Sadovnikova, 1902.

Greenblatt, Stephen. *Hamlet in Purgatory*. Princeton: Princeton University Press, 2001.

Grossman, Joan Delaney. 'Alternate Beliefs: Spiritualism and Pantheism among the Early Modernists.' In *Christianity and the Eastern Slavs*, edited by Boris Gasparov, Robert H. Hughes, Irina Paperno, and Olga Raevsky-Hughes, vol. 3. Berkeley: University of California Press, 1995.

Grossman, Leonid. *Biblioteka Dostoevskogo. Po neizdannym materialam. S prilozheniem kataloga biblioteki Dostoevskogo.* Odessa: A.A. Ivasenko, 1919.

– *Leskov. Zhizn' – Tvorchestvo – Poetika.* Moscow: Goslitizdat, 1945.

Grot, Ia.K. 'Rech'.' In *Venok na pamiatnik Pushkinu. Pushkinskie dni v Moskve, Peterburge i provintsii.* St Petersburg: Tipografia A. Transhelia, 1880.

Güldenstubbe, L. de. *La realite des esprits et le phenomene merveilleux de leur ecriture directe.* Paris: Librairie A. Franck, 1857.

Gustafson, Richard. *Leo Tolstoy: Resident and Stranger.* Princeton: Princeton University Press, 1986.

Hallengren, Anders. 'Russia, Swedenborg, and the Eastern Mind.' *New Philosophy* 43, no. 4 (1990): 391–407.

Hare, Robert. *Opytnye issledovaniia o spiritualizme Roberta Gera,* translated by Alexander Aksakov and Vladimir Dal'. Leipzig: F. Wagner, 1866.

Herman, Luc. *Concepts of Realism.* Columbia: Camden House, 1996.

Hess, David J. *Spirits and Scientists: Ideology, Spiritism, and Brazilian Culture.* University Park: Penn State University Press, 1991.

Högy, Tatjana. *Jung-Stilling und Russland.* Siegen: Selbstverlag der J.G. Herder-Bibliothek, 1984.

Holquist, Michael. 'The Supernatural as Social Force in *Anna Karenina.*' In *The Supernatural in Slavic and Baltic Literature: Essays in Honor of Victor Terras,* edited by Amy Mandelker and Roberta Reeder, 176–90. Columbus: Slavica, 1988.

Horowitz, Brian. *The Myth of A.S. Pushkin in Russia's Silver Age: M.O. Gershenzon, Pushkinist.* Evanston: Northwestern University Press, 1996.

Houghton, Walter E. *The Victorian Frame of Mind, 1830–1870.* New Haven: Yale University Press, 1957.

Iaroshevskii, M.G. *Istoriia psikhologii ot antichnosti do serediny XX veka.* Moscow: Mysl', 1996.

Iezuitova, R.V. 'Evoliutsiia obraza Pushkina v russkoi poezii XIX veka.' *Pushkin: Issledovaniia i materialy,* V:113–39. Leningrad: Nauka, 1967.

Ignatii (Brianchaninov D.A.). 'Slovo o smerti.' In *Sochineniia episkopa Ignatiia Brianchaninova* [Reprintnoe izdanie]. Moscow: P.S., 1991.

Iliushin, Aleksandr. 'Ivan Barkov i drugie.' In *Tri veka russkogo Erosa. Publikatsii i issledovaniia,* sostaviteli A. Shchuplov and A. Iliushin. Moscow: Piat' vecherov, 1992.

Il'in-Tomich, A.A. 'Dal' Vladimir Ivanovich.' In *Russkie pisateli. 1800–1917. Biograficheskii slovar'*, vol. 2. Moscow: Bol'shaia rossiiskaia entsiklopediia, 1992.

Istoriia russkoi literatury, vols. 1–4. Leningrad: Nauka, 1980–3.

Jackson, Robert Lewis. *The Art of Dostoevsky: Deliriums and Nocturnes*. Princeton: Princeton University Press, 1981.

Jahn, Gary R. 'The Aesthetic Theory of Leo Tolstoy's *What Is Art?*' *Journal of Aesthetics and Art Criticism* 34, no. 1 (1975): 59–65.

Jakobson, Roman. *Language in Literature*, edited by Krystyna Pomorska and Stephen Rudy. Cambridge, MA: Belknap, 1987.

– *Puškin and His Sculptural Myth*, edited and translated by John Burbank. The Hague: Mouton, 1975.

Johnson, W. Stacy. 'The Genesis of Ariel.' *Shakespeare Quarterly* 2, no. 3 (1951): 205–20.

Jones, Malcolm V. *Dostoevsky after Bakhtin: Readings in Dostoevsky's Fantastic Realism*. Cambridge: Cambridge University Press, 1990.

Joravsky, David. *Russian Psychology: A Critical History*. Oxford: Oxford University Press, 1989.

Jung-Stilling, Johann Heinrich. *Theorie der Geisterkunde*. Reading: Gedruckt und verlegt von Heinrich B. Sage, 1816.

Kallash, V. *Puschkiniana*, vols. 1–2. Kiev: Tipografiia I.I. Chokolova, 1902–3.

Kallash, V., ed. *Russkie poety o Pushkine. Sbornik stikhotvorenii*. Moscow: Tipografiia G. Lissnera i A. Geshelia, 1899.

Kandinskii, V.Khr. *Obshcheponiatnye psikhologicheskie etiudi*, Moscow: A. Lang, 1881.

Karamzin, N.M. *Istoriia gosudarstva Rossiiskogo*, vols. 1–3. Moscow: Kniga, 1988–9.

Karatygin, P.A. 'Vecher u generala Katenina.' *Russkaia starina* 11 (1880): 753–7.

Kardec, [Allan]. *Dukhovnaia filosofiia. Kniga dukhov*, 3 vols., translated by Apollon Boltin, OR RGB, fond 344 (Shibanov), no. 351.

Kardec, Allan. *Opytnyi spiritizm. Kniga mediumov ili rukovodstvo dlia mediumov i vyzyvanii*, translated by Apollon Boltin. OR RGB, fond 344 (Shibanov), no. 352.

– *Spiritizm v samom prostom ego vyrazhenii. Kratkoe ob'iasnenie ucheniia dukhov i ikh proiavleniia*, translated by Apollon Boltin. Leipzig: Franz Wagner, 1864.

– *The Spirits' Book*, translated by Anna Blackwell. New York: Arno, 1976.

Kaufman, L. 'Sovremennyi Kaliostro.' *Volny* 8 (1912): 73–80.

Kazanskii, D.L. 'Issledovanie o lichnosti pervogo Lzhedimitriia.' *Russkii vestnik* 8–10 (1877).

Kavelin, Konstantin. *Zadachi psikhologii. Soobrazheniia o metodakh i programme psikhologicheskikh issledovanii*. St Petersburg: Tipografiia F. Sushchinskogo, 1872.

Keeble, Ida M. Everett. *Beyond Earth's Fears: Talks Dictated by Ivan Sergevitch Turgenev to Ida M. Everett Keeble*. Ipswich: W.E. Harrison, 1936.

Kerr, Howard. *Mediums, and Spirit-Rappers, and Roaring Radicals: Spiritualism in American Literature, 1850–1900*. Urbana: University of Illinois Press, 1972.

Khartman [Hartman], Ekhbert. 'Elena Ivanovna Molokhovets,' *Zvezda* 3 (2000): 107–11.

Kholodov, E.G. 'Repertuar.' In *Istoriia russkogo dramaticheskogo teatra*, vol. 3, edited by E.G. Kholodova. Moscow: Nauka, 1980.

Khrisanf [V.N. Retivtsev]. 'Emmanuil Svedenborg i ego verouchenie.' *Khristianskoe chtenie* 1 (1866).

Kiiko, E.I. 'Realizm fantasticheskogo v glave "Chert. Koshmar Ivana Fyodorovicha,"' In *Dostoevskii. Materialy i issledovaniia*, vol. 4, 256–62. Leningrad: Nauka, 1980.

Kostomarov, N.I. *Izbrannye proizvedeniia. Avtobiografiia*. Kiev: Izdatel'stvo pri Kievskom gosudarstvennom universitete, 1989.

– *Kto byl pervyi Lzhedimitrii?* St Petersburg: Tipografiia V. Bezobrazova, 1864.

– *Russkaia istoriia v zhizneopisaniiakh ee glavneishikh deiatelei*, vols. 1–3. St Petersburg: 1873–88.

Kovalevskii, P.I. *Generalissimus Suvorov. Orleanskaia deva. Magomet. Svedenborg. Psikhiatricheskie eskizy iz istorii v dvukh tomakh*, 6th ed., vol. 2. St Petersburg: Tipografiia M.I. Akinfieva, 1908.

Kselman, Thomas. *Death and the Afterlife in Modern France*. Princeton: Princeton University Press, 1993.

Lacassagne, Jean-Pierre, ed. *Histoire d'une amitié (d'après une correspondance inédite 1836–1866): Pierre Leroux et George Sand*. Paris: Klincksieck, 1973.

Lann, Evgenii. *Literaturnye mistifikatsii*. Moscow and Leningrad: Gosizdat, 1930.

Lazarev, V.Ia., and O.E. Tuganova. 'Transformatsiia obraza Pushkina v tainikakh sovremennogo soznaniia.' In *Pushkin i sovremennaia kul'tura*, 199–206. Moscow: Nauka, 1996.

Leatherbarrow, William J. *A Devil's Vaudeville: The Demonic in Dostoevsky's Major Fiction*. Evanston: Northwestern University Press, 2005.

Lebedev, Mikhail. 'Spirity i spiritizm.' *Khristianskoe chtenie*, nos. 2–7 (1866): 24–101, 265–315, 615–707.

Lebon, G. *Psikhologiia narodov i mass*, translated by Ia. Fridman and E. Pimenova. St Petersburg: Izdatel'stvo F. Pavlenkova, 1896.

Ledkovsky, Marina. *The Other Turgenev: From Romanticism to Symbolism*. Würzburg: Jal-Verlag, 1973.

Leighton, Lauren G. *The Esoteric Tradition in Russian Romantic Literature: Decembrism and Freemasonry*. University Park: Penn State University Press, 1994.

Lesevich, V. 'Modnoe sueverie. ("Chto takoe spiritizm i ego iavleniia" A. Sumarokova). *Otechestvennye zapiski* 199, no. 12 (1866): 181–210.

Leskov, Andrei. *Zhizn' Nikolaia Leskova: po ego semeinym i nesemeinym zapisiam i pamiati*, 2 vols. Moscow: Khudozhetsvennaia literatura, 1984.

Leskov, Nikolai. 'Modnyi vrag tserkvi. (Spiritizm pod vzgliadom nashikh dukhovnykh pisatelei).' In N.S. Leskov, *Polnoe sobranie sochinenii v 30 tomakh*, VII:261–7, 270–300.

– 'Pis'mo v redaktsiiu. Mediumicheskii seans 13-go fevralia.' *Grazhdanin* 9 (1876).

– *Polnoe sobranie sochinenii v 30 tomakh*. Moscow: Terra, 1996.

– 'Velikie mira v budushchem ikh sushchestvovanii. Fantasticheskii polk na Marse.' In: N.S. Leskov, *Polnoe sobranie sochinenii v 30 tomakh*, VIII:117–27.

Levine, George. *The Realistic Imagination: English Fiction from Frankenstein to Lady Chatterley*. Chicago: University of Chicago Press, 1981.

Leving, Iurii. 'Vladimir Nabokov i Sasha Chernyi.' *Literaturnoe obozrenie* 2 (1999): 52–7.

Levitt, Marcus. *Russian Literary Politics and the Pushkin Celebration of 1880*. Ithaca: Cornell University Press, 1989.

Likhachev, Dmitry. *A History of Russian Literature, 11th–17th Centuries*, translated by K.M. Cook-Horujy. Moscow: Raduga, 1989.

Linton, Eliza Lynn. 'Modern Magic.' *All the Year Round*, 28 July (1860).

Littré, E. 'Govor'ashchie stoly i stuchashchie dukhi.' *Sovremennik* 58 (1856): 24–47.

Lotman, Iu.M. *Izbrannye trudy*, vols. 1–3. Tallinn: Aleksandra, 1992–3.

– 'K probleme raboty s nedostovernymi istochnikami.' In *Pushkin. Biografiia pisatelia – Stat'i i zametki. 1960–1990 – "Evgenii Onegin." Kommentarii*. St Petersburg: Iskusstvo, 1995.

– 'Tema kart i kartochnoi igry v russkoi literature nachala XIX veka.' In *Trudy po znakovym sistemam* 7 (1975): 120–42.

Lotman, Iu.M., and B.A. Uspenskii. 'Rol' dual'nykh modelei v dinamike russkoi kul'tury (do kontsa XVIII veka).' In B.A. Uspenskii, *Izbrannye trudy*. Moscow: Iskusstvo, 1996–7.

Lotman, L. 'Stikhotvornaia dramaturgiia Ostrovskogo (1866–1873).' In A.N. Ostrovskii, *Polnoe sobranie sochinenii 7*. Moscow: Iskusstvo, 1977.

Luk'ianov, S.M. *O Vl. Solov'eve v ego molodye gody. Materialy k biografii*, 4 vols. Moscow: Kniga, 1990 [reprint of the 1916–21 edition].

Maiakovskii, V.V. *Polnoe sobranie sochinenii*, 13 vols. Moscow: Gosudarstvennoe izdatel'stvo khudozhestvennoi literatury, 1955–61.

Maiorova, Ol'ga. 'Tsarevich-samozvanets v sotsial'noi mifologii poreformennoi epokhi.' *Rossiia/Russia* 3 (1999): 210–29.

Makoveeva, Irina. 'Gospoda Golovlevy as Devastated Idyll.' *AATSEEL. Program of the 2004 Annual Meeting* (Philadelphia).

Maley, Willy. 'Specters of Engels.' In *Ghosts: Deconstruction, Psychoanalysis, History*, edited by Peter Buse and Andrew Stott, 23–49. London: Macmillan, 1999.

Markevich, A. 'Kostomatov, Nikolai Ivanovich.' In *Russkii biograficheskii slovar'*, vol. 9. St Petersburg: Tipografiia Glavnogo upravleniia udelov, 1903.

Markov, E. 'Magiia pod krylom nauki.' *Golos* 152 (1875).

Martinsen, Deborah A. *Surprised by Shame: Dostoevsky's Liars and Narrative Exposure*. Columbus: Ohio State University Press, 2003.

Marx, Karl, and Friedrich Engels. *The German Ideology: With Selections from Parts Two and Three, Together with Marx's 'Introduction to a Critique of Political Economy.'* New York: International Publishers, 1970.

Masing-Delic, Irene. *Abolishing Death: A Salvation Myth of Russian Twentieth-Century Literature*. Stanford: Stanford University Press, 1992.

Matlock, John. 'Ghostly Politics.' *Diacritics* 3 (2000): 53–71.

Mazour, Anatole G. *Modern Russian Historiography*. Westport: Greenwood, 1975.

McLaughlin, Sigrid. 'Tolstoy and Schopenhauer.' *California Slavic Studies* 5 (1970): 187–245.

McLean, Hugh. *Nikolai Leskov: The Man and His Art*. Cambridge, MA: Harvard University Press, 1977.

McNair, John. 'Dostoevsky, "Bobok," Pierre Bobo, and Boborykin.' In *Dostoevsky on the Threshold of Other Worlds: Essays in Honour of Malcolm V. Jones*, edited by Sarah Young and Leslie Milne, 84–96. Ilkeston: Bramcote, 2006.

Mel'nikov-Pecherskii, P.I. 'Vospominaniia o Vladimire Ivanoviche Dale.' In *V.I. Dal' i Obshchestvo Liubitelei Rossiiskoi Slovesnosti*. St Petersburg: Zlatoust, 2002.

Mendeleev, D.I. *Materialy dlia suzhdeniia o spiritizme*. St Petersburg: Tipografiia tovarishchestva Obshchestvennaia pol'za, 1876.

– *Sochineniia*, vol. 24. Moscow and Leningrad: GONTI, 1954.

Meyer, Marvin W. 'Introduction.' *The Secret Teachings of Jesus: Four Gnostic Gospels*, translated by Marvin Meyer. New York: Vintage, 1984.

Miller, Robin Feuer. 'Dostoevsky's "The Dream of a Ridiculous Man."' In Elizabeth Cheresh Allen and Gary Saul Morson, eds, *Freedom and Responsibility in Russian Literature: Essays in Honor of Robert Louis Jackson*. Evanston: Northwestern University Press, 1995.

Miłosz, Czeslaw. 'Dostoevsky and Swedenborg.' In *Emperor of the Earth: Modes of Eccentric Vision*. Berkeley: University of California Press, 1977.

Minaev, Dmitri. 'Komy na Rusi zhit' khorosho.' *Iskra* 12 (1873).

Mochul'skii, Konstantin. *Gogol'. Solov'ev. Dostoevskii*. Moscow: Respublika, 1995.

Monroe, John Warne. *Laboratories of Faith: Mesmerism, Spiritism, and Occultism in Modern France*. Ithaca: Cornell University Press, 2008.

– 'Making the Seance "Serious": "Tables Tournantes" and Second Empire Bourgeois Culture, 1853–1861.' *History of Religions* 38, no. 3 (1999): 228–9.

Mordovtsev, D.L. *Samozvantsy i ponizovaia vol'nitsa*, 2 vols. Moscow: M.O. Vol'f, 1867.

Morogues, Inès Muller de. 'Leskov et le Spiritisme.' In *Schweizarische Beitrage zum IX. Internationalen Slavistenkongress in Kiev, September 1983*, 113–32. Bern, Frankfurt, New York: 1983.

– *'Le Probléme feminine' et les portraits de femmes dans l'ouevre de Nikolaj Leskov.* Bern: Peter Lang, 1991.

Morson, Gary Saul. 'Introductory Study: Dostoevsky's Great Experiment.' In *Fyodor Dostoevsky, A Writer's Diary*, vol. 1. Evanston: Northwestern University Press, 1993.

Moskovskaia izobrazitel'naia pushkiniana. Moscow: Izobrazitel'noe iskusstvo, 1975.

Moskovskaia izobrazitel'naia pushkiniana. Moscow: Izobrazitel'noe iskusstvo, 1991.

Murav, Harriet. *Holy Foolishness: Dostoevskii's Novels and the Politics of Cultural Critique.* Stanford: Stanford University Press, 1992.

Musorgskii v vospominaniiakh sovremennikov. Moscow: Muzyka, 1989.

Nabokov, Vladimir. *Sobranie sochinenii v 4 tomakh.* Moscow: Pravda, 1990.

Nekliudov, S.Iu. 'Tsyplionok zharenyi, tsyplionok parenyi.' *Fol'klor i post-fol'klor: Struktura, tipologiia, semiotika.* http://www.ruthenia.ru/folklore/neckludov19.htm.

Nikolaev, D.P. *Smekh Shchedrina. Ocherki satiricheskoi poetiki.* Moscow: Sovetskii pisatel', 1988.

Obatnin, Gennadi. *Ivanov-mistik: Okkul'tnye motivy v poezii i proze Viacheslava Ivanova.* Moscow: Novoe literaturnoe obozrenie, 2000.

Oduar [Audouard], Olimpiia. *Spiritizm. Mir dukhov ili zhizn' posle smerti*, translated from French by Samarina. St Petersburg: Tipografiia Transhelia, 1875.

Olcott, Henry S. *People from the Other World.* Hartford: American Publishing, 1874.

Oppenheim, Janet. *The Other World: Spiritualism and Psychical Research in England, 1850–1914.* New York: Cambridge University Press, 1985.

Orwin, Donna Tussing, ed. *Cambridge Companion to Tolstoy.* Cambridge: Cambridge University Press, 2002.

– 'Did Dostoevsky or Tolstoy Believe in Miracles?' In *A New Word on The Brothers Karamazov*, 125–41. Evanston: Northwestern University Press, 2004.

Osinin, I.G. 'Shvedenborg i ego uchenie.' *Khristianskoe chtenie* 29 (1859): 80–94.

Ostrovskii, A.N. *Polnoe sobranie sochinenii v 12 tomakh.* Moscow: Iskusstvo, 1973–80.

Otechestvo: Kraevedcheskii al'manakh 17 (1999).

Owen, Alex. *The Darkened Room: Women, Power, and Spiritualism in Late Victorian England.* Philadelphia: University of Pennsylvania Press, 1990.

Owen, R.D. *The Debatable Land Between This World and the Next*. New York: G.W. Carlton & Co., 1872.

Panchenko, A. 'Spiritizm i russkaia literatura: iz istorii sotsial'noi terapii.' In *Trudy otdeleniia istoriko-filologicheskikh nauk RAN*. Moscow: Nauka, 2005.

Paperno, Irina. 'Pushkin v zhizni cheloveka Serebrianogo veka.' In *Cultural Mythologies of Russian Modernism: From the Golden Age to the Silver Age*, edited by Boris Gasparov, Robert P. Hughes, and Irina Paperno, 19–51. Berkeley: University of California Press, 1992.

– 'Nietzscheanism and the Return of Pushkin in Twentieth-Century Russian Culture.' In *Nietzsche and Soviet Culture: Ally and Adversary*, edited by Bernice Glatzer Rosenthal, 211–32. Cambridge, MA: Harvard University Press, 1994.

Pavlishchev, L.N. *Vospominaniia ob A.S. Pushkine: Iz semeinoi khroniki*. Moscow: Universitetskaia tipografiia, 1890.

Petrovo-Solovovo, M. 'Obituary: Mr A.N. Aksakoff.' *Journal of the Society for Psychical Research* 11 (1903): 45–9.

– *Prilozheniia k perevodu sochineniia F. Podmora 'Spiritizm.'* St Petersburg: Slovo, 1905.

Phillips, Roger W. 'Dostoevskij's "Bobok": A Dream of a Timid Man.' *Slavic and East European Journal* 18, no. 2 (1974): 132–42.

Pisarev, D.I. 'Skholastika XIX veka.' *Polnoe sobranie sochinenii i pisem v 12 tomakh*, vol. 2. Leningrad: Nauka, 2000.

– 'Realisty.' *Polnoe sobranie sochinenii i pisem*, vol. 6. Leningrad: Nauka, 2003.

Platt, Kevin M.F. *History in a Grotesque Key: Russian Literature and the Idea of Revolution*. Stanford: Stanford University Press, 1997.

– *Terror and Greatness: Ivan IV and Peter I as Russian Myths*. Ithaca: Cornell University Press, forthcoming.

Pletnev, P.A. 'Iz perepiski s Ia. K. Grotom.' In *Pushkin v vospominaniiakh sovremennikov*, II:290–2. St Petersburg: Akademicheskii proekt, 1998.

Podmore, Frank. *Modern Spiritualism: A History and Criticism*, 2 vols. London: Methuen, 1902.

Poddubnaia, R.N. 'Stanovlenie kontseptsii lichnosti u N.S. Leskova. (Raznovidnosti i funktsii fantasticheskogo v romane "Na Nozhakh."' In *Tvorchestvo N.S. Leskova*, 2–32. Kursk: Kurskii GPI, 1988.

Pogodin, M.P. 'O stat'e V.A. Zhukovskogo o privideniiakh.' *Russkaia beseda* 1 (1856).

– *Prostaia rech' o mudrenykh veshchakh*. Moscow: V.M. Frish, 1873.

Polkanov, Ivan. 'O zhizni dushi po vossoedinenii eia s telom, vo vseobshchem voskresenii mertvykh.' *Strannik* 14, no. 1 (1873): 13–40.

Polonskii, Ia.P. 'Starye i novye dukhi.' *Polnoe sobranie sochinenii v 10 tomakh*, vol. 1. St Petersburg: Zh.A. Polonskaia, 1885.

Poluektova, I.V. 'M.E. Saltykov-Shchedrin: Skazki i filosofiia.' *Soffia: Rukopisnyi zhurnal Obshchestva revnitelei russkoi filosofii* 2–3 (2001). http://www.eunnet .net/sofia/02-3-2000/text/0215.htm.

Portnova, N.A. 'K probleme paradoksal'nosti stilia Dostoevskogo.' In *Dostoevskii: Materialy i issledovaniia*, VII:91–101. Leningrad: Nauka, 1987.

Potulov, N. 'Otvet na vopros.' *Domashniaia beseda* 43 (1869).

– *Prodolzhenie 'Bor'by s Igushchei uchenost'iu.'* St Petersburg: V tipografii I.I. Glazunova, 1874.

– 'Spiritizm i ego znachenie.' *Domashniaia beseda* 30 (1869).

Pozdiejew, Wiaczeslaw. 'Mistika i satira v sviatochnom rasskaze.' In *Satyra w literaturakh wschodnioslowianskich. IV. Studia*, pod. red. Wandy Supy, 136–43. Bialystok, 2000.

Preminger, Alex, and T.V.F. Brogan, eds. *New Princeton Encyclopedia of Poetry and Poetics*. Princeton: Princeton University Press, 1993.

Pribytkov, V.I. *Legenda starinnogo baronskogo zamka: Ne byl' i ne skazka*. St Petersburg: Rebus, 1883.

– *Spiritizm v Rossii: ot vozniknoveniia ego do nastoiashchikh dnei*. St Petersburg: Rebus, 1909.

Primak, Thomas M. *Mykola Kostomarov: A Biography*. Toronto: University of Toronto Press, 1996.

'Protokoly zasedanii russkogo obshchestva eksperimental'noi psikhologii.' *Voprosy filosofii i psikhologii* 22 (1894): 4–10.

Prutkov, Koz'ma. *Sochineniia*. Moscow: Khudozhestvennaia literatura, 1976.

Pumpianskii, L.V. 'Gruppa "tainstvennykh povestei."' In. I.S. Turgenev, *Sochineniia*, vol. 8, v–xx. Moscow and Leningrad: GIKHL, 1929.

Pushkin, A.S. *Polnoe sobranie sochinenii v 19 tomakh*. Moscow: Voskresen'e, 1994–7.

– *Collected Narrative and Lyrical Poetry*, translated by Walter Arndt. Ann Arbor: Ardis, 1984.

– *Sochineniia*, izdanie P.V. Annenkova, 2 vols. St Petersburg: Sovremennik, 1855.

– *'Ten' Barkova': Teksty. Kommentarii. Ekskursy.* Moscow: Iazyki slavianskoi kul'tury, 2002.

Rabaté, Jean-Michel. *Ghosts of Modernity*. Gainesville: University Press of Florida, 1996.

Rachinskii, S. 'Po povodu spiriticheskikh soobshchenii g. Vagnera, pomeshchennykh v Russkom vestnike za 1875 god.' *Russkii Vestnik* 5 (1875): 380–99.

Raevskii, N.A. *Drug Pushkina Pavel Voinovich Nashchokin*. Leningrad: Nauka, 1976.

Rainov, T. 'Estetika Tolstogo i ego iskusstvo.' In *Estetika L'va Tolstogo. Sbornik statei*, pod redaktsiei P.N. Sakulina, 27–99. Moscow: Gosudarstvennaia Akademiia khudozhestvennykh nauk, 1929.

Reitblat, A.I. 'Kryzhanovskaia.' *Russkie pisateli, 1800–1917*. Biograficheskii slo-var', vol 3. Moscow: Sovetskaia entsiklopediia, 1994.

Robinson, Douglas. 'Tolstoy's Infection Theory and the Aesthetics of De- and Repersonalization.' *Tolstoy Studies Journal* 19 (2007): 33–53.

Rose, Seraphim. *The Soul after Death: Contemporary "After-Death" Experiences in the Light of the Orthodox Teachings on the Afterlife*. Platina: St Herman of Alaska Brotherhood, 1994.

Rosenthal, Bernice, ed. *The Occult in Russian and Soviet Culture*. Ithaca: Cornell University Press, 1997.

Roshchin, Mikhail. 'Svedenborg v Rossii.' In E. Svedenborg, *Novyi Ierusalim i ego nebesnoe uchenie*, 15–20. Voronezh: 1996.

Rossetti, William Michael. *Rossetti Papers: 1860 to 1870*. New York: Ams, 1903.

Rozenbach, P. 'Gipnotizm.' *Entsiklopedicheskii slovar'*. St Petersburg: 1893.

S.A. *Zhivye rechi otzhivshikh liudei*. St Petersburg: 1905.

Sakulin, P.N. *Iz istorii russkogo idealizma: Kn. V.F. Odoevskii. Myslitel'. Pisatel'*, vol. I, part 1. Moscow: Izdanie M. i S. Sabashnikovykh, 1913.

Saltykov-Shchedrin, M.E. *Sobranie sochinenii v 20 tomakh*. Moscow: Khudo-zhestvennaia literatura, 1965–77.

– *The Golovlyov Family*, translated by Natalie Duddington. New York: NYRB Press, 2001.

– *The History of a Town*, trans. by I.P. Foote. Oxford: Willem A. Meeuws, 1980.

Samuels, Maurice. *The Spectacular Past: Popular History and the Novel in Nine-teenth-Century France*. Ithaca: Cornell University Press, 2004.

Sandler, Stephanie. *Commemorating Pushkin: Russia's Myth of a National Poet*. Stanford: Stanford University Press, 2004.

Sechenov, I.M. 'Zamechaniia na knigu Kavelina *Zadachi psikhologii*.' In *Izbran-nye filosofskie i psikhologicheskie proizvedeniia*. Moscow: Gosudarstvennoe izda-tel'stvo politicheskoi litaratury, 1947.

– 'Refleksy golovnogo mogza.' *Izbrannye proizvedemiia*, vol. 1. Moscow: Izda-tel'stvo Akademii nauk SSSR, 1952.

– *Reflexes of the Brain*. Russian text edited by K. Koshtoyants, translated by S. Belsky, edited by G. Gibbons, notes by S. Gellerstein. Cambridge, MA: MIT Press, 1965.

Selivanov, I.V. *Vospominaniia proshedshego: Byli, rasskazy, portrety, ocherki i proch.*, vol. 2. Moscow: Tipografiia V. Got'ie, 1868.

Senderovich, Savely. 'On Pushkin's Mythology: The Shade-Myth.' In *Alexander Pushkin: II Symposium. New York University Slavic Papers*, III:103–15. Columbus: Slavica, 1980.

Shepard, Jesse. 'Experiences in High Life in Russia.' *Religio-Philosophical Journal* 18, nos. 12/13 (1875).

Shepard, Leslie A., ed. *Encyclopedia of Occultism and Parapsychology,* 4th edition. New York: Gale, 1996.

Sherson, Erroll. *London's Lost Theatres of the Nineteenth Century; with Notes on Plays and Players Seen There.* London: John Lane, 1925.

Shkliarevskii, A. 'Chto dumat' o spiritizme; Kritika togo berega.' *Vestnik Evropy* 6–7 (1875).

Shleiden, M.Ia. *Etiudy: Populiarnye chteniia M.I. Shleidena, avtora "Rastenie i ego zhizn'."* Moscow: A.I. Glazunov, 1861.

Sholomova, T.V. 'Dostoevskii i Svedenborg.' In *Dostoevskii i sovremennost'. Materialy VIII Mezhdunarodnykh starorusskikh chtenii,* 248–51. Novgorod, 1994.

Šilbajoris, Rimvydas. *Tolstoy's Aesthetics and His Art.* Columbus: Slavica, 1991.

Sirotkina, Irina. *Diagnosing Literary Genius: A Cultural History of Psychiatry in Russia, 1880–1930.* Baltimore: Johns Hopkins University Press, 2002.

Soderholm, James. *Fantasy, Forgery, and the Byron Legend.* Lexington: University Press of Kentucky, 1996.

Sokolov, N.P. 'Kostomarov, Nikolai Ivanovich.' In *Russkie pisateli. 1800–1917. Biograficheskii slovar',* vol. 3. Moscow: Bol'shaia Rossiiskaia entsiklopediia, 1994.

Solov'ev, V.S. *Sochineniia v 2 tomakh.* Moscow: Mysl', 1990.

– 'Svedenborg.' In *Entsiklopedicheskii slovar',* edited by F.A. Brokgauz and I.A. Efron, vol. 10. St Petersburg, 1890.

Solovyoff, Vs. *A Modern Priestess of Isis.* London: Longmans, Green, 1895.

Sperrle, Irmhilde Christien. *The Organic Worldview of Nikolai Leskov.* Evanston: Northwestern University Press, 2002.

Stark, Henry S. 'Psychical Infection: Remarks upon the Probability of a Mental Contagium.' *Medical Record* 49 (1896).

Stasov, V.V. 'Modest Petrovich Musorgskii.' In *M.P. Musorgskii v vospominaniiakh sovremennikov.* Moscow: Muzyka, 1989.

Stepanian, K.A. 'K ponimaniiu "realizma v vysshem smysle."' In *Dostoevskii i mirovaia kul'tura,* X:54–64. Moscow: Klassika Plius, 1998.

Stepanov, N. 'Idei i plany.' In *Vospominaniia o Iurii Tynianove: Portrety i vstrechi.* Moscow: Sovetskii pisatel', 1983.

Stepanova, G. 'Stikhotvornaia dramaturgiia Ostrovskogo (1866–1873).' In A.N. Ostrovskii, *Polnoe sobranie sochinenii,* vol. 6. Moscow: Iskusstvo, 1976.

Stockenström, Göran. '"The Great Chaos and the Infinite Order": The Spiritual Journeys of Swedenborg and Strindberg.' In *Swedenborg and His Influence,* edited by Erland J. Brock, 47–76. Bryn Athyn: Academy of the New Church, 1988.

Strakhov, N. *O vechnykh istinakh. (Moi spor o spiritizme).* St Petersburg: Tipografiia brat'ev Panteleevykh, 1887.

– 'Tri pis'ma o spiritizme.' *Grazhdanin,* 41–4 (1876).

Struve, Gleb. *Russkie rasskazy.* New York: Bantam, 1963.

Suchkov, S.V. 'Aksakov Aleksandr Nikolaevich.' In *Russkie pisateli. 1880–1917,* vol. I. Moscow: Izdatel'stvo Rossiiskaia entsiklopediia, 1989.

Sushkov, N.V. *Zapiski o zhizni i vremeni sviatitelia Filareta, mitropolita Moskovskogo.* Moscow: Tipografiia A.I. Mamontova, 1868.

Swedenborg, Emanuel. *Heaven and Its Wonders and Hell: From Things Heard and Seen,* translated by John C. Ager. New York: Swedenborg Foundation, 1978.

– *O nebesakh, o mire dukhov i ob ade: Kak slyshal i videl E. Svedenborg,* translated by Aleksandr Aksakov. Leipzig: F. Wagner, 1863.

– *The True Christian Religion Containing the Universal Theology of the New Church.* New York: Swedenborg Foundation, 1972.

Sword, Helen. *Ghostwriting Modernism.* Ithaca: Cornell University Press, 2002.

Tanika, Tatyana. *Channeling Vysotsky: A Poet's Journey from Limbo into the Light.* Encino: Spirit Communicator's Press, 2005.

Taruskin, Richard. *Musorgsky: Eight Essays and an Epilogue.* Princeton: Princeton University Press, 1993.

Thrailkill, Jane F. *Affecting Fictions: Mind, Body, and Emotion in American Realism.* Cambridge, MA: Harvard University Press, 2007.

Tiutcheva, A.F. *Pri dvore dvukh imperatorov: Vospominaniia – Dnevnik,* 2 vols. Cambridge: Oriental Research Partners, 1975.

Tkachev, P.N. 'Belletristy-empiriki i belletristy-metafiziki.' *Delo* 5 (1875).

Todd, William Mills Todd III. 'The Anti-Hero with a Thousand Faces: Saltykov-Shchedrin's's Porfiry Golovlev,' *Studies in the Literary Imagination* 9, no. 1 (1976): 87–106.

Todorov, Tzvetan. *The Fantastic. A Structural Approach to a Literary Genre,* translated by Richard Howard. Ithaca: Cornell University Press, 1975.

Tokarskii, A.A. *K voprosu o vrednom vliianii gipnotizirovaniia.* St Petersburg: Tipografiia M.M. Stasiulevicha, 1899.

Tolstoi, A.K. *Dramaticheskaia trilogiia.* Moscow: Pravda, 1986.

Tolstoi, A.K., and Nikolaj Strakhov. *Complete Correspondence,* 2 vols., edited by A.A. Donskov. Ottawa: Slavic Research Group at the University of Ottawa, 2003.

Tolstoi, L.N. *Polnoe sobranie sochinenii v 90 tomakh (Iubileinoe izdanie).* Moscow: Gosudarstvennoe izdatel'stvo khudozhestvennoi literatury, 1928–59.

– *The Complete Works,* translated by Leo Wiener, vol. 28. New York and Boston: Colonial Press, 1909.

– *The Kreutzer Sonata and Other Stories,* translated by L. and A. Maude. Oxford: Oxford University Press, 1997.

– 'Neskol'ko slov povodu knigi "Voina i mir".' *Russkii arkiv* 3 (1868).

– *What Is Art?,* translated by Almyer Maude. Indianapolis: Liberal Arts Press, 1960.

- *Tolstoi, L.N. – N.N. Strakhov. Polnoe Sofranie perepiski.* Ed. A.A. Donskov. Moscow: Slavic Research Group at the University of Ottawa and State L.N. Tolstoy Museum, 2003.

Tomashevsky, B. *Pushkin.* Moscow: AN SSSR, 1961.

Trail, Nancy. *Possible Worlds of the Fantastic: The Rise of the Paranormal in Fiction,* Toronto: University of Toronto Press, 1996.

Tunimanov, V.A. 'Portret s "borodavkami" ("Bobok") i vopros o 'realizme' v iskusstve.''' In *Dostoevskii. Materialy i issledovaniia,* vol. 14. St Petersburg: Nauka, 1997.

Turgenev, I.S. *Polnoe sobranie sochinenii i pisem v 30 tomakh. Pis'ma v 19 tomakh,* vol. 3. Moscow: AN SSSR, 1997.

Tur'ian, M. 'Predislovie: K voprosu o pozitivistskikh vozzreniiakh pozdnego V.F. Odoevskogo.' In *Pushkin. Issledovaniia i materially,* 16–17. Moscow: Rossiiskaia Akademiia nauk, 2004.

Tynianov, Iu.N. 'Mnimyi Pushkin.' *Poetika. Istoriia literatury. Kino.* Moscow: Nauka, 1977.

Udimova, N.I. 'Stikhotvorenie Pushkina pamiati syna S.G. Volkonskogo.' In *Literaturnoe nasledstvo,* vol. 60, book 1, 405–10. Moscow: Izdatel'stvo Akademii nauk SSSR, 1956.

Utevskii, B.S. *Vospominaniia iurista.* Moscow: Iuridicheskaia literatura, 1989.

Vagner, N.P. 'Mediumizm.' *Russkii vestnik* 10 (1875): 806–951.

- *Nabliudeniia nad mediumizmom.* St Petersburg: F. Vasiberg, P. Gershunin, 1902.
- 'Otvet na prigovor spiriticheskoi komissii.' *Grazhdanin* 101 (1876).
- 'Po povodu spiritizma. Pis'mo k redaktoru.' *Vestnik Evropy* 4 (1875): 855–75.
- 'Vospominan'e ob Aleksandre Mikhailoviche Butlerove.' In A.M. Butlerov, *Stat'i po mediumizmu,* I–LXVII. St Petersburg: Tipografiia V. Demakova, 1889.

Vaiskopf, Mikhail. *Siuzhet Gogolia. Morfologiia. Ideologiia. Kontekst.* 2-e izdanie, ispravlennoe i rasshirennoe. Moscow: Rossiskii gosudarstvennyi gumanitarnyi universitet, 2004.

Vartier, Jean. *Allan Kardec, la naissance du Spiritisme.* Paris: Hachette, 1971.

Vatsuro, V.E. *Lirika pushkinskoi pory: 'Elegicheskaia shkola.'* St Petersburg: Nauka, 1997.

Venok na pam'atnik Pushkinu. Pushkinskie dni v Moskve, Peterburge i provintsii. St Petersburg: Sostavil F. Bulgakov Tipografiia A. Transhelia, 1880.

Vinitskii, I.Iu. *Dom tolkovatelia. Poeticheskaia semantika i istoricheskoe voobrazhenie V.A. Zhukovskogo.* Moscow: Novoe literaturnoe obozrenie, 2006.

- 'Dukhovnyi kartser: N.S. Leskov i "Palata nomer 6" A.P. Chekhova,' *Voprosy literatury* 4 (2006): 311–22.
- 'Russkie dukhi: Spiritualisticheskii siuzhet romana N.S. Leskova "Na nozhakh" v ideologicheskom kontekste 1870-kh godov.' *Novoe literaturnoe obozrenie* 87 (2007): 184–213.

Volgin, Igor'. *Poslednii god Dostoevskogo: Istoricheskie zapiski.* Moscow: Sovetskii pisatel', 1991.

Volgin, Igor', and V.L. Abramovich. 'Dostoevskii i Mendeleev: antispiriticheskii dialog.' *Voprosy filosofii* 11 (1971): 103–15.

Vries, Ad de. *Dictionary of Symbols and Imagery.* Amsterdam and London: North-Holland, 1976.

Wachtel, Andrew Baruch. *An Obsession with History: Russian Writers Confront the Past.* Stanford: Stanford University Press, 1994.

Warner, Marina. *Phantasmagoria: Spirit Visions, Metaphors, and Mediums into the Twenty-First Century.* Oxford: Oxford University Press, 2006.

Washington, Peter. *Madame Blavatsky's Baboon: A History of the Mystics, Mediums, and Misfits Who Brought Spiritualism to America.* New York: Schocken, 1995.

Weiner, Adam. *By Authors Possessed: The Demonic Novel in Russia.* Evanston: Northwestern University Press, 1998.

Wellek, Rene. 'Realism in Literature.' In *The Dictionary of the History of Ideas: Studies of Selected Pivotal Ideas,* edited by Philip P. Wiener, vol. 4, 51–6. New York: Scribner, 1973–4.

Wolfe, N.B. *Startling Facts on Modern Spiritualism.* Cincinnati: [n.p.], 1874.

Zen'kovskii, V. V. *Istoriia russkoi filosofii,* vol. 1, part 2. Leningrad: Ego, 1991.

– 'Problema bessmertiia u L.N. Tolstogo.' In *L.N. Tolstoi: Pro et Contra,* 500–27. St Petersburg: 2000.

Zielinski, Ludmila. 'Russia.' In *Abnormal Hypnotic Phenomena: A Survey of Nineteenth-Century Cases,* vol. 3, 2–105. London: Churchhill, 1968.

Zholkovskii, A.K. 'Malen'kii metatekstual'nyi shedevr Leskova.' *Novoe literaturnoe obozrenie* 5 (2008): 155–76.

Zhukovskii, V.A. 'Pis'mo k S.L. Pushkinu.' In *Pushkin v vospominaniiakh sovremennikov,* II:423–36. St Petersburg: 1998.

– *Polnoe sobranie sochinenii v 12 tomakh.* St Petersburg: Izdanie A.F. Marksa, 1902.

Zubov, V. 'Tolstoi i russkaia estetika 90-kh godov ("Chto takoe iskusstvo i ego kritiki").' In *Estetika L'va Tolstogo. Sbornik statei,* edited by P.N. Sakulin. Moscow: Gosudarstvennaia Akademiia khudozhestvennykh nauk, 1929.

Index

Abaza, Y.F., 39
Abveka, 'spirit of spirits,' 13
Addams Family, film, 103
Adon'eva, S.B., 193
afterlife, 3, 9, 13–14, 59, 100, 111, 115–16, 120–1, 176; Pushkin on, 74–5; Swedenborg on, 121–9, 131, 203, 206; Tolstoy on, 138–9
afterlife poetry, 13–14, 58; and 'posthumous authorship,' 58–62; Russian 'spirit mail,' 65–9; spiritualist poem as a genre, 62–5
Akhmatova, A.A., 186
Aksakov, A.N., xvii, 18, 19, 26, 27, 28, 32, 33, 34, 37, 41, 91, 94, 101, 126, 141, 162, 165, 175, 176, 178, 180, 181, 188, 189, 203, 206, 209, 216; *Animism and Spiritualism*, 177, 186, 187, 194; 'Mediumism and Philosophy,' 29; *Psychische Studien*, 29, 194
Aksakov, S.T., 28
Aldanov, Mark, 84
Alexander II, Emperor, 17, 45, 47, 169
Alexei Mikhailovich, Tsar, 55, 56
Anacreon (a shade of), 77
animal magnetism (mesmerism), 4, 5, 6, 7, 31; and hypnotism, 141–3
Annenkov, P.V., 52, 67, 79, 190, 210

Antokol'skii, Pavel, 193
Apukhtin, A.N. (a spirit of), 65
Aristotle, 104, 198
Audouard, Olympe, 61, 187
Augustine, Saint (a spirit of), 11

Bacon, Francis, 112
Bakhtin, Mikhail, 119, 124, 178, 201, 202, 203
Bakthin, N.I., 12
Banner of Life, 172, 196
Barkov, Ivan, 162, 188, 189, 191, 216
Barsukov, Nikolai, 181
Barthes, Roland, xv, 182, 185, 186
Batiushkov, K.N., 78
Baudelaire, Charles, 130
Bayer, G.Z., 181
Beast with Five Fingers, film, 103
Beer, Daniel, 147, 212
Beethoven, Ludwig van, 148, 215
Behrs, S.A., 140
Belinsky, V.G., xv, 11, 111, 166
Bell, Robert, 27, 174
Belov, E., 180
Belyi, Andrei, xiv, 202, 203
Benjamin, Walter, 'The Storyteller,' 214, 217, 218
Benz, Ernst, 124

Berg, N.V., 17, 18, 70
Berkov, P.N., 189, 190
Bernheim, Hippolyte, 141
Berry, Thomas, 166, 168, 169, 173, 201
Bestuzhev-Riumin, K.N., 181
Betanelli, Michael C., 195
Bibinov, Ivan, 13
Birkin (a scrivener), 46
Bitov, Andrey, 103
Bitsilli, P.M., 208, 210
Bitsyn. *See* N.M. Pavlov
Blake, William, 164
Blavatskaya (Blavatsky), E.P., 29, 66, 67, 94, 95, 98, 99, 106, 137, 171, 172, 180, 194–6, 210; *Isis Unveiled*, 141
Blok, A.A., xiv, 83
Boborykin, P.N., 26, 27, 30–5, 40, 41, 174, 176, 177, 180, 202; 'Neither Backward nor Forward,' 34; *Vespertine Sacrifice*, 30
Boccaccio, Giovanni (a spirit of), 59
Boileau-Despréaux, Nicolas, 202
Boltin, A.P., 4, 10, 14, 15, 110, 167, 169, 170, 171, 176, 198, 207
Boratynskaia, E.I., 209
Boris I (Godunov), Tsar, 47, 50–4, 184
Borodin, A.P., 52
Borodulin, Rygor, 86
Botkin, V.P., 197
Bouget, Édouard Isidore, 19, 173, 194
Bramwell, John Milne, 211
Brédif, Camille, 19, 24, 91, 92, 98, 100, 194
Brewern, Baron, 80
Brierre de Boismont, Alexander, 8, 169
Britten, Emma Hardinge, 168, 170, 198, 210
Briusov, Valery, 171

Brodie, Mary. *See* Saint Claire
Bulgarin, F.V., 6
Butlerov, A.M., 24, 26, 29, 30, 33–4, 41, 94, 101–2, 105, 139, 140, 142, 144, 175, 177–8, 180, 194, 196, 198, 210–11
Bykov, V.P., 168, 170, 172, 186
Byron, George Gordon, Lord, 59, 60, 62, 78, 180, 188, 191
Byurger, A., 14

Cagliostro, Alessandro, 144, 145
Calmet, Agustine, 159; *Dissertation sur les apparitions*, 159, 168, 215
Carlson, Maria, 166, 191, 196
Carlyle, Thomas, 49, 182
Castle, Terry, 49, 105, 116, 167, 182
Catherine II (a spirit of), 215
Chaadaev, P.Ya., 200
Chaev, N.A., 52, 53, 54, 184
Charcot, Jean-Martin, 141, 211
Charlemagne (a spirit of), 45
Chateaubriand (a spirit of), 59
Chekhov, A.P., 183
Chenier, Andre (a spirit of), 45
Chernyi, Sasha, 83, 192
Chernyshevsky, N.G., xv, xvi, xvii, 129, 166; *What Is To Be Done*, xv, xvi, 169
Chizhevsky, Dmitry, 166, 205
Christmas stories, genre, 159
clairvoyance, 5, 108, 132, 142, 206
Clayton, Douglas, 183
Commission of Mendeleev, 24–5, 27–8, 34–7, 41, 171, 179
Comte, Auguste, 29, 30
Cook, Florence (medium), 91, 95, 104
Corneille, Pierre (a spirit of), 59
Craddock, Patricia B., 214
Cromwell, Oliver, 45, 95

Crookes, William, 19, 27, 29, 91, 95, 174, 194

Dal', V.I., 7, 17, 18, 28, 29, 130, 173, 189, 204, 206
Dante Alighieri, 59, 131
Darwin, Charles, 30
Davis, Andrew Jackson, 9, 28, 29, 100, 131, 207
Davydov, N.V., 137, 138
Debolsky, G., Archpriest, 14
Delvig, A.A., 78, 191, 209
Denner, Michael, 212
Derrida, Jacques: *On Touching*, 198; *Specters of Marx*, 166, 198
Derzhavin, G.R. (a shade of), 78
Despine, Prosper, *De la contagion morale*, 147
Diamond Arm (Brilliantovaia ruka), film, 103
Dimitry, False (The Impostor), 48, 50–1, 53–5, 180, 183–5
Dimitry Donskoy, Prince, 46
Dixon, W.H., 17
Dobrolyubov, N.A., xv, xvi, 46
Dobrotvorsky, M.M., 183
Domashnyaya beseda (Household Talk), 17, 178
Dostoevskaya, A.G., 42, 89, 90, 93, 197
Dostoevsky, F.M., xv–xvii, 19, 26, 27, 30, 32–41, 65, 102, 122, 124–35, 137, 153, 155, 157, 163, 164, 172, 174–80, 188, 193, 195, 197, 200–5, 207, 208, 209, 216, 218; 'Bobok,' 119–25, 128, 131–9, 201–5, 208, 231, 233, 238; *The Brothers Karamazov*, xvi, 37, 38, 39, 125, 132, 178, 195, 203, 209; *Crime and Punishment*, 126, 132; *The Devils* (The Possessed), 127, 132, 133, 134,
205; 'Dream of a Ridiculous Man,' 128, 132, 204, 208; *The Idiot*, 204, 207; 'Just a Bit More about Spiritualism,' 36, 37; 'Modern Spiritualism: Something about Devils: The Extraordinary Cleverness of Devils, If Only These Are Devils,' 31, 32, 36, 38, 125; *Writer's Diary*, 31, 32, 35, 36, 38, 41, 125, 131, 192, 195
Dostoevsky, M.M., 125
Dotten, Lizzie, 60
Doyle, Arthur Conan, 196
Drug yunoshestva i vsyakikh let (The Friend of Youth and All Ages), 200
Dryden (a spirit of), 59
Du Deffand, Mme, 158, 214
Dumas, Alexandre, 61
Dunning, Chester, 183
Dushechkina, E.M., 215

Eckhartshausen, Karl, *The Key to the Mysteries of Nature*, 116
Eddy, William and Horatio (mediums), 94–5, 104, 195
Efremov, P.A., 69, 70, 72, 189
Egarev, V.N., 103
Eikhenbaum, B.M., 157, 183, 214
Ekaterina, martyr (a spirit of), 11
Elizabeth I of England (a spirit of), 215
Emerson, Caryl, 54, 179, 183, 184, 185, 207, 209, 212
Epstein, Mikhail, 217
Epstein-Matveyev, Rebecca, 185

Fanger, Donald, 201
fantastic, 26, 39, 120, 163, 166–7, 177, 202, 204
'fantastic realism.' *See* realism
Feldman, Osip, 139, 144–6, 151, 153–5

Felkner, V.I., 12
Feodora, the Blessed, 130
Feofan (Govorov), Bishop, 165
Feuerbach, Ludwig, 112
Filaret (Drozdov), Metropolitan, 8, 15
Flammarion, Camille, 196
Florovsky, Georgy, 130
Fontenelle, Bouvier de, 202
Fonvizin, D.I., *The Minor*, 139
Fourier, Charles, xv, 9
Frank, Joseph, 201
Franklin, Benjamin (a spirit of), 45
Freeborn, Richard, 175–6, 199
Freud, Sigmund, xiii, 103, 144, 166, 197; *Das Unheimliche* (The Uncanny), 116
Furst, Lilian R., 166, 213

Gaevsky, V.P., 110
Gagarin, Ivan, 214
Galberg, S.I., 79
Gall, Franz Joseph, 5
Gangelin, A., 82
Garber, Marjorie, 86
Garin-Vinding, D.V., 211
Gasparin, Agénor, comte de, 7
Gasparov, Boris, 86, 186, 191
Gauld, Alan, 210
Gegidze, Mikhalko (a spirit), 96, 97, 98, 106, 195
Genlis, Stéphanie Félicité, 156–63, 168, 214–18
Gershenzon, M.O., 166, 186, 190, 191
Gibbon, Edward, 158, 214
Giliarov, A.N., 151, 213
Gluck, Christoph Willibald Ritter von (a spirit of), 215
Goethe, Johann Wolfgang von, 21, 59, 100

Gogol, N.V., xiv, 11, 49, 102, 130, 149, 164, 166, 189, 201, 208, 217, 218; *Dead Souls*, xvi, 25, 65, 114, 200, 202; 'The Nose,' 134; *Selected Passages from Correspondence with Friends*, 114; 'A Terrible Vengeance,' 114; 'Vii,' 199
Goncharov, I.A., *Oblomov*, 158, 214
Goncharov, Vasily, *Life and Death of Pushkin*, 83
Gordin, Michael, 173–4
Gossman, Lionel, 49
Gothic tradition, xv, 103, 113–14
Gradovsky, G.K. (Gamma), 101
Grazhdanin (Citizen), 31, 35, 44, 46, 120, 134
Greenblatt, Stephen, 165, 185, 188
Grossman, Leonid, 125, 126
Grot, N.Ya., 146
Grot, Ya.K., 190, 211
Güldenstubbe, Ludwig von, 7, 80, 81, 186, 192
Gustafson, Richard, 149, 150, 212
Gustav (a spirit of Blavatsky's uncle), 98

Hare, Robert, 19, 29, 91
Hellengren, Anders, 205
Hess, David, 10
historical drama, 52–5
Hoffman, E.T.A., 30
Home, Daniel Dunglas, 9, 19, 28, 29, 91, 139
Homer (a spirit of), 59, 77
'Homo Mysticus,' 129–30
Honto (a spirit), 95, 100, 102
Horace, 97
Hugo, Victor, 8, 45, 169
hypnotism 137, 141–3, 145–6, 151, 154; Blavatsky on the dangers of, 141–2; artistic, 146–52, 163

Ignaty (Brianchaninov), Bishop: *Sermon on Death*, 15, 16, 172, 173, 177, 203
infection (contagion): artistic, 146–8, 212; moral, 146, 149–50, 152–3, 155; psychic, 136, 142, 147–8, 151–2. *See also* hypnotism
Ioann, Damaskin (a spirit of), 13
Isakov Ya.A., 69
Iskra (Spark), 133–4
Ivan the Terrible, 11, 45, 47, 48, 50, 170
Ivanitsky, A., 189
Ivanov, Vyacheslav, xiv, 166, 171

Jackson, Robert Louis, 201
Jahn, Gary R., 212
Jakobson, Roman, 93, 192, 193
John of Kronstadt, 145
Jung-Stilling, Johann-Heinrich, xv, 5, 107, 116, 130, 200, 206

Kallash, V.V., 189
Kandinsky, V.Kh., 147, 148, 151, 153
Kant, Immanuel, 208
Kappes, A.R., 94
Karamzin, N.M., 42, 44, 182
Karatygin, P.A., 12, 71, 72, 74
Kardec, Allan (real name Léon-Dénizarth-Hippolyte Rivail), xv, 9–15, 18, 19, 21, 51, 100, 110–11, 121, 137, 157, 160–2, 167, 169, 172, 180, 196, 207, 215–16; *Le livre des esprits* (Book of Spirits), 9, 31, 170; *Le livre des mediums* (Book of Mediums), 9, 170, 216
Katenin, A.A., 71
Katkov, M.N., 94
Kavelin, K.D., 90, 165, 181, 194, 195
Kazanskii, P.S., 183

Keats, John (a spirit of), 170
Kerner, Justinus, 5, 206
Khlebnikov, Velimir, 103
Khrisanf (V.N. Retivtsev), 205, 206
Khristianskoe chtenie (Christian Reading), 16, 129
King, Katie (a spirit), 45, 91, 95, 100, 194, 195
Kireevsky, Ivan, 50, 183
Konetsky, Viktor, 86
Korzhavin, Naum, 193
Kostomarov, N.I., 46–9, 51, 53, 54, 180–4; *Russian History through the Lives of Its Major Figures*, 47, 181
Kovalevsky, P.A., 130
Krestovsky, V.V., 183
Krylov, I.A. (a spirit of), 189
Kryzhanovskaya V.I (Rochester), 171
Kukolnik, N.I., 52
Kuprin, I.A., 215
Kuzmin, Mikhail, 171

Labzin, A.F., 200
Lavrov, V.M., 189, 190
Leatherbarrow, William J., 178, 179, 205, 218
Lebedev, M., 16
Le Bon, Gustave, 153, 213; *Psychologie des foules*, 153, 213
Lelut, L.F., 8
Lenin, V.I., 84
Lermontov, M.Yu., xiv, 65, 130
Leroux, Pierre, 9, 169
Lesevich, V.V., 15, 187; 'Fashionable Superstition,' 111
Leskov, A.N., 215
Leskov, N.S., xv, 16–18, 26, 31–5, 40, 41, 50, 130, 156–64, 168, 170, 172–3, 176, 177, 183, 207, 209, 214–17; 'The Apparition of the Spirit,' 161;

Cathedral Folk, 31; *At Daggers Drawn*, 17, 31, 50, 51, 161, 162, 168, 215; 'On the Edge of the World,' 161; 'The Enchanted Pilgrim,' 31; 'Laughter and Woe,' 31, 161, 162; *No Way Out*, 31; 'The Sealed Angel,' 31, 214; 'The Spirit of Mme Genlis,' 156–63, 168, 218; 'White Eagle,' 161

Letkova, E.P., 213

Levine, George, xiv, xv, 165, 166, 167

Leving, Yu., 192

Lewis, Matthew, 114

Liébault, Jean, 141, 211

Likhachev, D.S., 56

Likhonin, N.O., 194

Literaturnaya gazeta (Literary Gazette), 85

Littré, Émile, 8, 169

Lokhvitskaya, M.A. (a spirit of), 65

Lombroso, Cesare, 213

Lomonosov, M.V. (a shade of), 78

Lotman, Lidia, 53, 184, 185

Lotman, Yu.M., 55, 65, 179, 188, 207, 217

Lubianovsky, F.P., 200

Lucas, Prosper, *De l'imitation contagieuse ou de la propagation sympathique des névroses et des monomanies*, 147

Lucian, 202

Ludovic, Saint (a spirit of), 11

Luk'ianov, S.M., 209

Luys, Jules Bernard, 210

Lvov, N.A., 137–9, 151

Maikov, Apollon, 31, 130, 200

Maiorova, Olga, 183

Makoveeva, Irina, 199

Mamai (Khan), 46

Mamchich (a medium), 137, 138

Mandorsky, Anatoly, 188

Marat, Jean-Paul (a spirit of), 45

Markov, E.L., 19, 92, 102

Marshall, Emmanuel, 27

Marshall, Mary (Mrs Claire's mother-in-law), 27. *See also* Saint Claire

Marx, Karl, 112, 168, 198

materialism, xii, 9, 14, 32, 38, 59, 90, 110, 112, 199–200, 213

materializations, 18, 53–6, 60, 63, 79, 90–100, 102–4, 195; materialized hands, 100–6. *See also* soul; spiritualism

Mayakovsky, V.V., 103, 106, 192

McLaughlin, Sigrid, 210

McLean, Hugh, 160

mediums and mediumship, xiii, 3–5, 7, 10, 12, 19, 25, 26, 40, 45, 58, 63–4, 94, 100, 162, 164, 168–70; Blavatsky as, 66–7, 94–9; Brédif as, 19, 24, 91, 92, 98, 100, 194; Cook, 91, 95, 104; Eddy, 94–5, 104, 195; Home as, 9, 19, 28, 29, 91, 139, 140, 169, 175, 194; and hypnotists, 139–45; Mamchich as, 137–8; Saint Claire (Mary Marshall) as, 25–8, 31–5, 40, 41, 174; and writing, 187, 194, 196

Mel'nikov-Pechersky, P.I. 169, 206

Mendeleev, D.I., xvii, 24–5, 27, 28, 34, 40, 41, 63, 93, 171, 173, 174, 177–80, 187, 194, 196

Menippea, 120, 121, 135, 201–3

Meshchersky, V.P., 43–8, 181

Mesmer, Franz, 5, 7, 141, 143

Meyer, Marvin, W., 200

Michelet, Jules, 182

'middle world,' xvi, 116–17

Mikhail I (Romanov), Tsar, 46

Milioti, K.Yu., 138
Miller, Robin Feuer, 204
Milosc, Czeslaw, 126
Minaev, Dmitry, 133
Minin, Kozma, 46, 185
Mirville, Eudes de, 7, 167; *Des esprits et les leurs manifestations fluidiques*, 6
Mochulsky, Konstantin, 121, 201
Molière, Jean-Baptiste (a shade of), 62
Molokhovets, E.I., 180
Mordovtsev, D.L., 183
Morgan, Henry, 45
Morogues, Inès Muller de, 160
Morson, Gary Saul, 177, 178, 179, 208
Moskovskie vedomosti (Moscow Gazette), 6
Moskvitianin (The Moscovite), 7, 169, 173
Mozart, Wolfgang Amadeus (a spirit of), 215
Murav, Harriet, 208
Musorgsky, M.P., 52; *Boris Godunov*, 73, 184

Nabokov, Vladimir, 83, 103; *The Eye*, 162; *The Gift*, 72, 192
Napoleon (a spirit of), 45
Nashchokin, P.V., 12, 71, 72, 74, 171
Nekrasov, N.A., 111, 131
Nekrasova, E.S., 178
Nérval, Gerard de, 130
Nevrev, N.V., 184
Newton, Isaac, 169
Nicholas I, Emperor, 5, 11, 169
Nikodim, Bishop, 84
Nikolaev, D.P., 199
Novalis, 49

Odoevsky, V.F., xiv, 130, 169
Olcott, Henry, 91, 94–5, 98, 104, 194–6

ontological realism. *See* realism
Origen, 161, 215
Orthodox Church: attitudes towards spiritualism, 9, 16–18, 35, 36, 121, 124–5; and Swedenborg, 130, 177
Orwin, Donna Tussing, 178, 179, 209
Osipova, P.A., 73
Ostrovsky, A.N., 52–5, 183, 184, 185; *A Comedian of the Seventeenth Century*, 55; *Dimitry the Pretender and Vasily Shuisky*, 53
Otechestvennye zapiski (Fatherland Notes), 111
Otrep'ev, Grishka, Pretender, 47, 51, 54
Ovid (a shade of), 78

Panchenko, A.A., 193
Panyutin, L.K., 134
Paracelsus, 164
Paul I (a spirit of), 45, 51
Pavlishchev, L.N., 71
Pavlishcheva, O.S. (née Pushkina), 66, 73, 169, 189
Pavlov, I.F., 189
Pavlov, N.M. (Bitsyn), 183
Perov, Vasily, 208
Perovo Solovovo, M., 168, 174
Perovsky, Sofia (a spirit of), 45
Peter I, the Great, Emperor, 11, 45, 48, 50, 51
Petrarch, Francesco (a spirit of), 59
Petty, Joseph and William, mediums, 25
Phillips, Roger W., 205
Pisarev, D.I., xvii, 9, 112, 169, 199; 'Realists,' 9, 87; 'Scholasticism of the Nineteenth Century,' 107, 199
Pisemsky, A.F., xvi
Platt, Kevin M.F., 203, 229

Pobedonostsev, K.P., 36, 92, 149, 153, 211
Podmore, Frank, 174, 194
Poe, Edgar Allan, 59, 60
Pogodin, M.P., 46, 47, 53, 54, 168, 177, 181; *History in Characters about Dimitry the Pretender*, 53
Pogorzhinsky, priest, 84
Polkanov, Ivan, 128, 205
Polonsky, Ya.P., 102, 105, 130, 193
Polozov, Nikolai, 53
Poluektova, I.V., 199
positivism, xii–xiii, 9, 15, 19–20, 29–30, 35, 64, 90, 104–5, 121, 125, 129, 135, 140, 193–4
Potulov, N.I., 17, 18, 172, 178, 216
Powelstock, David, 192
Pozdiejew, W., 161
Pribytkova, V.I., 38
Proudhon, P.-J., 111
Prutkov, Koz'ma, xvii, 65, 187, 188
Puccini, Giacomo (a spirit of), 215
Pushkin, A.S., xiv, 11, 12, 21, 39, 50, 52–4, 57, 58, 64–75, 77–86, 101, 162–4, 169, 171, 182–6, 188–93, 198, 199, 202, 209; *Boris Godunov*, 50, 52–4; 'Elegy,' 74; 'Epitaph to an Infant,' 75; *Eugene Onegin*, 78; *Feast during the Plague*, 202; 'But Flying Off to Other Worlds,' 75–7; *Gabrieliad*, 74; 'I Love Your Unknown Twilight,' 75–7; 'Monument,' 75; 'Queen of Spades,' xiv, 39, 179; *Ruslan and Ludmila*, 78, 101
Pushkin, A.S. (a spirit), 'Entering the Heavenly Realms,' 66, 69, 71–5, 77, 190
Pushkin, S.L., 7

Rachinsky, S.A., 19, 92, 93, 176
Radcliffe, Anne, 114

Raduga (The Rainbow), 14
Raevsky, N.N., 190
Rainov, T., 212, 213
realism, xii–xiii, xvii, 26, 44, 51, 163, 165–6; age of, xvii, 26, 51; 'fantastic,' 121, 130, 200–1; 'in a higher sense,' 155; and history, 49–53, 56; inner kinship with spiritualism, xvi–xvii, 26, 56, 93, 100, 157, 164; ontological, xvii, 130–3, 163; psychological, 131, 166; realist exorcism, xv, 24, 93, 111–13, 155 (in Tolstoy); and Shchedrin, 107, 117–18; spiritualist, xvii, 89, 93–100, 107; and Tolstoy, 155–6
realist exorcism. *See* realism
Rebus, 65, 66, 142, 144, 170, 179, 198, 209, 215
Repin, Ivan, 52
Revue Britannique, 6
Revue spirite, 170, 215, 216
Rimbaud, Arthur, 130
Rimsky-Korsakov, N.A., 52
Robespierre, Maximilien (a spirit of), 45
Robinson, Douglas, 212
Roshchin, M.M., 186
Roshchin, Mikhail, 206
Rossetti, William Michael, 27
Rousseau, Jean Jacques (a spirit of), 170
Russian Psychological Society, 146
Russkii Invalid (Russian Veteran), 69
Russkii Vestnik (The Russian Herald), 19, 29, 94

Saadi (a spirit of), 59
Sade, Marquise de, 120
Saint Claire, Mrs (real name Mary Marshall, neé Brodie), 25–8, 31–5, 40, 41, 174

Sakulin, P.N., 166
Saltykov-Shchedrin, M.E., xvi, xvii, 107–15, 117, 119, 155, 163, 198–200, 213, 224; *The Golovlyov Family*, 108, 113–16, 199–200; *The History of a Town*, 109, 117, 118; *Life's Trifles*, 109–10; 'Modern Phantoms,' 87, 109, 112; *The Whole Year*, 11
Saltykova, E.A., 110
Samarin, P.F., 138
Sand, George, 169
Sandler, Stephanie, 186, 192
Sankt-Peterburgskie Vedomosti (St Petersburg Gazette), 41
Sarovsky, Seraphim (a spirit of), 11
Schlegel, August von, 164
Schlotzer, August Ludwig, 181
Schopenhauer, Arthur, xv, 29, 98, 210
seances: at Aksakov's, 26–36; of Bredif, 91–2; as a cultural metaphor, xvi; of the Eddy brothers, 95–9; as hermeneutic trap, 25–6, 39; as a mystery play, xiv, 19, 39–41, 56; and phantasmagoria, 49; at Samarin's, 138; spiritualist and hypnotic, 139–41, 149–50, 153; as test, 36–9; as zone of contact between the material and spiritual worlds, 104
Sechenov, Ivan Mikhailovich, xvii, 90, 94, 165, 194, 195; *Reflexes of the Brain*, 15, 198
Senderovich, Savely, 186, 191
Sergius of Radonezh (a saint), 46
Serov, A.N., *Dmitrii samozvanets* (Dmitry the Impostor), 184
Severnaya pchela (The Northern Bee), 6, 209, 210
Shakespeare, William, 6, 21, 56, 59–61, 78, 86, 164, 166, 170, 171, 188, 193, 217

Shakhovskaia, K.M., 206
Sham Pushkin (*mnimy* Pushkin), 72–3
Shchapov, A.P., 181
Shelley, Percy Bysshe (a spirit of), 170
Shepard, Jesse (Francis Grierson), 45, 170
Shevyrev, S.P., 81
Shklyarevsky, A., 102, 176, 197
Shleiden, M.Ya., 206
Shuisky, Vasily, Prince and Tsar, 47, 50
Šilbajoris, Rimvydas, 212
Sinyavsky, A.D., 103
Sionskiy vestnik (Messenger of Zion), 200
Sirotkina, Irina, 213
Skabichevsky, A.M., 36
Slavnikov, G., 193
Sluchevsky, Konstantin, 130
Smirnov, Archpriest, 84
Solovyov, S.M., 181
Solovyov, V.S., xiv, 17, 31, 98, 171, 175–6, 181, 193, 201, 202, 206, 207–9
soul: of the dead poet, 64–5, 69, 75–7; debates about, xii, 15–17, 25–6, 90, 94, 195; Dostoevsky on, 27, 36–42, 130–1, 135, 155; and hand, 104; Kardec on, 10–11, 111; Leskov on, 31, 35; transmigration of, 137; tribulations of, 121. *See also* afterlife; materializations; 'middle world'; spiritualism
Souriau, Étienne, *La suggestion dans l'art*, 151
Sovremennik (The Contemporary), 8, 184
spectralization, 55, 105, 107, 113, 116, 117, 119
Spiridon (a spirit), 162
spirit communication. *See* spiritualism

spirit photography, 19; the Bouget scandal, 54, 173, 194
spirit writing. *See* table writing
spiritual realism. *See* realism
spiritualism, modern: Aksakov on, 18–19, 28–9, 41, 94, 162, 186–9, 194, 206, 209; artistic, 157, 163–4; Boborykin on, 27–8, 30–1, 34–5, 40–1, 174, 177; Butlerov on, 24, 29–30, 41, 140, 144; critique of, 15–18, 19–20, 92–3, 102–3, 144; definition, xii, 3–4; Dostoevsky on, 31–2, 35–40, 125–6; experimental (scientific, empirical), xvi, 18–20; 'historical,' 44–8; Leskov on, 31, 34–5, 160–3; Mendeleev on, 24–5, 27–8, 34, 40–1, 63, 93, 171–2, 177–80, 194, 196; 'philosophical,' xvi, 10, 14–18; and realism, xiv–xvii; Romantic, 172; Russian spiritualism compared to American and French, 11–12; Shchedrin on, 108–11; Strakhov on, 19, 29, 140, 144; Tolstoy on, 19–20, 137–42, 153–4; Vagner on, 12–14, 24–5, 30, 41–2, 90–5, 124. *See also* materializations; realism; spectralization; spirit photography; table writing
Stalin, Joseph, 85
Stasov, V.V., 184
Strablin, N.D., medium, 13
Strakhov, N.N., xvii, 29, 139, 140, 144, 165, 173, 183, 187, 196, 202, 209, 210; *Three Essays on Spiritualism*, 19
Strannik (Wanderer), 128
Strekoza (Dragonfly), 69, 103, 189
Struve, Gleb, 203
Struve, Heinrich, 165
Surikov, Ivan, 171
Surikov, Vasily, 52
Susanin, Ivan, 46

Suvorin, A.S., 53, 54; 'Progulka v adu' (Promenade in Hell), 201
Swedenborg, Emanuel, xv, 5, 7, 9, 28, 59, 60, 100, 121–35, 177, 202–8; *On Heaven, the World of Spirits, and on Hell*, 121–3, 125–8; *The White Horse*, 207
Sword, Helen, xiii, 63, 166, 186, 187, 188

table writing 7–8, 11–4, 79, 92. *See also* afterlife poetry
Taruskin, Richard, 183, 184
Tasso, Torquato (a shade of), 78
Tchaikovsky, P.I., 52
Thomas, Apostle, 37, 38, 178
Thrailkill, Jane F., 213
Thury, M., 7
Tikhonravov, N.S., 55
Todd, William Mills III, 219
Todorov, Tzvetan, 39, 162, 167
Tokarskii, A.A., 210
Tolstoy, A.K., 52, 183, 184, 197; *Tsar Boris*, 54–5, 185
Tolstoy, L.N., xv, xvii, 19, 49, 52, 130–55, 163, 165, 173, 178, 179, 182, 183, 196, 197, 208, 209–13; *Anna Karenina*, 19, 140, 167, 197, 212; 'Death of Ivan Ilich,' 137; *The Fruits of Enlightenment*, 138, 140–1, 145–7, 211; 'The Kreutzer Sonata,' 145, 148, 212; *War and Peace*, 49, 209; 'On What Art Is and What It Isn't,' 146–7; *What Is Art?* 146, 149, 150, 212, 213
Tournier, Victor, 110
Tredyakovsky, V.K. (a spirit of), 65
Tserkovnyi Vestnik (The Church Herald), 18
Tsvet, Professor, 102
Tsvetaeva, M.I., 103, 186
Tunimanov V.A., 126, 134, 201, 202

Turgenev, I.S., xv, xvii, 26, 139, 162, 173, 174, 188, 210, 215; *Fathers and Sons*, 112, 199; 'Klara Milich,' 194, 199
Tyminskaya, E.D., 180
Tynianov, Yu.N., 87, 218; 'Sham Poetry,' 63
Tyucheva, A.F., 169, 203
Tyutchev, F.I., 8, 45, 169

Uspensky, Boris, 207
Uspensky, G.I., xvi
Utevskii, B.S., 211

Vagner, N.P., xvii, 12, 24, 26, 30, 34, 37, 41, 42, 89, 90, 91, 95, 98, 100, 105, 107, 112, 130, 139, 141, 142, 143, 151, 155, 162, 163, 171, 173, 175, 176, 177, 179, 180, 188, 189, 193, 194, 195, 196, 197, 198, 210, 211, 216; 'In the Darkness,' 196; 'God's Furrow,' 30; 'Mediumship,' 94–5, 98–100, 194, 195; *Observations on Mediumship*, 12, 171; 'Old Diks,' 196; 'On Spiritualism,' 90–2
Vaiskopf, Mikhail, 200
Vatsuro, V.E., 191, 199
Veinberg, P.I. (a spirit of), 65
Venevitinov, D.V. (a spirit of), 65
Verne, Jules, 90
Vestnik Evropy (The Herald of Europe), 24, 46, 90, 180, 182, 214
Villiers de L'Isle-Adam, Comte Jean-Marie, 130
Vinitskii, I.Yu., 216
Virgil (a spirit of), 59, 77

Voeikov, A.F., 173
Volkonskaya, Maria, 190
Volkonsky, S.G., 190
Voprosy filosofii i psikhologii (Questions of Philosophy and Psychology), 151
Vrach (Physician), 211
Vsemirnaya illiustratsiya (Worldwide Illustration), 15

Wachtel, Andrew Baruch, 16, 49
Wagner, Richard, 143, 150, 196, 213
Wallace, Alfred Russel, 27, 91
Walpole, Horace, 114; *The Castle of Otranto*, 103
Washington, George (a spirit of), 45
Weiner, Adam, 179, 218
Williams, T.W., 94
Wittgenstein, Emile, Prince, 11
Wolfe, N.B., 91

Yurkevich, P.D., xvii, 29, 165, 175, 176, 178, 206, 208

Zabelin, I.E., 55, 181
Zenkovsky, V.V., 165, 195, 210
Zheke (a spirit), 91, 92, 100, 102
Zhelikhovskaya, V.P., 66, 67
Zholkovsky, Alexander, 215, 217
Zhukovsky, V.A., 11, 17, 18, 65, 73, 78, 103, 173, 191, 199; 'Something about Ghosts,' 172
Zhuravskii, D.I. (Jouravski), 170
Zielinski, Ludmila, 210
Zola, Émile, 30, 176
Zubov, V., 211